JUNIOR SCHOOL SCIENCE EDUCATION IN ENGLAND AND WALES SINCE 1900

JUNIOR SCHOOL SCIENCE EDUCATION IN ENGLAND AND WALES SINCE 1900

From Steps to Stages

E.W. Jenkins

B.J. Swinnerton

Routledge
Taylor & Francis Group
LONDON AND NEW YORK

First published 1998 by Woburn Press

Published 2020 by Routledge
2 Park Square, Milton Park, Abingdon, Oxon OX14 4RN
52 Vanderbilt Avenue, New York, NY 10017

Routledge is an imprint of the Taylor & Francis Group, an informa business

British Library Cataloguing in Publication Data

Jenkins, E. W. (Edgar William), 1939–
Junior school science education in England and Wales since 1900 : from steps to stages. – (The Woburn education series)
1. Science – Study and teaching (Elementary) – England – History – 20th century 2. Science – Study and teaching (Elementary) – Wales – History – 20th century
I. Title II.Swinnerton, B.J.
372.3'5'0942'0904

Library of Congress Cataloging-in-Publication Data

Jenkins, E. W. (Edgar William)
Junior school science education in England and Wales since 1900 : from steps to stages / E.W. Jenkins, B. Swinnerton.
p. cm. – (Woburn education series)
Includes bibliographical references and index.
ISBN 0-7130-0202-6 (cloth). – ISBN 0-7130-4023-8 (pbk.)
1. Science – Study and teaching (Elementary) – England – History 2. Science – Study and teaching (Elementary) – Wales – History. I. Swinnerton, B. (Bronwen), 1964– . II. Title. III. Series.
LB1585.5.G7J46 1998
372.3'5'0941–DC21 97-52231
CIP

Typeset by Vitaset, Paddock Wood, Kent

ISBN 13: 978-0-7130-4023-4 (pbk)
ISBN 13: 978-0-7130-0202-7 (hbk)

Contents

Foreword

In 1900, there will have been few, if any, teachers working in public elementary schools in England and Wales who were not acquainted with at least the name of Herbart and who did not know, however imperfectly, something of his educational ideas. Those ideas, developed in the early nineteenth century, identified education as an essentially moral undertaking and ascribed to the teacher a central and directing role in pupils' intellectual and spiritual development. By the end of that century, however, Herbart's philosophy of education had become strongly associated with a series of steps or stages (*Stufen*) to be used in organising instruction, although Herbart himself did not distinguish these with the precision and finality subsequently claimed by his followers. These steps of preparation, presentation, association, generalisation and application were widely used to structure lessons, the *Journal of Education* commenting in 1911 that 'all students of education were stepping to the tune of the five steps' not long after they had been introduced.[1] Herbartianism sustained a minor publishing industry[2] and its emphasis upon moral education and upon feeding the mind 'with a rich repast of historical and biographical ideas' brought its proponents into conflict with those, notably Henry Armstrong and Philip Magnus, who sought to advance the cause of practical and scientific studies within elementary education[3] where science found accommodation only as object teaching or nature study.

The work of public elementary schools was governed by a series of *Regulations* issued annually by the Board of Education, established in 1899. In 1904, these *Regulations* required[4] that such schools provide a 'graduated course of instruction, suitable to the age and capacity of the scholar', in English Language, arithmetic, geography, history, drawing, singing, physical exercises, plain needlework for girls and 'knowledge of the common phenomena of the external world'. In the following year, this last element of the public elementary school curriculum was changed to 'Observation Lessons and Nature Study', taught, as far as possible, with special reference to the surroundings of the pupils and to the natural features, industries and plant life of the locality.[5]

Almost a century later, primary school teachers in England and Wales find their work more, rather than less, defined by statute. It is framed by the first two of the four key stages which structure the national curriculum introduced following the passage of the Education Reform Act 1988. Key stages 1 and 2 cover respectively years 1 and 2 and 3, 4, 5 and 6 of compulsory schooling, and, at the end of each stage, teachers are required to make judgements, although not in all subjects, about pupils' attainment against a variety of statutory descriptions. The curriculum of the primary school embraces English, mathematics, science, design and technology, information technology, history, geography, art, music, physical education and, in Wales, Welsh. Although not a national curriculum subject, religious education is also a compulsory element of primary schooling, the Education Reform Act 1988 serving to reinforce the position established in the legislation of 1944. As a compulsory component of the primary school curriculum, the minimum statutory entitlement of pupils to a scientific education is set out in the programme of study specified for each key stage. Along with English and mathematics, pupils' attainment in science at Key Stage 2 is subject to statutory, external testing.

While reference to 'steps' and 'stages' is a pointed way of identifying the period with which this book is concerned, it runs the risk of masking, inadvertently, the much more profound changes which have taken place during the twentieth century in the publicly-funded education of children between the ages of 5 and 11. It would, for example, be a mistake to regard 'primary' and 'elementary' as readily interchangeable terms or to ignore the fact that, until the passage of the 1944 Education Act, only a very small number of pupils were able to transfer, by means of Free Place and Scholarship examinations, from elementary to secondary schools, almost all of which, until that Act, charged fees even when supported by Parliamentary grant. The construction of public elementary education in the nineteenth century ensured that, by 1900, it was distinguished from what has become known as secondary education largely in terms of social class. As Morant, the Permanent Secretary of the Board of Education, explained in 1909,[6]

> the idea that elementary and secondary schools (represented) not successive stages of education but alternative kinds of education for different social classes (was) deeply rooted and may be said to have dominated practice until recently.

Primary education, therefore, is a comparatively recent development within the education system of England and Wales.

Although the class dimension of elementary education was removed when the 1944 Act designated primary education as that which, for all pupils, preceded publicly-funded secondary education, elements of what might be called the elementary tradition within schooling survived and have continued to do so to the present day. Indeed, it is important to acknowledge that the reorganisation of compulsory schooling into primary and secondary phases was not completed until as late as 1965. Pupils in primary and secondary modern schools were taught by non-graduates, trained in teacher training colleges and, until the 1970s, paid less generously than their graduate colleagues. Primary teachers were not subject experts but 'experts in teaching children', and they taught in schools whose function was to lay the basis of some kind of secondary education. In addition, the elementary school tradition was marked by the teaching of classes as a whole, rather than in groups, and by a particular emphasis on reading, writing and arithmetic. The language of elementary education was that of 'Standards', pupils progressing from one to another to reach 'Standard 7' as the top class of the elementary school.

There is also, however, a different tradition within primary education in England and Wales. This is associated with child-centredness, manifest, at least at the level of curriculum rhetoric, by the furthering of experience at the expense of formal knowledge, and by disparaging references to the rote learning, rigidly timetabled days and the fixed desks associated with the elementary schooling to which it stands in opposition. As Alexander has pointed out,[7] the class teaching of elementary education required no justification in a system of mass public education, other than economic and administrative expediency. Child-centredness, in contrast, rests upon a commitment to, and an understanding of, children's intellectual, personal, social and spiritual development and to teaching that is responsive to their presumed individual needs. It is here that the expertise of the primary teacher is sometimes said to lie, an expertise different from, but of comparable status to, the subject knowledge of the secondary teacher. The language of child-centredness is cosy and consensual. The references are not to mass 'Standards' but to individual progress, freedom of expression, creativity and richness of experience.

The coexistence of these traditions within primary education, and the tensions between them, are, of course, only to be expected in an enterprise which is, of necessity, value-laden. Yet the tensions are much more evident at the level of rhetoric and discourse about primary education than within individual primary classrooms. In the twenty or so years following the publication of the seminal Plowden Report,[8] the evidence is of a continuing emphasis upon, rather than a significant neglect of, the teaching of numeracy and literacy, and a far from universal commitment to so-called progressive methods of teaching.[9]

It might be expected that the tensions between a subject-based and a child-centred approach to primary education would be particularly acute in the case of science, a discipline which is commonly presented as paradigmatic of secure, objective knowledge. How far this is the case, and the extent and manner in which any such tensions were accommodated or resolved is an important sub-theme of this book. Such tensions were present in the long-standing commitment to the teaching of nature study and they re-emerged both in the primary science curriculum development projects of the 1960s and in the more recent debates surrounding the accommodation of science as a compulsory component of the statutory primary curriculum. Equally, they were manifest in the report, *The Primary School*, prepared by the Consultative Committee of the Board of Education under the chairmanship of Sir Henry Hadow and published in 1931.

Following an account of the nineteenth century background (Chapter 1), Chapter 2 explores the way in which this 1931 Hadow report constructed primary education in terms of a curriculum 'thought of in terms of activity and experience, rather than knowledge to be acquired and facts to be stored'. Chapter 3 offers an account of the teaching of nature study in elementary and primary schools since the early years of this century. Here, as throughout the book, an attempt is made to explore some of the complex social, political, educational and other factors which have been influential in shaping both rhetoric and practice relating to the education of young children. Chapter 4 examines two major attempts to introduce science into primary education by means of large-scale, centrally-directed curriculum initiatives, the *Nuffield Junior Science Project* and the *Science 5–13 Project*.

With science, as with any other element of the primary curriculum, what can be achieved with pupils is critically dependent upon the knowledge and expertise of those who teach them. The preparation of those who teach young children has undergone a number of major changes during the twentieth century and the nature of these changes and their implications for primary science education are examined in Chapter 5. Important in the training of these teachers and their subsequent work in the classroom have been ideas about how children learn and how teachers might best facilitate their intellectual development. Not surprisingly, these ideas have also changed throughout the century and Chapter 6 examines a number of learning theories and the role they have played in the scientific education of young children. The book concludes with a brief 'Afterword'.

The studies that comprise this book are not offered as a history of twentieth-century primary science education in England and Wales. Rather they are offered as an exploration of the factors which have shaped it and of some of the fundamental problems relating to the educational function of science. It is our hope that the book will be of interest to primary teachers, to historians of science education and, more widely, to all those who seek to promote the interest of young children in the science which, in conjunction with technology, has done so much to structure the physical and mental world within which they are growing up.

Edgar W. Jenkins
Bronwen J. Swinnerton

Centre for Studies in Science and Mathematics Education, University of Leeds

NOTES

1 *Journal of Education*, XXXIII, Jan. 1911, p. 39.
2 R.J.W. Selleck, *The New Education 1870–1914* (London, 1968), p. 243.
3 F.H. Hayward, *The Secret of Herbart* (London, 1904), p. 76. Hayward was a leading exponent of Herbartian ideas. For criticism of the Herbartian emphasis upon historical and literary studies, see W.H. Brock (ed.), *H.E. Armstrong and the Teaching of Science 1880–1930* (Cambridge, 1973), and P. Magnus, *Educational Aims and Efforts 1890–1910* (London, 1910).
4 Board of Education, *Code of Regulations for Public Elementary Schools with Schedules, 1904* (HMSO, 1904), chapter 1, p. 1.
5 Board of Education, *Code of Regulations for Public Elementary Schools with Schedules, 1905* (HMSO, 1905), chapter 1, p. 2.
6 Board of Education, *Report for the Year 1908–9* (HMSO, 1909), pp. 31–2.
7 R.J. Alexander, *Primary Teaching* (London, 1984), p. 14.
8 Central Advisory Council for Education (England), *Children and Their Primary Schools* (HMSO, 1967).
9 See, for example, N. Bennett, *Teaching Styles and Pupil Progress* (London, 1976) and B. Simon and J. Willcocks (eds), *Research and Practice in the Primary Classroom* (London, 1981).

Acknowledgements

It is a pleasure to record our thanks to the librarian and staff of the following for their help and for permission to consult the sources listed.

Institute of Education, London, back issues of the journal of the School Nature Study Union and other SNSU material, together with some Schools Council material.

King's College London, archival material from the Nuffield Junior Science Project (prefixed JSP) and some sources relating to the work of the Schools Council (prefixed SC or C).

Public Record Office, Kew, evidence and correspondence relating to the Hadow Report on the Primary School, 1931.

University of Leeds, Brotherton Library, minute books and other papers relating to the Association of Public School Science Masters, the Science Masters' Association, the Association of Women Science Teachers and the Association for Science Education; papers relating to the School Nature Study Union and the School Natural Science Society.

University of Leeds Archives, examination papers for the Teachers' Certificate in the interwar years.

We are also indebted to the following who generously gave of their time and allowed themselves to be interviewed about their involvement in a number of primary science curriculum initiatives: Wynne Harlen, Roy Richards, Ron Wastnedge and John Williams. The tapes of the interviews are held by the authors. We have drawn upon these interviews at several places in this book, notably in Chapter 4. We hope that we have done so in ways that do justice to the interviewees' recollection of the events with which they were closely involved and to their subsequent judgement of them.

Acknowledgements

In writing Chapter 2, we are grateful to Taylor and Francis for permission to draw upon material relating to the Hadow report of 1931 which appeared in a paper by one of us (BJS), published in *History of Education*, 1996, Volume 25, No. 1, pp. 73–90.

Several of our colleagues or former colleagues at the University of Leeds have offered advice and comments on drafts of various parts of the text or made helpful suggestions about source material. We would wish to acknowledge particularly the advice of Professor Peter Gosden, Professor David Layton and Professor Anne Edwards. Phil Sheffield, Manager of the British Education Index, and Nicola Rathbone, Librarian in the School of Education, have been courteous and unfailing sources of bibliographic help.

Finally, our thanks go to the School of Education for funds which have made possible our collaboration in writing this book.

List of tables

List of figures

1

The nineteenth century background

Despite the striking contemporary achievements in science, engineering and the industrial arts, the evidence suggests that science was almost totally absent from the curriculum of the 15,000 or so public elementary schools which existed in England and Wales in 1851. The object teaching promoted in the 1830s by Charles and Elizabeth Mayo at Epsom and Cheam[1] and dedicated to promoting the 'faculty of observation' among young children might have formed the basis of an elementary education in science grounded in experience rather than words. However, the relationship envisaged by the Mayos between 'object teaching' and scientific education was not always understood and, for many young children, object lessons became a sterile experience, with the work sometimes all too easily subverted to the cause of moral education or religious improvement. Nonetheless, the work of the Mayos in England and, in Scotland of David Stow,[2] was important in seeking to relate the scientific education of young children to the realities and experiences of their everyday world.

The attempts made in the 1850s to establish the teaching of science in elementary schools, notably by Richard Dawes, J.S. Henslow and Henry Moseley, have been well described by Layton.[3] In particular, he has characterised the movement for teaching 'the science of common things' and explored why, despite substantial initial progress, the fate of the movement was decided as early as July 1856. The reasons for the eventual failure of this movement are complex, but important among them are the lack of a cohesive view among the individuals seeking to promote the teaching of the science of common things, the opposition of a number of influential scientists to the teaching of 'applied science' within general elementary education, and a rejection of the community-related curriculum upon which the movement rested.

Robert Lowe's Revised Code of 1862, with its emphasis on the teaching of reading, writing and arithmetic, effectively excluded science, along with other subjects, from the curriculum of the public elementary school until subsequent revisions of that Code permitted change. In 1867, government grants were offered, on the result of individual examination of pupils, to schools which introduced a three-year course of instruction extending over Standards IV, V and VI in one or two so-called 'specific subjects' (for example, geography, grammar, history) which could be taught in addition to the compulsory '3 Rs'. In the Code of 1871, the list of specific subjects was extended to include algebra, geometry, natural philosophy, physical geography, the natural sciences, political economy and languages, together with any other subject approved by HMI. In the passage referring to these specific subjects, the following two sentences are of interest in the light of later developments.[4]

> It is not improbable that new plans may be proposed by which children may be enabled to gain scientific ideas from the study of natural objects and from careful direction of their power of observation. Such plans would necessarily differ in town and country, and the suitability of each to the school in which it is adopted must be a matter of discretion.

Table 1.1 summarises the entries in a number of specific subjects between 1872 and 1898.[5]

In 1875, the curriculum of public elementary schools was reorganised[6] to provide for *elementary/obligatory subjects* (reading, writing and arithmetic, together with needlework for girls), *class subjects* and *specific subjects*. The class subjects, if taught at all, had to be taught throughout the schools above Standard I, and not more than two might be taken at the same time. The specific subjects could be taught to individual pupils in Standards IV to VI, provided that no child offered more than two of them for examination. The specific subjects were listed in 1875 as Algebra, Euclid, Mensuration, Latin, French, German, Mechanics, Animal Physiology, Physical Geography, Botany and Domestic Economy (for girls). Five years later, the list of class subjects was expanded beyond the original four (Grammar, Geography, History and Plain Needlework) to include 'any others that can be reasonably accepted as special branches of elementary instruction and properly treated in reading books'. In 1882, the list of class subjects was further amended to include English (Literature and Grammar) and Physical Geography, together with a new subject called 'Elementary Science'. This last was defined as a 'progressive course of simple lessons' on selected topics, adapted to 'cultivate habits of exact observation, statement and reasoning'. The Code also extended the list of specific subjects to include Chemistry, Principles of Agriculture, Sound, Light and Heat, and Magnetism and Electricity.

TABLE 1.1 NUMBER OF DAY SCHOLARS PRESENTED IN THE VARIOUS SCIENTIFIC SUBJECTS 1872–98

Year ending 31 August	Geography	English Literature	Physical Geography	Algebra	Euclid	Mensuration	Mechanics	Animal Physiology	Botany	Chemistry	Sound, Light and Heat	Magnetism & Electricity
1872	59,774	11,085	1,036	2,884	17	33	–	901	–	9	8	
1873	61,361	19,817	658	3,681	–	53	–	725	–	14	70	
1874	62,070	26,881	1,088	4,653	77	89	37	660	45	41	115	
1875	68,451	39,211	2,087	5,913	78	28	–	966	58	26	11	
1876	47,200	34,931	8,553		5,860		299	5,936	483	27	20	
1877	–	44,790	18,936		3,806		584	13,032	913	–	–	
1878	–	58,966	23,126		3,820		884	15,866	928	–	–	
1879	–	80,137	29,459		5,253		1,621	20,506	1,332	–	–	
1880	–	113,193	34,288		5,628		2,109	24,725	1,853	–	–	
1881	–	127,313	34,382		6,174		2,458	25,866	1,903	–	–	
1882	–	140,772	34,207		6,422		3,933	27,683	2,149	–	–	
1883	–	109,485	22,521	8,236	4,750	604	4,136	29,027	2,672	368	196	1,133
1884	–	–	–	24,787		2,010	3,380	22,857	2,604	1,047	1,253	3,244
1885	–	–	–	25,347		1,269	3,766	20,869	2,415	1,095	1,231	2,864
1886	–	–	–	25,393		1,247	4,972	18,523	1,992	1,158	1,334	2,951
1887	–	–	–	25,103		995	6,348	17,338	1,589	1,488	1,158	2,250
1888	–	–	–	26,448		1,006	7,292	16,940	1,598	1,808	978	1,977
1889	–	–	–	27,465		928	9,651	15,893	1,944	1,531	1,076	1,669
1890	–	–	–	30,035		977	11,662	15,842	1,830	2,007	1,183	2,293
1891	–	–	–	31,349	870	1,489	15,559	15,050	2,115	1,847	1,085	2,554
1892	–	–	–	28,542	927	2,802	18,000	13,622	1,845	1,935	1,163	2,338
1893	–	–	–	31,487	1,279	3,762	20,023	14,060	1,968	2,387	1,168	2,181
1894	–	–	–	33,612	1,399	4,018	21,532	15,271	2,052	3,043	1,175	3,040
1895	–	–	–	38,327	1,468	5,614	23,806	17,003	2,483	3,850	914	3,198
1896	–	–	–	41,846	1,584	6,859	24,956	18,284	2,996	4,822	937	3,168
1897	–	–	–	47,225	2,059	8,619	26,110	19,989	3,377	5,545	1,040	3,431
1898	–	–	–	53,081	2,471	10,828	27,009	22,877	4,031	6,978	1,155	3,905

The scheme of work in Elementary Science in the 1882 Code[7] was different from that originally envisaged, largely as a result of pressure from the British Association for the Advancement of Science which, from 1879 until the end of the century, monitored the position of science in the public elementary schools and kept a careful watch on the Annual Code and its effects. The Association had been particularly concerned that the elementary work in science did not articulate with the more specialised specific courses in the science subjects taken by some of the older pupils. Not surprisingly, therefore, the Association broadly welcomed the provisions of the 1882 Code.

The active interest of the British Association in elementary education in the 1880s paralleled its initiative in the 1860s in encouraging debate about the form and content of scientific education in the public schools. The immediate origin of this earlier debate lay with a paper presented to the Biology Section of the Association at its Annual Meeting in Nottingham in 1866 by the Reverend F.W. Farrar, the author of *Eric, or Little by Little* and a teacher of classics at Harrow who had been elected to Fellowship of the Royal Society in the same year. At Farrar's initiative and with the support of Thomas Huxley, the British Association set up a committee of scientists and public school science teachers which presented its report to the Annual Meeting held in Dundee in 1867. The report, entitled *On the Best Means of Promoting Scientific Education in Schools*,[8] was widely circulated and publicised, and proved an important point of reference for advocates of scientific education for at least half a century. One element of the case presented by the British Association for teaching science deserves particular mention, namely the distinction drawn between scientific *information* and scientific *training*, that is, between general 'literary acquaintance' with scientific facts and the knowledge of scientific methods that may be gained by studying those facts at first hand under the guidance of a competent science teacher. While both of these aspects were recognised as important, the principal benefit of a scientific education was never in doubt. It was identified as the 'scientific habit of mind', and justified as 'of incalculable value, whatever ... the pursuits of after life'. The distinction drawn in the Report between 'content' and 'process' and the relative importance to be ascribed to these two aspects of scientific education provide a useful framework for the discussion of the practice and rationale of school science education down to the present day.

It is not difficult to understand why, in the 1880s, those within the British Association with an interest in science education focused their attention upon elementary schooling. Forster's Education Act had led to the building of large numbers of elementary schools, and in some parts of the country, notably in London and the larger cities, enterprising School Boards were seeking to provide for the education of pupils who wished to continue their education beyond about 12 years of age. These initiatives were soon to lead to the setting up of a number of Higher Grade Schools, earning grants under the Elementary School Code and supplementing their income by entering small numbers of older pupils for the examinations conducted by the Department of Science and Art. Some of these Higher Grade Schools incorporated an 'Organised Science School' and several functioned as secondary schools in all but name, providing a post-elementary education, sometimes of a high quality, for the children of parents drawn principally from an emerging lower middle class.[9] The report of the Devonshire Commission on *Scientific Instruction and the Advancement of Science* published in several volumes[10] between 1872 and 1875 had recommended that older pupils in elementary schools be taught more science than the Code of 1871 allowed and had put forward a variety of suggestions for the training, recognition and payment of qualified science teachers. The Samuelson Commission[11] on *Technical Instruction*, reporting between 1882 and 1884, recommended more object lessons in schools and more teaching of science in the training colleges. The Cross Commission[12] specifically concerned with elementary education, produced a deeply divided report in 1888 but, by this time, the British Association had initiated a number of activities which were to have a significant, if ultimately transient, influence on elementary school science education.

Central to these initiatives were the biologist, Thomas Huxley,[13] and the chemists, John Hall Gladstone[14] and Henry Edward Armstrong.[15] As a member of the London School Board, Huxley pressed strongly for the introduction of elementary science into the curriculum of those schools for which the Board was responsible. Frustrated by the limitations of the Elementary School Code in the 1870s, he encouraged the use of the examinations and grants of the Department of Science and Art to promote the scientific education of senior pupils in elementary schools. Although he resigned from the London School Board in 1872, Huxley's connections with the Department of Science and Art enabled him to exert a powerful influence on the work of the schools, particularly in London. The case of physiography is a striking practical example. In 1876, it was realised that some pupils were earning grants twice by being successfully examined in physical geography under the provisions of both the Science and Art Department and the Elementary School Code. Accordingly, in 1877, a distinction was introduced by the government between physical geography as a grant-earning element of the Code and a more broadly conceived subject, physiography, to be examined exclusively by the Department of Science and Art.[16] Huxley's response was to augment a series of lectures he had given in 1869–70 on the 'Thames and its Basin' and publish these as a book entitled *Physiography*. The book[17] was a major publishing success and the numbers of papers examined in physiography rose from 4,958 in 1879 to 21,408 20 years later to become, over that period, the second most popular subject funded by the Department of Science and Art.[18] It should, however, be noted that the Department's syllabus in physiography was not drawn up by Huxley but by Lockyer,[19] and that Huxley's own book was soon followed by a variety of competing volumes. It should also be noted that Huxley's motive in campaigning for the teaching of science 'as part of the day's work' within elementary education reflected his concern to advance the cause of science itself. As he advised his fellow members of the Devonshire Commission in June 1870, 'the great object' was to 'construct such a scheme as should enable you to sift out, and to get hold of, the men (*sic*) who have real scientific ability'. Such a scheme, argued Huxley, would also meet the additional responsibility placed upon mass scientific education of raising the level of technical competence of those leaving school.[20]

John Hall Gladstone, a former student of Liebig and a man of independent means, was elected to the London School Board in 1873, effectively as Huxley's successor. He remained a member of the Board until 1894. In 1878, when the upper standards in the elementary schools were beginning to fill, Gladstone persuaded the Board to issue a detailed science syllabus. This dealt with Object Lessons in the lower Standards and with Elementary Science derived from the specific subjects of the Elementary Code in the upper Standards, augmented for individual pupils at the top of the school by the specialised subjects examined by the Department of Science and Art. The success of Gladstone's attempt to provide a degree of curriculum coherence was inevitably limited by the complex system of funding of individual subjects based upon payment by results and involving two separate government departments. Nonetheless, it was an important initiative and one which, when adopted across a larger number of subjects, provided the financial basis of Higher Grade Education until the Cockerton judgement of 1900. It is interesting to note that almost the only specific science subject taught in the London elementary schools was Animal Physiology, taught entirely by lecturing with the aid of a few diagrams. In 1881, for example, 6,901 children took this subject, compared with 411 in Botany and 51 in Mechanics.[21] In at least some schools, this may have owed less to any benefits that may have accrued to the pupil from the study of animal physiology than to an estimation of the income that might accrue to the school from the pupil's success in the relevant examination. One HMI commented[22] as follows:

> I wish that I could think that the choice of a specific subject was more often determined by a special fitness for teaching, or any special aptitude for learning it. It is too much regarded as a possible streamlet from the Parliamentary milch-cow, towards which the teacher is guided by an intelligent forecast of its grant-earning capacity. Having established the probable advantage ... the boys are set to work upon diagrams of the human skeleton, or illustrations of the phases of the moon, upon a calculation of their *remunerative*, rather than their scientific and educational value.

Under Gladstone's influence, the London School Board forwarded a Memorial to the Education Department in 1881, urging a number of changes which were accepted and introduced in the Code of 1882. However, the class subject of Elementary Science, introduced in 1882, had little immediate impact on the work of the public elementary schools in London and, almost certainly, elsewhere in England and Wales. The Code allowed a maximum of two class subjects to be taken and, of these, English was obligatory. The other class subject was almost invariably History, Geography or Needlework. When, prompted by Gladstone, the London School Board issued in 1882 a revised syllabus of 'Object Lessons in Elementary Science', only a few schools, denied the stimulus of a class subject in science, took up the subject. Gladstone was also responsible for introducing into the London schools an inexpensive box of simple science apparatus for teaching experimental physics and chemistry to the relatively small numbers of pupils involved.

To help its teachers incorporate experiments into their teaching, the London School Board followed the example of the Liverpool and Birmingham School Boards and appointed in 1885 a peripatetic demonstrator who carried apparatus from school to school and organised what would today be called short in-service courses in elementary chemistry and mechanics, the latter being directed towards helping teachers to teach the specific subject with this title.[23] The appointee, W.H. Grieve, worked in Tower Hamlets and Hackney, visiting each of 21 schools in a fortnight and conducting, on each occasion, a lecture demonstration which was observed by the class teacher. The class teacher then repeated the demonstration in between Grieve's visits. The Board's inspectors reported favourably on Grieve's work with his 2,090 pupils whose attendance improved significantly on 'science days'. Three additional demonstrators were appointed in the capital in 1887, although not without opposition from some of the more cost-conscious members of the Board, and their influence is indicated by a rise in the number of entries for examination in the specific subject of mechanics, from 174 in 1885 to 3,610 in 1890 and 12,652 in 1898, a year in which the chemistry entries reached 1,482 and Animal Physiology 5,650.

Gladstone was also particularly active within the British Association for the Advancement of Science. He was responsible for setting up a Committee under the auspices of Section F, Economic Science and Statistics, a section of the Association not unused to receiving papers on educational subjects. When Henry Armstrong wrote to Gladstone suggesting that science teaching should be discussed within Section F, Gladstone replied that the reports of his elementary school committee provided ample opportunity to do so. One outcome of the exchange between Gladstone and Armstrong was the co-option of the latter onto the former's committee.[24] Despite persuading the British Association in 1887 to establish a committee to enquire into the teaching of chemistry in a variety of types of schools, Armstrong was characteristically impatient and he undertook to produce some suggestions for a course of elementary instruction in physical science. These suggestions were presented to the Newcastle Meeting of the Association in 1889 and subsequently incorporated in Armstrong's book,[25] *The Teaching of Scientific Method and Other Papers on Education*, published in 1903.

Like Gladstone and many other chemists of his generation, Armstrong had studied in Germany. His experience of working in Kolbe's laboratory in Leipzig was an important formative influence, both in helping Armstrong to undertake significant research in organic chemistry and in encouraging him to follow Kolbe in adopting a critical stance towards scientific theorising. He also shared with Kolbe a sharp tongue and a readiness to challenge the orthodox views of those in positions of authority. In the present context, however, the most important legacy of Armstrong's time in Leipzig was his conviction that education in science depended fundamentally upon the skilful use of laboratory teaching to find out for oneself. He initiated his campaign to establish science teaching along heuristic lines in a lecture delivered to an International Conference on Education held at South Kensington in 1884. As a Fellow of the Royal Society, Secretary of the Chemical Society and, in the following year, President of the Chemistry Section of the British Association for the Advancement of Science, Armstrong had a wide range of professional contacts and was able to exert considerable influence. He used the Association as a platform for his developing ideas, presenting the Newcastle meeting with the suggestions for a course of instruction in elementary physical science, referred to above. For Armstrong, chemistry, as usually taught, lost much of its educational value because pupils were told, more often than not, that 'such and such *is* the case', instead of being taught *how it has been found out* that such is the case'.[26] It was Armstrong's distinctive achievement that he developed a clear role for the laboratory in the teaching of school science, derived from his own teaching experience and those who shared his views. His belief that good science teaching is essentially investigative and concerned to promote 'scientific method' is a legacy which was to endure to find explicit expression in the first Attainment Target of the version of the national curriculum introduced in England and Wales in 1991. His 'British Association course' began with lessons on common and familiar objects and were followed by 'lessons in measurement'. The third stage involved investigating the effect of heat on a number of common materials so that 'pupils may see that profound changes take place on burning substances and that these changes involve something more than the destruction of the things burnt'. These three stages laid the foundations for a further three which Armstrong referred to as 'chemical studies proper' and identified as the problem and quantitative stages, and studies involving the molecular and atomic theories and their application.

From 1890 onwards, Armstrong engaged in most of the activities now associated with curriculum development, addressing meetings, writing articles for the educational press, conducting in-service courses for teachers and serving on numerous committees.[27] The Board of Education published,[28] as one of its *Special Reports on Educational Subjects*, his account of the 'Heuristic Method of Teaching or the Art of Making Children Discover Things for Themselves'. In 1903, Armstrong served as a member of a British Association Committee appointed to advise upon the 'course of experimental, observational and practical studies most suitable for elementary schools' and his influence, not least in the emphasis to be given to exact measurement, 'the basis of all true science' is clear in the syllabuses which the Committee eventually produced.[29]

The last decade of the nineteenth century was a period not without some promise for science education in public elementary schools. Armstrong's campaign to introduce his heuristic method was meeting with some success, a small nucleus of teachers had been trained, mainly in London, and some advertisements for teaching appointments even specified that a knowledge of the 'Armstrong method' was desirable or essential. In addition, the Code of 1890 introduced further changes in the wake of the Cross Commission on Elementary Education which had reported in 1886. In specifying the essential subjects of the elementary school curriculum, the Commissioners had included lessons on common objects in the lower Standards, leading up to a knowledge of elementary science in the higher standards. Accordingly, in the 1890 Code, the Regulation making English compulsory if any class subject were taken was relaxed, and a number of alternative courses in Elementary Science were introduced.[30] Taken together, these changes led to a significant increase in the amount of time given to science in the curricula of some public elementary schools.

However, even after the 1890 Code, which identified science as a subject to be developed,[31] there remained several factors which severely limited the scope of science teaching in the elementary school. The poor scientific background of teachers, together with a lack of suitable equipment, meant that science was, in the main, limited to the study of common objects, and 'completely lacked purpose and system', especially for younger children.[32] Nonetheless, science teaching had expanded, from 51 departments of English elementary schools in 1884 to 1,396 by 1895 (Table 1.2).[33]

The 1890 Code also removed a number of other restrictions on the elementary school curriculum and, by 1897, both the individual examination of pupils and the system of payment by results had been abandoned. Furthermore, in 1896, Elementary Science was made compulsory,[34] although it is likely that this was taught, for the most part, by simple object lessons. In 1898, the last year which allows straightforward comparison with earlier data, Elementary Science was taught as a class subject in 2,143 'departments', compared with 17,049 for geography, 5,780 for history and 13,456 for English. Even so, as Table 1.3 indicates, there had been a considerable growth in the teaching of elementary science in the public elementary schools during the last decade of the nineteenth century. Table 1.4 records[35] a similar growth in the number of day pupils presented for examination in specific subjects during the same period, and indicates that the rate of increase in the number qualifying for grants in respect of these subjects was particularly marked after 1897.

It is convenient to examine in a little more detail the position of elementary science in 1899, the last year in which the Committee of the Privy Council on Education was responsible for elementary education in England and Wales. Elementary Science remained in the list of approved class subjects and several alternative schemes of work were available. In each case, the instruction of the first three Standards was

TABLE 1.2 NUMBER OF DEPARTMENTS TEACHING THE VARIOUS CLASS SUBJECTS

Year ending 31 August	English	Geography	History	Elementary Science	Needlework (for girls only)	Domestic Economy (for girls only)	Welsh	Object lessons
1884	19,080	12,775	382	51	5,929	–	–	–
1885	19,431	12,336	386	45	6,499	–	–	–
1886	19,688	12,055	375	43	6,809	–	–	–
1887	19,917	12,035	383	39	7,137	–	–	–
1888	20,041	12,058	390	36	7,424	–	–	–
1889	20,151	12,171	386	36	7,620	–	–	–
1890	20,304	12,367	414	32	7,758	–	–	–
1891	19,835	12,806	750	173	8,026	–	–	–
1892	18,175	13,485	1,627	788	7,655	–	–	–
1893	17,394	14,256	2,209	1,073	7,612	–	–	–
1894	17,030	15,250	2,972	1,215	7,675	–	1	–
1895	16,272	15,702	3,597	1,396	7,396	316	8	–
1896	15,327	16,171	4,143	2,237	7,219	471	–	1,079
1897	14,286	16,656	5,133	2,617	7,397	633	–	8,321
1898	13,456	17,049	5,780	2,143	7,252	784	–	21,882
1899	13,194	17,872	5,879	21,301	6,952	866	–	–
1900	12,993	18,632	5,338	19,998	6,396	981	–	–

TABLE 1.3 NUMBER OF DEPARTMENTS IN DAY ELEMENTARY SCHOOLS IN WHICH ELEMENTARY SCIENCE WAS TAUGHT AS A CLASS SUBJECT, 1890–1900

Year	Number of departments in which Elementary Science was taught
1890	32
1891	173
1892	788
1893	1,073
1894	1,215
1895	1,396
1896	2,237
1897	2,617
1898	2,143
1899	(21,301)*
1900	(19,998)

* It is not possible to compare these figures with those for earlier years. The marked increase is explained by alterations to the Elementary Code in 1895, 1896 and 1898. For details see Board of Education, *Report for the year 1900–1*, Vol. 2, p. 468.

TABLE 1.4 NUMBER OF SCHOLARS PRESENTED IN SPECIFIC SUBJECTS UNDER THE ELEMENTARY CODE, 1890–1900

Year	Animal Physiology	Botany	Chemistry	Sound, Light and Heat	Magnetism & Electricity
1890	15,842	1,830	2,007	1,183	2,293
1891	15,050	2,115	1,847	1,085	2,554
1892	13,622	1,845	1,935	1,163	2,338
1893	14,060	1,968	2,387	1,168	2,181
1894	15,271	2,052	3,043	1,175	3,040
1895	17,003	2,483	3,850	914	3,198
1896	18,284	2,996	4,822	937	3,168
1897	19,989	3,377	5,545	1,040	3,431
1898	22,877	4,031	6,978	1,155	3,905
1899	41,244	8,833	14,737	1,943	7,697
1900	36,810	8,905	13,557	1,730	7,026

to be based on object lessons, although the Committee of Council advised that the teaching in general should be 'mainly by experiment and illustration' rather than by 'definition and verbal description'.[36] To encourage such teaching, Her Majesty's Inspectorate was required to examine pupils in Elementary Science in a manner likely to elicit from them, 'as far as possible in their own language', the ideas they had formed of what they had seen. Further insight into the object lessons taught to the younger pupils attending public elementary schools is available from the large numbers of books offering advice to elementary school teachers on how to organise this aspect of their work. The writing of Louisa Walker, headmistress of Hampstead Board School in London, is typical of its genre. Her book,[37] likened by an HMI to a 'good bag of tools' from which a pupil teacher 'could always pick out a lesson' suitable to his or her needs, catalogued a large number of objects from 'apple' to 'zinc', each of which formed the basis of a standardised lesson. Every lesson was divided into three sections, qualities named and described, uses, and sources, and each was prefaced by a clear statement of aims coupled with a list of the apparatus required. In some instances, facts were woven 'together in rhyme' in order to help pupils retain the necessary information. The following extract from the object lesson on 'cork' illustrates the procedure.[38]

> Shew a large piece of cork. Ask what it is (a piece of cork). Where do we find bark? (On trees). On what part of trees? (On the stem). Teacher to shew the stem of a tree on which the bark still remains. Tell the children the bark before them is from the cork oak and is called 'cork bark'. Repeat together 'Cork is the bark of a small oak tree' Write on blackboard, etc.

The versified mnemonic began thus:

> *Teacher*:
> This cork which I hold is part of a tree
> *Which* part? and where found, on mountain or sea?
> From whence and for what? How, why and wherefore
> Was this beautiful substance first brought to our shore ?
>
> *Children*:
> Cork is the *bark* of a little oak tree,
> Which grows on the shores of a very blue sea.

The contribution of the Board of Education to the teaching of object lessons was published as an Appendix to the 1901 Regulations for Elementary Schools. The lessons were divided into seven categories, covering plant life, animal life, the sky, object lessons for town schools and for country schools, the science of common things, and measuring, weighing and testing. Elementary school teachers were invited to select topics other than those listed in the Appendix but such selection was subject to approval by the Inspectorate. The following extracts indicate the kind of work encouraged officially at this time.[39]

Sunrise, noon and sunset (Note the object over which the sun is seen to rise from month to month. Note sun's position at noon and its varying height above the horizon).
Mole – shape, snout, teeth, paws, claws, eyes, ears, fur, food.
Volcanic rocks, lava, brimstone, pumice stone, basalt or whinstone (According to the nature of the district).
Measurements of length – first by eye, then with rule.

As far as the Board of Education was concerned, object lessons were to be distinguished from instruction in natural science, the former constituting elementary science only in so far as they helped pupils 'to observe some of the facts of nature upon which Natural Science depended'.[40] It is clear from the reports of HMI that this distinction was not always appreciated by elementary school teachers and that many of the topics suggested by the Board could be taught adequately only by those with a sound knowledge and understanding of scientific principles.

The quality of the work done in object lessons varied widely. Some very good object lessons were given in the best elementary schools, but many were clearly inadequate and often seriously so. The interests of the pupils were often ignored and the sequence of lessons often lacked coherence. For Armstrong,[41] the conventional object lesson in 1902 provided a model of 'what should be avoided' and, by 1908, the British Association judged[42] that the object lesson had often deteriorated to become little more than a 'laborious elucidation of the obvious'. Lowndes has described some of the objects used. 'In the case of urban schools or the remoter rural schools a bird's nest full of assorted eggs was usually the *pièce de resistance*, but stuffed dogs and even alligators were not unknown'.[43] H.G. Wells described an equally bizarre variety of 'sealing-wax and silkworms and potato-bugs and ginger and iron and such-like things'.[44]

In 1899, specific subjects, such as Chemistry, Mechanics, Animal Physiology and Botany, were taken only by small numbers of the older pupils attending public elementary schools. It was possible for a school to submit its own scheme of work for approval in this category but there is no evidence that schools did so in significant numbers. As in earlier Codes, the Code for 1899 specified the rate of grant to be paid for each of the various components of the public elementary school curriculum, for example, one shilling or sixpence for specific subjects, and one or two shillings for class subjects.[45] The relevant syllabuses were elaborated in a series of Schedules to the various Codes and these are exemplified for a class and some specific subjects in Figures 1.1 and 1.2 respectively.

FIGURE 1.1 SCHEME OF WORK IN ELEMENTARY SCIENCE, A CLASS SUBJECT UNDER ARTICLE 101(E) OF THE ELEMENTARY CODE, 1898

	Standard I	Standard II	Standard III
Elementary Science (Scheme A)	Thirty object lessons on the chief tribes of animals and their habits, on common plants and their growth, and on common inorganic substances and their properties.		
or			
Elementary Science (Scheme B)	Thirty lessons on common objects, *e.g.*: A postage stamp; the post; money; a lead pencil; a railway train. Foods and clothing materials, such as bread, milk, cotton, wool. Minerals; natural phenomena, such as gold, coal, the day, the year.	Thirty lessons on common objects, such as animals, plants, and substances employed in ordinary life, *e.g.*: Horse, Leaves, Sparrow, Candles, Roots, Soap, Stems, Cork, Buds, Paper.	Simple principles of classification of plants and animals. Substances used in the arts and manufactures. Phenomena of the earth and atmosphere.

Standard IV	Standard V	Standard VI	Standard VII
Simple mechanical laws in their application to common life and industries. Pressure of liquids and gases.	Simple chemical laws in their application to common life and industries.	Outlines of physiology in its bearing on health and work.	Familiar illustrations of applied science: *e.g.* the dwelling; fabrics and clothing; food; warming; lighting, etc.
A more advanced knowledge of special groups of common objects, such as: (a) Animals, or plants, with particular reference to agriculture; *or* (b) Substances employed in arts and manufactures; *or* (c) Some simple kinds of physical and mechanical appliances: *e.g.* the thermometer, barometer, lever, pulley, wheel and axle, spirit level.	(a) Animal or plant life; *or* (b) the principles and processes involved in one of the chief industries of England; *or* (c) The physical and mechanical principles involved in the construction of some common instruments, and of some simple forms of industrial machinery.	(a) Animal and plant life; *or* (b) The commonest elements and their compounds; *or* (c) The mechanical powers.	(a) Distribution of plants and animals, and of the races of mankind; *or* (b) Properties of common gases; *or* (c) Sound, or light, or heat, or electricity, with applications.

FIGURE 1.2 SCHEME OF WORK IN SPECIFIC SCIENCE SUBJECTS,* UNDER ARTICLE 101(F) OF THE ELEMENTARY CODE, 1898

	Mechanics	Animal Physiology	Botany	Principles of Agriculture	Chemistry
1st stage	Matter in three states; solids, liquids, and gases. The mechanical properties peculiar to each state. Matter is porous, compressible, elastic. Measurement as practised by the mechanic. Measures of length, time, velocity, and space.	The build of the human body. Names and positions of the internal organs. The properties of muscle.	Characters of the root, stem, leaves and parts of the flower. Illustrated by specimen of common flowering plants.	The principles influencing the supply of plant food in the soil, and necessity for cultivation, and the circumstances making tillage more or less effective.	Elementary and compound matter, illustrations of combination and decomposition in such bodies as hydrochloric acid, water, oxide of mercury, and rust of iron.
2nd stage	Matter in motion. The weight of a body, its inertia and momentum. Measures of force and work.	The mechanism of the principal movements of the limbs and of the body as a whole. The organs and functions of alimentation, circulation, and respiration. The use and abuse of foods and drinks.	Structure of wood, bark, and pith. Cells and vessels. Food of plants and manner in which a plant grows. Functions of the root, leaves, and different parts of the flower.	The principles regulating the more or less perfect supply of plant food; manures as supplemental sources of plant food.	Preparation and properties of the common gases, such as oxygen, hydrogen, nitrogen and chlorine. The chemical character and constituents of pure air, and pure water and the nature of the impurities sometimes found in both. Effects of plants and animals on air.
3rd stage	The simple mechanical powers, viz., (1) the lever; (2) the wheel and axle; (3) pulleys; (4) the inclined plane; (5) the wedge; (6) the screw. Liquid pressure; the hydrostatic press; liquids under the action of gravity. The parallelogram of velocities. The parallelogram of forces. Examples commonly met with illustrating the mechanical powers. N.B. – *Instruction in this subject should be purely descriptive and experimental.*	The general arrangements of the nervous system. The properties of nerve. Reflex action. Sensation. The organs and functions of touch, taste, smell, hearing, and sight. N.B. – *Instruction in this subject should be illustrated by diagrams or models only.*	The comparison of a fern and a thorn with a flowering plant. The formation of different kinds of fruits. The structure of a bean and of a grain of wheat or barley. The phenomena of germination.	The principles regulating the growth of crops, and the variations in their yield and quality.	The properties of carbon and its chief inorganic compounds. Differences between metallic bodies. Combination by weight and volume. The use of symbols and chemical formulae.

	Physics			
	Sound, Light, and Heat	Magnetism and Electricity	Elementary Physics and Chemistry	Domestic Economy (Girls)
1st stage	The three modes in which heat may be conveyed from place to place. Effects of heat on solids, liquids, and gases. Expansion by heat. The thermometer. Latent heat. Elementary notions of specific heat. Heat produced by mechanical, chemical, and vital action.	Attraction, repulsion and polarity, as illustrated by the magnet. Terrestrial magnetism, and the mariner's compass.	Properties of common stuffs: relative density of solids and liquids: flotation of solids. The barometer and thermometer; their use; graphic representation of daily readings. Solution. Water as a solvent: solubility of metals, etc., in acids: crystallisation of salt, soda, alum.	Food: its composition and nutritive value. Clothing and washing.
2nd stage	Sources and propagation of light. Intensity, shadows, shadow photometer. Reflection, mirrors. Refraction, lenses. Elementary explanation of the microscope, camera obscura, and magic lantern. Dispersion, prisms. The rainbow. Reflecting and refracting telescopes.	Attraction of light bodies by rubbed sealing wax and glass. Experimental proof that there are two forms of electricity. Attraction and repulsion. Gold-leaf electroscope. Construction of electrophorus, electrical machine, and Leyden jar. Explanation of atmospheric electricity.	Evaporation and distillation: heat absorbed in fusion of ice and in conversion of water into steam: density of ice; change in density of water on heating: moisture in air: wet and dry bulb thermometer. Study of iron rusting and of combustion of candle, gas, oil, phosphorus: effect on metals of heating in air: discovery of active constituent of air.	Food: its functions. The dwelling: warming, cleaning and ventilation.
3rd stage	Propagation of sound. Elementary notions of vibrations and waves. Reflection of sound echoes. Musical notes, simple instruments. Simple explanation of beats and nodes.	Voltaic or chemical electricity. The voltraic battery and notions of a current. Chemical effect of a current. Electrolysis. Magnetic effect of a current. Galvanometer. Induced currents. Electro-magnets. The electric telegraph.	Chalk and lime: the burning of chalk or limestone: action of muriatic acid on chalk or limestone: carbonic acid: reformation of chalk. Discovery of carbonic acid in air: its formation by combustion of carbonaceous materials and in respiration. Study of action of muriatic and vitriolic acids on zinc; combustion of the gas obtained and discovery of the composition of water. Presence of air and solids dissolved in water: sea-water; hardness of water.	Food: its preparation and culinary treatment. Rules for health; the management of a sick room.

* The three stages of 'such of these subjects as admit of it' could be taken in any order.

In 1900, the elaborate system whereby different grants had been paid for different parts of the curriculum was replaced by an average attendance grant and the tripartite classification of the curriculum abolished. The latter was reduced to a two-fold division between subjects taught 'as a rule' in all public elementary schools, although not necessarily to all classes, and a second group to be taught when, 'in the opinion of the Inspector', circumstances made this desirable. Science was represented in the first group only by a reference to 'lessons, including object lessons, on ... common things'. It was accommodated in the second group as the former specific subjects, although no additional grant was now of course payable for teaching them. Unfortunately, a change in the way that the official statistics were presented prevents a direct comparison of the position of individual science subjects in the public elementary schools shortly before and after 1900. The difference is essentially between the numbers of 'departments' on the one hand and of pupils on the other. In 1898–99, 2,876 'departments' prepared pupils for examination in specific subjects. Of those pupils presented, 'nearly 70 per cent' were examined in algebra, mechanics, animal physiology and domestic economy. Recognising that some candidates entered for the maximum of two specific subjects and that some 'departments' taught more than one specific subject, an approximate figure of 500 may be conjectured for the number of public elementary schools which taught specific science subjects, other than those mentioned, in 1898. This, tentatively, may be compared[46] with the 574 'departments' in which science was taught in 1902.

In 1903, the newly-established Board of Education issued[47] a provisional Code of Regulations for public elementary schools to cover a period which was essentially transitional in character since a number of schools were still managed by School Boards which had not yet given way to the local education authorities being set up following the passage of the 1902 Education Act. In the following year, the distinction between subjects commonly taught in all public elementary schools and those taught in appropriate circumstances was abolished and the 1904 Code 'attempted to exhibit, without undue elaboration, the course of instruction as a connected and coherent whole'.[48] While allowing for local variation, public elementary schools were expected to provide a 'graduated course of instruction, suitable to the age and capacity of the scholar', in English Language, arithmetic, geography, history, drawing, singing, physical exercises, plain needlework for girls and 'knowledge of the common phenomena of the external world'. In the Regulations[49] for 1905, this last component of the elementary school curriculum was replaced by 'Observation Lessons and Nature Study' which, ideally, were to be taught with special reference to the surroundings of the pupils and to the natural features, industries and plant life of the locality, with the view of forming 'the habit of intelligent and accurate observation'. Further advice was offered in the Board of Education's *Suggestions to teachers and others concerned in the work of Public Elementary Schools*, also published[50] in 1905.

In the opinion of the Board, the 1904 Regulations introduced no 'important changes of substance' into the Elementary School Code and the Prefatory Memorandum advised against any far-reaching and sudden change in the instruction given in the schools.[51] The introductory statement about the purpose of the public elementary school, written by Robert Morant, the Permanent Secretary to the Board, was widely regarded by his contemporaries as 'excellent'[52] and described by his biographer[53] as 'ennobling'. Several historians have brought a harsher judgement to bear, seeing his 1904 Code as providing an elementary education which amounted[54] to the 'training in followership, rather than leadership' which he deemed suited to the majority of the population, particularly the working class. Their formal education was, in almost all cases, to be confined to an elementary school throughout the next forty years.[55]

As for the promise of Armstrong's investigative course of elementary physical science, it is clear that by the end of the century, heurism was already under attack. There were a number of factors which contributed to the decline of heuristic teaching, if not of the commitment to 'finding out' as an essential feature of school science education. These were the undermining of faculty psychology, principally by Herbartian ideas, an increased scepticism of the validity of the transfer of training accepted by Armstrong and a growing awareness of the limitations of the teaching of 'scientific method' as an educational objective.

Although the doctrine of phrenology was largely discredited by Armstrong's day, a faculty psychology was used widely to legitimise the aims, methods and content of school curricula. This is not to imply that such curricula were determined logically by the ideas of a faculty psychology or that practising teachers were much concerned with faculty psychology as a dominant theory of learning. It does mean, however, that Armstrong, like many of his contemporary 'new' educationists, was obliged to argue his case in terms of a faculty psychology which was widely accepted and generally understood. Heuristic methods 'trained the faculties of thoughtfulness and power of seeing: accuracy of thought, of word and deed'.[56] As a practical educationist, arguing for the teaching of experimental science, Armstrong claimed that these faculties could be developed only if pupils were made to reason for themselves. He therefore carefully distinguished scientific facts from scientific method, a distinction with antecedents not only in the British Association Report of 1867 but also in the writings of the secular educationist and phrenologist, George Combe.[57]

By the end of the nineteenth century, the philosophy of science which underpinned Armstrong's heurism was also encountering serious difficulty, although it is unlikely that the issues involved engaged the attention of the teachers themselves. Acknowledging his intellectual debt to the ideas of Herbert Spencer and T.H. Huxley, Armstrong saw scientific method as the methodical, logical use of systematised knowledge. It was 'a game' which could be learned and in which 'trumps' were rarely turned up and 'low cards prevailed'.[58] Moreover, scientific method could be applied to a wide range of human endeavour, a view shared by many at the end of the nineteenth century, notably by W.K.Clifford and Karl Pearson. The title of Clifford's book, *The Common Sense of the Exact Sciences* is sufficient indication of a claim, elaborated by Pearson in his own volume, *The Grammar of Science*, published seven years later in 1892.

> The scientific method ... is not peculiar to one class of phenomena and to one class of workers ... the material of science is co-extensive with the whole life, physical and mental of the Universe.[59]

Although these claims for the nature of science and its 'methods' were to linger, the notion of science as 'organised common sense' was already untenable by the early twentieth century. The fundamental obscurity of the apparently simple foundations of Newtonian mechanics was exposed by Mach and Hertz. Einstein's Theory of Relativity raised the important question of how science could claim to progress by accumulating knowledge if major advances required the destruction of previously held theories. The conception of science implicit in heurism could not account for developments such as thermodynamics or quantum theory, any more than it could accommodate Newton's assertion that a body is at rest only because there are forces acting upon it or Galileo's rape of the senses in advocating a heliocentric universe. As the concepts and imagery of science were seen to be removed further and further from 'common sense', it became increasingly difficult to argue convincingly that pupils must be put in the position of an original discoverer and to maintain that science owed its achievements to a 'game' whose rules could be learnt and applied.

Within the first few years of the twentieth century, School Boards were abolished and their responsibility for public elementary education handed over to the newly-created local education authorities working, not always harmoniously, with the Board of Education. Public elementary schools, freed from the cumbersome funding arrangements that had for so long governed and distorted their work, were encouraged to consider their curriculum as a coherent whole. In doing so, they were inevitably both prisoners of their subject teaching past and of the pressures of the contemporary present which sought, often in beguiling and ultimately unhelpful language, to assert the importance of activity, imagination, organic growth and natural development unconstrained by subject boundaries or the formality of a rigid timetable. These and other tensions were to be evident in the rhetoric and work associated with elementary and, later, primary schools throughout the twentieth century. They were to be entangled with the spurious contrast of teaching children and not subjects, with debates about class and group teaching, and with such notions as child-centred and progressive education. More particularly, the alliance of science as investigation/discovery with discovery methods of teaching was to become a noteworthy element of the case for developing the primary science curriculum in the 1960s.

As far as science in public elementary schools is concerned, the legislative and administrative initiatives of central government between 1899 and 1904, broader social concerns about matters as diverse as moral welfare and the ongoing drift from the land to the towns, and more practical matters relating to accommodation, facilities[60] and teacher competence,[61] all helped to ensure that this component of the curriculum found no more substantial expression than object teaching and nature study in the Code of 1904. Such expression seemed able to accommodate the concerns of both the naturalists in education and those who still sought to encourage investigative teaching and promote children's powers to observe and record accurately. These concerns and the nature of their accommodation receive particular attention in the next three chapters.

NOTES

1 For an indication of the Mayos' work, see F. Smith, *A History of English Elementary Education* (London, 1931), 128–30 and H.M. Pollard, *Pioneers of Popular Education 1760–1850* (London, 1956).

2 F. Smith, op. cit., 98–102.
3 D. Layton, *Science for the People. The origins of the school science curriculum in England* (London, 1973).
4 Committee of Council on Education, *Minute Establishing a New Code of Regulations*, PP 1871, LV, 293–312.
5 The figures are taken from the Report of the Committee of Council on Education for each of the years in question.
6 Committee of Council on Education, *New Code of Regulations for Elementary Schools*, PP 1875, LVIII, 1–36.
7 Committee of Council on Education, *Minute Establishing a New Code of Regulations*, PP 1882, XXIII, 111–44.
8 British Association for the Advancement of Science (hereafter BAAS), *Report of the (Dundee) Meeting 1867* (London, 1868).
9 For an account of the work of some Higher Grade Schools, see *Royal Commission on Secondary Education, Report, Volume III*, PP 1895, XLVIII, 1 *et seq*.
10 Royal Commission on Scientific Instruction and the Advancement of Science, *Report*, 1872–5 (London, HMSO). The sixth report, 1875, deals with schools. Together with the seventh and eighth reports it appears in PP 1875, XXVIII, 59–473.
11 Royal Commission on Technical Instruction, *First Report*, PP 1882, XXVII, 401 *et seq*.
12 Royal Commission appointed to inquire into the Elementary Education Acts, *Final Report*, PP 1888, XXXV, 1 *et seq*.
13 For Huxley, see C. Bibby, *T.H. Huxley, Scientist, Humanist and Educator* (New York, 1960) and A. Desmond, *Huxley: The Devil's Disciple* (London, 1994) and *Huxley: Evolution's High Priest* (London, 1997).
14 D. Coleman, *The Life and Work of John Hall Gladstone (1827–1902) with particular reference to his contribution to elementary science education at the London School Board*, Unpublished Ph.D. thesis, King's College London, 1991.
15 W.H. Brock, *H.E. Armstrong and the Teaching of Science 1880–1930* (Cambridge, 1973).
16 Physiography and Physical Geography, *Nature*, LXIII, 27 Dec. 1900, 207–8.
17 T.H. Huxley, *Physiography: An Introduction to the Study of Nature* (London, 1877).
18 H. Butterworth, *The Development and Influence of the Science and Art Department 1853–99*, Unpublished Ph.D. thesis, University of Sheffield, 1968. Table XIVA, based upon figures from the Annual Reports of the Department of Science and Art.
19 *Nature*, LXIII, 27 Dec. 1900.
20 Royal Commission on Scientific Instruction and the Advancement of Science, *Report, Volume 1*, PP (1872), pp. 53–60.
21 *The Final Report of the School Board for London, 1870–1904* (London, 1904), deals (102–22) with object lessons and science in the Board's schools.
22 PP (1888), XXXVIII, p. 122, quoted in M. Waring, 'To make the mind strong, rather than to make it full' : 'Elementary School Science Teaching in London 1870–1904'. In I. Goodson (ed.), *Social Histories of the Secondary Curriculum: Subjects for Study* (London, 1985), 121–44.
23 M. Waring, op. cit., 126–9 and *Final Report of the School Board for London 1870–1904*, 104.
24 W.H. Brock, op. cit., 22–3.
25 H.E. Armstrong, *The Teaching of Scientific Method and Other Papers on Education* (London, 1903). Arthur Smithells, reviewing the book for *Nature* (LXIX, 1903, 289) noted a 'want of system and co-ordination' in the volume and expressed his regret that Armstrong had not 'mixed the twenty-three outpourings and ... subjected the mixture to fractional distillation'.
26 H.E. Armstrong, 'Suggestions for a course of elementary instruction in Physical

Science'. In BAAS, *Report of the (Newcastle) Meeting 1889* (London, 1980) and reproduced in part in W.H. Brock, op. cit., 90–8.

27 E.W. Jenkins, *From Armstrong to Nuffield. Studies in twentieth century science education in England and Wales* (London, 1979), 41–57.

28 Board of Education, *Special Reports on Educational Subjects*, Vol. 2 (London, HMSO, 1898) and reprinted in G. van Praagh (ed.), *H.E. Armstrong and Science Education* (London, 1973), 60–79.

29 BAAS, *Report of the Annual Meeting 1908* (London, 1909), 495–526.

30 Committee of Council on Education.

31 R.J.W. Selleck, *The New Education. The English Background, 1870–1914* (London, 1965), 123.

32 P. Uzzell, 'The changing aims of science teaching', *School Science Review*, 210, (Sept. 1978), 8–9.

33 R.J.W. Selleck, op. cit., 123.

34 P. Uzzell, op. cit., 9.

35 The figures in the Tables are taken from Committee of Council on Education, *Report 1898–99* (London, HMSO, 1899), Schedule II 574–5, Schedule IV 114–16 and Board of Education, *Report for the Year 1900–01* (London, HMSO), 468–9.

36 Committee of Council on Education, *Report 1898–9* (London, HMSO, 1898), 540 and 582–3.

37 L. Walker, *Cusack's Object Lessons* (London, 1895).

38 Ibid., Part II, 169, 172.

39 Board of Education, *Report for the Year 1900–01*, Vol. III (London, HMSO, 1902), 270–80.

40 Ibid. 268.

41 H.E. Armstrong, 'Training in Scientific Method as a Central Motive in Elementary Schools'. In G. van Praagh, op. cit., 104.

42 BAAS, *Report of the Annual Meeting 1908* (London, 1909), 503.

43 G.A.N. Lowndes, *The Silent Social Revolution* (London, 1937), 35.

44 Quoted in J. Lawson and H. Silver, *A Social History of Education in England* (London, 1973), 381.

45 Committee of Council on Education, *Report 1898–9*, 558–9.

46 Ibid. and Board of Education, *Report for the Year 1910–11* (London, HMSO, 1912), 20.

47 Board of Education, *Provisional Code of Regulations for Public Elementary Schools and Training Colleges with Schedules 1903* (London, HMSO, 1903).

48 Board of Education, *Code of Regulations for Public Elementary Schools with Schedules 1904* (London, HMSO, 1904), iv.

49 Board of Education, *Code of Regulations for Public Elementary Schools with Schedules 1905* (London, HMSO, 1905), chs 1, 2.

50 The function of the *Suggestions* was to 'spread as widely as possible a knowledge of the best that was being thought and done in the whole sphere of elementary education throughout the country'. Board of Education, *Report for the Year 1910–11* (London, HMSO, 1912).

51 Board of Education, op. cit., 1904, Prefatory Memorandum.

52 For example, *The Record of Secondary and Technical Education*, XIII, No. 55 (1904), 278.

53 B.M Allen, *Sir Robert Morant, A Great Public Servant* (London, 1934).

54 E. Eaglesham, *Foundations of Twentieth Century Education* (London, 1967), 52.

55 Ibid. and C. Birchenough, *History of Elementary Education in England and Wales from 1800 to the Present Day* (London, 1938).

56 H.E. Armstrong, op. cit. (1903), 196.

57 Combe's distinction was between *positive* instruction and *instrumental* instruction. For Combe's educational ideas, see W. Jolly, *Education: its Principles and Practice as*

Developed by George Combe (London, 1879). For a biography, see C. Gibbon, *The Life of George Combe* (London, 2 volumes, 1878).

58 F.H. Hayward, *Day and Evening Schools* (London, 1910), 211–12.

59 H.E. Armstrong, *The Heuristic Method etc.*, reproduced in van Praagh, op. cit., 68.

60 E.W. Jenkins, op. cit., ch. 4.

61 D.M. Turner, *A History of Science Teaching in England* (London, 1927).

2

Authorising child-centred education

The Primary School was the title of the second of three reports prepared by the Consultative Committee of the Board of Education, under the chairmanship of Sir Henry Hadow.[1] Published in 1931, it presented radical recommendations for the reorganisation and reform of elementary education in England. The terms of reference for this second Hadow study were

> To inquire and report as to the course of study suitable for children (other than children in Infants' Departments) up to the age of 11 in Elementary Schools with special reference to the needs of children in rural areas,[2]

and part of its remit was to carry out

> an enquiry conducted with reference to the specific part to be played by the primary schools in shaping and fostering the life of a people under modern economic and social conditions.[3]

Although the eventual report was replete with contradictions and tensions, the deliberations of the Hadow Committee were strongly coloured by progressive educational views and its recommendations came to be seen as an official endorsement of a child-centred approach to the education of young children. In particular, the frequently-quoted assertion that the curriculum of the primary school should henceforth be thought of in terms of 'activity and experience, rather than of knowledge to be acquired and facts to be stored' was a direct challenge to the subject-based formalism of traditional elementary schooling. A commitment to 'activity and experience' permeated the entire report and translating this commitment into professional practice became the responsibility of primary school teachers, and those who trained them, for at least the next half century. This chapter examines the forces that shaped the Hadow recommendations and traces the development of radical ideas from a position marginal to official educational policy prior to the First World War to one of influence less than twenty years later.

It is appropriate to begin by examining how the Consultative Committee came to inquire into education for children up to 11 with a particular emphasis on rural education.

THE CONCERN OVER RURAL EDUCATION

Historians have traditionally viewed the relationship between the official educational establishment and its committees, such as the Consultative Committee of the Board of Education, as one of master and servant. However, an alternative interpretation regards the educational arena as made up of various and competing interests, and presents the formulation of educational policy as the outcome of struggles between them.[4] According to Brehony, the Board's Consultative Committee, although in part intended to be a vehicle whereby different knowledge and experience could be utilised in determining educational policy, was actually a means of giving various educational interests the impression of meaningful rather than real engagement with the process of policy formation.[5] Established in 1900, the Consultative Committee contained representatives, appointed by the President of the Board of Education and drawn from all stages of education from primary school to the university. It was to be 'independent of the Board but to act as an advisory body which would study problems set by the President and report directly to him'.[6] The selection rather than the election of members of the Committee, allied with an advisory function, ensured that power always remained with the Board of Education. However, the relative strength and position of the Consultative Committee *vis-à-vis* the Board increased, after Lord Irwin, President of the latter in March 1923, granted the Committee authority to identify issues for investigation and suggest these and appropriate terms of reference to the Board.[7] From this time onwards, although only intermittently, members of the Consultative Committee were invited to make suggestions as to future areas of inquiry. In 1926, a comprehensive list was suggested, including among others a proposal that the Committee '... consider and report upon the organisation and curriculum of courses and study for children attending public elementary schools up to the age of eleven'.[8] The Board's reaction to this suggestion was predictably cautious, recognising that it would

> not only raise very wide issues all of which are under constant discussion, but issues involving administrative problems of organisation with which the Consultative Committee have little

> capacity to deal involving as they do political and religious difficulties.[9]

The Board also had its own preference for the next area of investigation, namely, rural education.

> I feel rather strongly that the moment is opportune for considering this problem and would coincide very conveniently with our thoughts on the training of teachers for the country districts. It seems to me a subject which would arouse public interests and one in which the present Government is peculiarly interested.[10]

Although the Consultative Committee had gained the right to make suggestions, there was, of course, no entailed guarantee that any suggestion would be accepted by the Board of Education. However, while the Board could not simply dictate to the Consultative Committee, neither could it completely ignore its wishes. The decision that the second Hadow Committee should inquire into the education of pupils up to the age of 11, but with an emphasis on rural education, was, therefore, a compromise that achieved the Board's aim of getting rural education put on the agenda whilst still allowing the Committee to have one of its suggestions accepted. It was also an outcome that lends some support to McCulloch's view that educational policy-making is better understood as an arena of conflicting interests struggling for supremacy, rather than as an exercise of authority by the state on behalf of the ruling class.[11]

The Board's insistence that particular reference be made to the needs of children in rural areas[12] reflected an official concern for rural education that was far from new. However, the raising of the school leaving age to 14 in 1918 had exacerbated the difficulties facing rural education, where small schools, often with only one teacher, and a lack of equipment and facilities, made streaming impossible, and the provision of more advanced teaching for older children required pupils to travel to larger schools in urban or semi-urban areas.[13] It was inevitable, therefore, that, in such schools, children of widely different abilities would have to be grouped together, which made teaching particularly difficult.[14] These difficulties were made even more acute by the fact that many of the teachers in small rural schools were untrained, so that where skilled teachers were especially needed they were all too often conspicuous by their absence.

The continuing exodus of the rural population to the towns, the influence of urban values on the countryside through widening and expanding systems of communication and transport, and the contrary movement of prosperous members of the urban population into the countryside, were long-standing matters of official concern.[15] The amount of land used for arable purposes and wheat production both declined in the inter-war period and the proportion of the country's food produced domestically fell to 39.3 per cent between 1924 and 1928. In Mowat's estimation, 'In the thirties this caused a new stirring of conscience over the nation's use of its land and its treatment of its farms and farmers.'[16] The proportion of the population of England and Wales living in rural areas halved between 1851 and 1901, and the relative decline of the rural population continued up to 1931, but at a slower rate. Although in real terms the rural population actually increased in the period 1911 to 1931,[17] there was still concern about the undermining of rural life by urban influences. While education did not cause these changes, it was seen as both a contributory factor and a potential mitigating influence. An added and particular difficulty was presented by the 1921 Education Act, which advocated the establishment of Central Schools, situated in towns and cities but recruiting pupils from surrounding rural areas.[18]

To counteract this urban influence, an increased emphasis was placed on giving education in rural areas a rural bias.[19] The official assumption was that if rural children were given a more practical and rural-based education, then this might lead to a greater understanding of rural needs and help stem the drift from the land to the towns and cities. In 1925, the Board of Education emphasised in a Circular to schools that rural children should not be diverted from rural occupations, claiming that 'It would be a misfortune if the bringing of country children into the towns for their schooling should involve any such result.' The same Circular suggested that rural education be investigated.[20] Three years later, in a pamphlet entitled *The New Prospect in Education*, the Board devoted a section to the problems of education in rural areas.[21] The types of responses from witnesses to the Board's Consultative Committee also reveal the extent of concern about the rural problem. The National Council of the Evangelical Free Churches noted that rural education should encourage rural pupils to remain in the countryside and should contribute to the improvement of country life.[22] E.G. Davies, the Headteacher of a school in Suffolk, hoped for the same role for rural education, although he doubted its effectiveness.

> In these days of overcrowded towns, and depleted villages, one should welcome every honest attempt to solve this very difficult

> problem of adapting the educational curriculum to the needs of the child, and to foster a natural love for the beauties of the countryside, but one fears that the spirit of adventure in some cases, and the urge of economic necessity in others, will be strong enough to counteract the influences of a 'rural' curriculum as expounded by 'rural' teachers.[23]

The problems faced by rural schools were summed up by a teacher in the following terms.

> Let the Consultative Committee demand from the Board for rural children the same opportunities for learning as are given to town children: let them have the same modern building: let them have the same amount of modern equipment: let them have the same qualified staff: let them be organised so that only one class (containing children of equal ability and attainment) is taught by one teacher: and there will be no need to consider a curriculum with special reference to rural schools.[24]

It was these concerns that led the Board to insist on rural education as an explicit element of the terms of reference of the inquiry to be conducted by its Consultative Committee.

CREATING THE PRIMARY SCHOOL

When, in 1922, the Labour Party called for 'Secondary Education for All' with a division between the stages of education at the age of 11, the ensuing debate inevitably focused attention on the relationship between elementary and secondary education, a relationship which, during the nineteenth century, had been largely defined in terms of social class.[25] The Consultative Committee responded to the issues surrounding this debate by suggesting to the Board of Education that it should undertake an inquiry into secondary education. The outcome was an inquiry which began in 1924 and led to the publication, two years later, of the first Hadow report, entitled *The Education of the Adolescent*. This report shared the view that access to post-primary education should not be restricted to intellectually able pupils or those from wealthy families, but should be available to all children. This, in the Committee's judgement, required different forms of post-primary education,[26] a first step towards which was the reorganisation of large elementary schools into distinct junior and senior elementary departments.[27] As Gordon and Lawton have observed, 'this resulted in a readily identifiable primary school population'.[28] Given that the notion of the 'primary school' as a recognisable, distinct and autonomous institution was legitimised by the first Hadow report, it was to some degree inevitable that the Consultative Committee would need to turn its attention to its role *vis-à-vis* the new types of post-primary institution. As a reviewer of the 1931 report noted:

> It was necessary that the Consultative Committee should issue a Report which would be complementary to the previous Hadow Report.[29]

In other words, the recommendations in the 1926 report and the action taken to implement them created the need for some examination of primary education, as the 1931 report itself acknowledged.

> ... the formal adoption of the primary school as an autonomous unit in the educational system renders necessary a fresh inquiry into the question what should be taught to children between the ages of seven and eleven.[30]

The implication in the 1931 report that primary education was autonomous, when in reality it was inextricably linked with, and to a large extent subordinate to, post-primary education and, in particular the grammar schools, coloured the whole of the 1931 report and created many of the tensions and contradictions that the inquiry ultimately failed to acknowledge and/or resolve. Persuaded by informal views about both the curriculum and organisation of primary education, the Committee retained the view that the purpose of primary education was to be a 'foundation' for post-primary education. This in essence was the view of the Board of Education which, in 1928, had re-emphasised that the function of the Junior School was

> to prepare children for the more diversified development of the senior stage, that is to give them a mastery of the tools and elements of instruction, and to enliven and open their minds and interests for the more complex courses of the post-primary stage ...[31]

This raised questions about the relative importance of the 3 Rs in the curriculum and whether, for older children in particular, there should be a gradual move towards the use of more formal methods to prepare for post-primary education. These questions were compounded by the system of Free Place Examinations, introduced in 1907, whereby a relatively small number of pupils aged 11 were selected for admission to grant-maintained secondary schools. When the Consultative Committee came to discuss the role and work of the primary school, its discussion was, therefore, always going to be coloured by the relationships between primary and post-primary schooling, and, in particular, by the demands of the free place and scholarship examinations taken by pupils at about the age of eleven.[32]

One of the obstacles to adopting an informal, child-centred approach in the primary school was the existence of a working environment designed to facilitate whole-class, formal methods of teaching. English public elementary school education in the early twentieth century was still very much a product of the assumptions and restricting influences which had been present in the nineteenth century. The system of payment by results, the introduction of which has been called 'one of the most retrograde steps ever taken in English education',[33] gave grants to schools according to the number of pupils who passed annual examinations in each standard in the 3 Rs,[34] and it ensured the predominance of these subjects, often narrowly conceived, within the curriculum. Although this system had been abolished in 1895, and replaced by a block grant, and some liberalisation of the curriculum followed the Regulations of 1904, the emphasis in the education of young children was still placed on the 3 Rs, sometimes almost exclusively so and to the comparative neglect of other subjects. Writing in 1911, Edmond Holmes, a former Senior Chief Inspector of Schools, offered a damning account of elementary education in a widely read and seminal book, *What is and What Might Be*. The 'might be' of the title is elaborated by Holmes in an account of 'good practice' thought to be based on teaching that he had observed in a school in Sussex, where children 'were offered that free and joyful schooling which he believed was their due'.[35] He claimed elementary education was still based on 'mechanical obedience', whereby pupils were taught rules to be learnt by rote, with the aim of passing examinations.[36] The timetable remained split into distinct separate subjects and classes were divided into standards I to VII, appropriate to a child's age, although pupils progressed through these standards according to attainment.[37] Furthermore, classes were large and were made up of children in different standards, often under one teacher. Lowndes has remarked that photographs of elementary school activities from this period often show an entire class, which could be as many as 70 or 80 children of all ages, doing exactly the same thing.[38] Under these conditions of mass education, formal teaching methods, rigid discipline and an emphasis on the recall of knowledge were almost inevitable. Individual or group work would have been all but impossible in schools built to accommodate the formal and didactic teaching of large classes of pupils.[39] Rows of desks in small, dark, often airless classrooms, designed for rote learning, where children listened and observed but rarely participated, in schools situated in the middle of industrial areas, were the norm. The National Union of Teachers (NUT), in its evidence to the Consultative Committee, pointed out that 'the benefit of good teaching could not be fully felt without suitable buildings'.[40] The 1931 report recognised this problem, commenting that

> the question of school buildings and of the size of the classes that may suitably be accommodated in them is inseparably bound up with the problem of the curriculum and methods of study for children at the primary stage, since group and individual work and modern methods of teaching can be applied only with difficulty in old-fashioned and unsuitable buildings.[41]

Not surprisingly, therefore, the 1931 Hadow report recommended that, where new schools were being built, they should have spacious, airy classrooms and be located on open and sunny sites. Wherever possible, existing schools were to be modified. However, the reality of the interwar school building programme, which was drastically affected by the National Government's restrictions on public expenditure after 1931, was that priority was given to post-primary forms of education, with the majority of new buildings being constructed for pupils over the age of 11.[42] In addition, 'Hadow reorganisation', as recommended in the 1926 report, was almost brought to a standstill, with some local authorities not yet having started, and others halting their programmes and leaving some of their schools on the former system and the remainder restructured to provide for primary and various forms of post-primary education. As late as 1938, 78 per cent of rural schools remained un-reorganised as all-age schools,[43] and even in several urban areas, typically with a significant number of denominational schools, the percentage of reorganised all-age schools often fell below 50. Likewise, significant progress in the use of child-centred methods in primary education, as advocated in the 1931 report, had to wait until after the Second World War when, despite enduring financial difficulties, large numbers of new and suitably-designed primary schools, catering for classes of more modest size and constructed to reflect the new 'primary philosophy', could be built.

CHILD-CENTRED AND PROGRESSIVE EDUCATION

Although *The Primary School* emphasised both a 'child-centred' and a 'progressive' approach, neither term appears in the published report of the Consultative Committee. In Selleck's judgement the idea of 'progressive education' emerged '... out of the confusing mixture of theories and beliefs and practices which was the "New Education"'.[44] These theories and practices and their influence upon primary education in England and Wales are considered in Chapter 6. It will be sufficient to note here, therefore, that the educational 'progressives' were a far from homogeneous group who occasionally gave the impression of being united by little more than their opposition to the authoritarian role of the teacher in traditional elementary schools. In broad terms, however, progressive educationists emphasised 'freedom' (for both the teacher and the pupil) and stressed the importance of the individual in the educative process. This led them to argue for flexibility (in the timetable and curriculum) and to value informality in all respects, including the teaching approach, the timetable, the curriculum, and the relationships between pupils and their teachers. Particular significance was attached to 'active learning' by the child, an idea perhaps best appreciated in contradistinction to the rote learning to which progressive educationists were so strongly opposed. Although agreement about how best to translate the various strands of educational progressivism into professional practice often proved elusive, the years following the end of the First World War saw a growth of interest in progressive ideas and the establishment of a number of experimental schools based upon progressive principles (see Chapter 6). Those principles were elaborated in T.P. Nunn's *Education: Its Data and First Principles*, a book which, following its publication in 1920, quickly established itself as a 'textbook for the progressives'.[45]

The Consultative Committee received evidence from hundreds of witnesses[46] who can be classified under a number of categories; teachers and teachers' organisations, training college lecturers, members of His Majesty's Inspectorate, rural-based organisations, educational pressure groups, local authorities, the labour movement, and individuals. However, since there was no hard and fast 'progressive' line, many of these witnesses cannot be equally readily categorised as progressive or traditional. At one end there were organisations such as the New Education Fellowship which proposed quite radical and far-reaching changes, and at the other, moderate teachers proposing very little change, or, in one or two cases, none at all.

Most of the witnesses, however, showed that they had some sympathy, although to different degrees, with 'progressive' ideas and these are much in evidence in the eventual report. Thus,

> Up to the age of eleven, the school subjects and their presentation should be kept closely related to the children's concrete knowledge and their own immediate experience.[47]
>
> ... no good can come from teaching children things that have no immediate value for them...[48]

and the aim of primary education should be

> to develop in a child the fundamental human powers and to awaken him to the fundamental interests of civilized life so far as these powers and interests lie within the compass of childhood...[49]

The application of this child-centred philosophy to primary schools contrasted sharply with the earlier policy of drilling pupils in the 3 Rs, with its scant regard for pupils' individual needs, and it is captured in the following, perhaps best known and most frequently quoted, extract from the report,

> ... the curriculum of the primary school is to be thought of in terms of activity and experience, rather than of knowledge to be acquired and facts to be stored.[50]

The key words in this phrase, 'activity' and 'experience', were expected to permeate the whole of the curriculum.

> We desire to see the child an active agent in his early schooling, making his approach to the activities necessary for an understanding of the body of human civilisation and for an active participation in its process, through his own experiences and his own activities, and relating his growing knowledge at all points to the world in which he lives.[51]

Although the evidence of a number of witnesses advocated a child-centred approach, none used this specific term. However, there is no mistaking the sentiment in many of the submissions to the Committee, of which the following extract from the evidence submitted by the National Union of Agricultural Workers may be taken as representative.

> We do not think that the child should be regarded as a receptacle to be crammed with facts, but rather as a personality to be developed to the full ...[52]
>
> We are most strongly convinced that the education of the child up to the age of 11 should be directed towards the development of what is in him and the encouragement of his interest in and curiosity concerning the world in which he lives.[53]

The evidence given by the Joint Committee of the Welsh Branches of the Incorporated Association of Assistant Masters in Secondary Schools identified the diminished importance of subject matter in primary education, an issue which was to acquire particular significance in the debate about progressivism in education which followed the publication of the so-called Black papers over thirty years later.

> The ideal and method of education are of greater importance than the content at this stage. We desire to see the child's self activity developed so that he may at the same time acquire the power and the habit of self-control and of independence of thought.[54]

For Ellen Healey, giving evidence in an individual capacity, the child was the beginning or the centre of any educational scheme[55] and Miss E.J. Cook, headteacher of a girls' school, claimed that the child's interests must occupy the most prominent place.[56]

It was these interests and the prominent place to be accorded to them that served to characterise the primary school as a distinct form of educational provision. In the words of the 1931 report, the defining criterion of primary education

> must above all be the requirements of its pupils during the years when they are in its charge, not the exigencies of examinations or the demands of the schools and occupations which they will eventually enter.[57]

In thus detaching the primary curriculum from a range of external considerations, including employment and examinations, the 1931 report stands in marked contrast to its predecessor, published five years earlier and concerned with the education of the adolescent. Here, the argument had been that the curriculum of post-primary schools should have a marked practical bias appropriate to the occupations that pupils would later take up.[58]

Accommodating and responding to children's interests within primary education had profound implications for the work of primary schools, and these were indicated in many of the submissions of evidence to the Committee. An integrated, rather than a subject-based timetable was widely favoured and, ultimately, received some support in the published report.

> The traditional practice of dividing the matter of primary instruction into separate 'subjects' taught in distinct lessons, should be reconsidered. The treatment of a series of central topics which have relations with many subjects, may be a useful alternative.[59]

Devising schemes of work which 'followed' children's interests required flexibility in the planning of topics to be covered and in the use of the time available within the school day. In its evidence, the National Union of Women Teachers claimed that in the Junior school, there was 'little need to systematise knowledge and still less to departmentalise it under the names of separate subjects'.[60] For the National Union of Teachers (NUT),

> No better indication of improving method could be provided than the growing elasticity of the school timetable.[61]

For many witnesses, this elasticity in the timetable was further justified on the grounds that, in the primary school, it was appropriate to make pupils aware of the interrelation of subjects,[62] and, as far as possible, to perceive knowledge 'as a whole'.[63]

It would be a mistake, however, to overlook some of the reservations about progressive education offered in evidence to the Consultative Committee. When the Committee's report was published, a reviewer claimed that

> The point of view of the Report in its examination of the problems of primary education is consistently that of the teacher...[64]

However, while the Committee may well have considered the problems that teachers were facing, its eventual advocacy of a child-centred approach can hardly be said to have reflected their views. Only one teacher out of twenty advocated such an approach,[65] in contrast with half the training college lecturers and all the witnesses associated with the labour movement. Interestingly, there seemed to be no explicit support for progressive educational ideas from the members of His Majesty's Inspectorate. Mr. T. Caden, a headteacher, was particularly critical of the emerging new methods, claiming that

> There is no doubt that the pupil, taught by what are called the new and intellectual methods, often leaves school with a pitiful store of exact knowledge and with little power of sustained thought.[66]

Interestingly, not least in the light of more recent controversies, almost all those who sought reform along progressive lines remained firmly committed to the teaching of the 3 Rs and recognised the need for some drill to master them. This was true even for the most radical witnesses, such as the Bradford Independent Labour Party (ILP) which encouraged activity in the Junior School and, in particular, recommended the use of the Playway method. While also advocating teacher freedom, a flexible and integrated timetable, and a child-centred approach, the ILP acknowledged that some 'fixed drilling' of pupils in writing, reading and arithmetic was necessary, as long as this did not last for long periods.[67] The Hadow report concurred with this view, acknowledging that while pupils' attainments in reading, writing and arithmetic could be improved while studying other elements of the primary curriculum, it was 'essential that provision ... be made for an adequate amount of "drill" in these subjects'.[68] There is, however, something of a tension between the Committee's claim that primary education should not be a preparation for the schooling that followed, and its commitment to ensuring that pupils reached a sufficiently high standard in the 3 Rs to allow them to take full advantage of later stages of education.

Some of the evidence submitted to the Consultative Committee advocated specific methods of teaching and classroom organisation as a progressive approach to promoting pupils' learning. The Education Section of the British Psychological Society suggested the adoption of the Dalton Plan for older junior school children, as did the Workers' Educational Association.[69] The Dalton Plan, first introduced at Dalton High School in Massachusetts in 1920 by Helen Parkhurst, abandoned the traditional timetable in favour of a programme of assignments split into sections, each to be completed by the child in a specified amount of time.[70] In suggesting the use of 'Playway', the Bradford ILP claimed that 'Play elicits the maximum activity, not only in immediate intensity, but draws the whole nature into the field of stimulation.'[71] The Playway method was introduced by Caldwell Cook in a book published in 1917, which stressed the importance of a child's own interests and the promotion of activity, and argued that a child learns naturally through play.[72] The so-called 'Automatic' method, whereby children used apparatus and books to teach themselves, and could each proceed at his or her own pace, was advocated by the Auto-Education Institute and by Miss H.E. Wix, one of His Majesty's Inspectors of schools.[73]

However, the most popular of the progressive methods advocated was the so-called 'Project' method, in which projects were used as a starting point for problem-solving activities undertaken on a cross-curricular basis.

> Starting with 'projects' connected with the pupils' immediate surroundings their horizon can gradually be widened so that they will come to realise the relationship of the life around them to the lives of the people in their own and other countries ...[74]

The Hadow report stressed that the project method should be practised only in moderation, concluding that 'We are ... definitely of the opinion that it would be unnecessary and pedantic to attempt to throw the whole of teaching of the primary school into the project form.'[75] This firm view derived from the Committee's concern that such an excessive commitment to project work ran the risk of leaving inadequate time for the teaching of, and drill in, the 3 Rs, and opened up the possibility that a number of important areas of work might be neglected or even made the focus of inappropriate specialisation.[76] Ideally, any introduction of this new, project method, should be gradual and cautious, and as children got older, should give way to direct subject teaching.

> Although, therefore, we are of the opinion, subject to the foregoing qualifications, that the teaching of children in the primary schools should be increasingly informed by the principles of the project method, we do not wish to see that transformation from the more usual subject method undertaken with dangerous haste or where conditions are not favourable to its success.[77]

Although the Consultative Committee was sympathetic to the measured use of the 'project' method and encouraged cross-curricular work, it devoted 50 pages of its report to suggestions on the teaching of what it called the 'various branches' of the curriculum of primary schools.[78] The 'suggestions' for science were almost entirely confined to nature study, although some elementary work in astronomy, such as observation of the apparent movements of the sun, moon and a few stars, was seen as 'arising naturally in the introductory work to geography'.[79] The report made great play of the 'added significance' of nature study 'in the development of the country child', claiming that

> In rural areas where the home life of the children generally centres around outdoor pursuits and where contact with nature is intimate and many sided, nature study should lead to that breadth of outlook and grasp of essentials which raises the value and increases the dignity of rural occupations.[80]

It might, perhaps, be thought that the 'dignity of rural occupations' depended upon rather more than the teaching of nature study. In town and city schools, although such study was thought to be 'heavily handicapped' by the lack of suitable materials and the reduced opportunity for pupils to explore and venture on their own account, the Committee convinced itself that 'Much can be done'. There was also a recognition that, while nature study 'would form the main part of the work in science of the primary school', it 'should not be the whole of that work'.

> Physical facts play so large and obvious a part in modern life that they cannot be neglected entirely in the school, and even young children can properly be introduced to those outstanding facts which come within their everyday experience ... 'How it works' is a good practical guide for the teacher in all this early work. The lever in its practical uses, the magnet and the mariner's compass, the effect of heat on water – these are the kinds of topic which seem suitable in the primary stage. But no attempt should be made to build up an organised body of science at this stage; the aim should be to interest children in just those physical phenomena which they meet in their ordinary experience.[81]

With the questionable benefit of hindsight, the 1931 Hadow report arguably represents something of a lost opportunity to extend the scientific education of young children beyond that encompassed by nature study. In defence of the Committee, however, neither the professional scientific organisations nor the two associations concerned with science teaching in grammar schools submitted evidence to it, and the attention of those who did so was focused on matters other than the scientific education of young children.

PROGRESSIVISM AND THE STREAMING OF PUPILS

The 1931 Hadow report was heavily influenced by psychological evidence, and especially that of Cyril Burt (who had also given evidence to the Committee that had produced the 1926 report). His central tenet that intelligence was innate and that education had to be adapted to each child's inborn level of intelligence underpinned much of the Committee's conclusions. For Burt, 'Intelligence, in the technical sense, may be defined as inborn, general, intellectual ability.'[82] One consequence of this view was that as children became older, the greater became the differences in their intellectual capabilities. For example, children aged five had a mental age ranging from three to seven, giving a spread of four years. By the age of ten, the mental spread had doubled, and 'by the age of 12' had 'become so wide, that a still more radical classification is imperative'.[83] Burt concluded, therefore, that 'Before this age is reached children need to be grouped according to their capacity, not merely in separate classes or standards, but in separate types of schools.'[84] His views were accepted by the Committee, which concluded that 'In view of the varying attainments of children it is specially important that there should be small classes or groups',[85] and recommended the formal adoption of streaming.

> In general we agree with our psychological witnesses in thinking that in very large primary schools there might, wherever possible, be a triple track system of organisation, viz.: a series of 'A' classes or groups for the bright children, and a series of smaller 'C' classes or groups to include retarded children, both series being parallel to the ordinary series of 'B' classes or groups for the average children.[86]

Streaming had been introduced in the 1920s in response to the difficulties of teaching children of very different ages who had reached the same standard of achievement. Separating the more able children from the less able, and thereby assigning appropriately different work, allowed all children of the same age to progress together through the standards. The support by the Committee for streaming had a further purpose, since streaming was also viewed as one of the ways of solving the problems of large mixed-ability classes in rural schools. However, as Galton, Simon and Croll have pointed out, the principle of a child-centred approach and support for the streaming of pupils do not sit comfortably together.

> It may be thought that the concepts underlying the 'child-centred' approach, and those underlying streaming are contradictory, yet both were accepted by the Consultative Committee in the report on The Primary School ...[87]

The contradiction lies in the seeming impossibility of marrying ideas on innate intelligence and the consequent whole-class teaching of groups of pupils of similar ability, with the need to respond, in ways that are both active and flexible, to the educational needs of children on an individual basis. The Hadow Committee effectively denied this contradiction by arguing that streaming offered an effective and empirically-based means of accommodating the needs of individual pupils in ways that could command the support of progressive opinion. Given an acceptance of the 'mental characteristics of children between the ages of 7 and 11' (described by Burt in a Memorandum published as an appendix to the report), 'What was necessary was to provide an education appropriate to the child's inborn, and measurable, intelligence level.'[88] In beguilingly simple terms, progressive education required that each child be put in the stream which most suited his or her inborn intellectual capacity.[89] P.B. Ballard, a former Divisional Inspector under the London County Council and a witness before the Committee, claimed that classification by chronological age could result in dull pupils progressing prematurely and clever pupils being held back. In contrast, classification by mental age could result in a situation where a 12 year old and an eight year old, each with a mental age of ten, were grouped together, but with the likelihood that the younger child was the better scholar. Ballard, therefore, favoured classification by chronological age, but with sub-classification by ability, that is, streaming, as a means of overcoming these difficulties, claiming that only by divisions into groups or streams could a child receive an appropriate education.[90] For both Burt and Ballard the appropriate stream for a particular child was to be determined by the results of mental or intelligence tests.

THE PROBLEM OF SELECTION

The 1931 report accepted the need for testing at two stages; first, on transfer from the infant to the primary stage, at age seven, to determine the appropriate stream for a child, and second, at age 11 to determine the appropriate type of post-primary school. This acceptance of the need for formal assessment, especially at the end of the primary stage, was significant and it generated a number of tensions and contradictions within the report. Free place examinations were used to select pupils from public elementary schools to proceed to grant-maintained secondary schools under arrangements first introduced in 1907. Since the demand for free places usually exceeded the supply, the examination was a competition as well as an attempt to classify pupils on the basis of ability.

Although the 1931 report concluded that 'some qualifying examination or test'[91] would always be needed to classify pupils, witnesses to the Committee were very critical of the existing scholarship examination and, in particular, of its effect on the upper primary curriculum.

> ... as our schools are undoubtedly judged on these results, and we are expected by the Local Education Authorities to help to fill these Schools, one feels that the curriculum in the Senior classes of our Junior Schools must be based on this as an end in view.

In addition,

> External examinations lead to serious distortion of the syllabus of the examination subjects, and to cramming the children on the supposed lines of the examination requirements.[92]

Many of those who submitted evidence to the Hadow Committee referred to the rivalry between schools based on success in the free place or scholarship examinations,[93] to the neglect of other subjects in favour of those to be tested, namely English and Arithmetic,[94] to the danger of encouraging private coaching,[95] and to the problems of 'cramming'.[96] The Froebel Society warned of the danger of the Junior School becoming the forcing house for selective schools[97] and others drew attention to the way in which judging teachers on their pupils' success in the selection examination reinforced its influence on the primary school.[98] Another witness argued that this examination and its influence on the curriculum prevented the junior school becoming a place of equal opportunity according to individual ability.[99] For HMI Richardson, the Junior School would never get a fair chance until the Free Place examination was altered.[100] In practice, however, it was difficult to lessen the influence of this examination on the primary curriculum when, as G. Owen of the Nursery Schools Association explained,

> The award of a high number of free place scholarships was felt to be an honour to the school, ...[101]

All of the witnesses save one who mentioned this issue criticised some aspect of the free place examination (Mr. F.E. Amos, a headteacher, described the scholarship examination as an 'admirable test').[102] Nonetheless, there was agreement that some sort of selection procedure was necessary,[103] so that attention inevitably turned to procedures which could produce valid and reliable results. Various alternatives were suggested, including a written examination, group intelligence tests, oral tests, and the use of school records.[104]

The report, again heavily influenced by the psychological witnesses, and in agreement with earlier Board statements,[105] advocated the use of tests which would show capacity rather than attainment. This was due in part to the acceptance that academic attainment could be retarded by external social factors such as continued absence due to illness, or adverse home conditions.[106] Acknowledgment of the influence of external factors upon achievement also led the Committee to recommend that any 'classification of young children should be regarded as merely provisional, and should be subject to frequent revision'.[107] Such a recommendation is difficult to reconcile with the belief that intelligence was innate and fixed.

The relevant tests were, in almost all cases, confined to English and arithmetic.[108] While this was thought to distort the primary curriculum by encouraging an undue emphasis upon these two subjects, extending testing to other areas of the curriculum presented considerable problems. A joint report by the Association of Education Committees and the National Union of Teachers (1930) argued that the inclusion of other subjects was possible only at the expense of standardisation, since there was a wide variation in the work covered in such subjects as history and geography.[109] In contrast, some witnesses to the 1931 Committee supported the inclusion of other subjects to test such qualities as artistic ability. The Board of Education had discussed this issue at some length in an earlier pamphlet, and after considering widening the subject areas to be included in free place examinations, had concluded that the difficulty of differing syllabuses in subjects such as History and Geography 'can only be overcome by imposing a common syllabus in these subjects with the grave danger of stereotyping the teaching in these schools'.[110] Nonetheless, it was widely thought to be unfair to test pupils on such a narrow basis. The Head Masters and Head Mistresses of Secondary Schools claimed that

> Most Heads imply that the free-place scholar's knowledge of Arithmetic and English is out of all proportion to his knowledge of other subjects, and that there is evidence that these two subjects are worked up by 'drill' methods.[111]

Burt's position, however, was that 'Between the ages of 7 and 11 all intellectual activities appear closely correlated with one another.'[112] He claimed that children up to 11 rarely showed any special abilities, so that the results of properly constituted tests in English and arithmetic were a reliable index of a child's overall ability. Ballard also believed that it was sufficient to test in just two subjects, English and arithmetic, as long as they were in the form of intelligence tests rather than tests of attainment because

> it can be proved mathematically that there is a positive correlation between all forms of native ability; they always tend to hang together; the odds are always in favour of high ability in any given function being accompanied by high ability in any other function.[113]

The Hadow Committee, persuaded by the views of Burt and Ballard, concluded that 'carefully devised papers in English and arithmetic should be sufficient as a basic test of capacity and attainment for children at the age of eleven',[114] although it warned against relying exclusively upon group tests of intelligence. The experience gained in the next thirty or so years was to lead many to question this conclusion and to express growing concern over the effects of testing upon the work of the primary schools. As progressive ideas gained a more secure place in at least the rhetoric of primary schooling, so did the testing and classification of pupils become increasingly unacceptable.

CONCLUSION

The tensions and contradictions apparent in the 1931 report arise from the attempt by the Hadow Committee to promote progressive education in a context which, in many respects, was at odds with some of the central tenets of a progressive ideology. While an accommodation of sorts was reached over the issue of streaming, the selection of pupils for secondary education, usually by means of tests based exclusively upon English and arithmetic, distorted the work of primary schools and linked them, and their status, with the work of the grammar schools. In addition, many newly-designated primary schools were quite unsuited, in architectural and other ways, for the kinds of project work advocated by the Hadow Committee, and many of the teachers within them were not only unfamiliar with progressive ideas but, if the evidence to the Committee reflects wider opinion, somewhat opposed to them. In these circumstances, it is hardly surprising that

> While the 1931 report developed the idea of universal popular education of a new, broader, child-centred activity type, the actual emergence of a junior school on a mass scale, which only took place *after* the Second World War, coincided precisely with the crystallization of the school system as primarily a sorting, classifying, selective mechanism.[115]

The Hadow Committee sought to structure primary education in ways that would allow pupils to realise their full potential, irrespective of class, social background, or of educational capability, and to create a system of education for all, rather than for a particular social class, the attribute which had so tainted public elementary school education in the nineteenth century. In the Committee's view,

> primary schools must be considered as in principle common schools: that is, institutions provided not for a particular section of the population, however large, but for all who choose to take advantage of them and to use them as the normal approach to institutions for secondary education.[116]

The primary school as it appeared in its 1931 report, therefore, 'was to be a school for all social classes'.[117] In these respects the report was radical, announcing 'a new conception of schooling for young children which broke decisively with previous practice in the elementary schools'.[118] However, as long as the Committee and its witnesses accepted that there should be different types of post-primary education which preserved the status and authority of the grammar school, its stance was essentially traditional. In practice, its recommendations not only perpetuated but also strengthened the role of the primary school in selection for secondary education. In addition, despite the weight of evidence about the malign effect of testing, and testing on a narrow basis, upon the primary curriculum, such testing not only continued but gained greater influence upon the work of the primary schools.

For as long as these conditions prevailed, primary education could never develop in the progressive ways envisaged in the Hadow report. A child could not be assigned to the appropriate type of post-primary school without some sort of selection procedure, and if a selection procedure existed towards the end of the primary stage, teaching at this stage would inevitably involve preparing pupils to do well in the selection process based upon English and arithmetic. The selection results would continue to reflect on the quality of the school and its teachers, and the warnings expressed in the report, or by the various witnesses, would be to no avail.

Using language that evoked a rather different image in 1933 than it does today, Ramsbottom, the Parliamentary Secretary to the Board of Education, warned that

> to throw secondary education open to all and sundry would very likely be the reverse of an educational advance and might easily

be an educational regression; we might easily turn the nation into something like an educational soup-kitchen.[119]

That 'educational soup kitchen' was to emerge only after the Second World War and, more particularly with the advent of comprehensive secondary education following Circular 10/65. It is, therefore, no accident that progressive ideas in primary education came into their own in the later 1960s and received a ringing endorsement in the report of the Plowden Committee, *Children and their Primary Schools*, published in 1967.

As for the Hadow Committee's response to the issues surrounding rural education, it claimed that the differences between rural and urban schools were 'often exaggerated', and its report did little more than recommend some differentiation between the curriculum of urban and rural schools, and the preparation of teachers to use group and individual work to cope with the wide range of ability likely to be found within them. In addition, the assumption seems to have been that all-age schools would quickly disappear. However, since any reorganisation of all-age schools would have led to new forms of post-primary education, accompanied by selection procedures, it is difficult to see how such reorganisation could have addressed the problems of rural education in the terms defined by the Board of Education.

NOTES

1 The first of these reports was that of the Consultative Committee of the Board of Education, *The Education of the Adolescent* (1926), which considered secondary education, and the third Hadow report was the Board of Education Consultative Committee, *Report on Infant and Nursery Schools* (1933).
2 Board of Education Consultative Committee, *The Primary School* (London, HMSO, 1931), xii.
3 Ibid., 91.
4 G. McCulloch, '"Spens v. Norwood": contesting the educational state?', *History of Education*, 22, 2 (1993), 163–80.
5 K. Brehony, 'The "school masters' parliament": the origins and formation of the Consultative Committee of the Board of Education 1868–1916', *History of Education*, 23, 2 (1994), 171–93.
6 R.J.W. Selleck, 'The Hadow Report: A Study in Ambiguity', *Melbourne Studies in Education* (1972), 145,148–51.
7 PRO ED 24/1226 Unconfirmed minutes of Board of Education Consultative Committee held 22 and 23 July 1926, 2.
8 PRO ED 24/1226 Summary of suggestions for the next Reference to the Consultative Committee, 20 July 1926, (signed but illegible).
9 PRO ED 24/1226 Board of Education, Richards to Secretary, 21 July 1926, 2.
10 PRO ED 24/1226 Board of Education, Richards to Secretary, 21 July 1926, 2–3.
11 But, as Selleck explains, the independence of the Consultative Committee of the

Board of Education meant that it had no powers to get its recommendations implemented. R.J.W. Selleck, op. cit., 145.

12 Particular interest in rural education was also signified by the enquiry into the training of rural teachers. *Report on the Training of Rural Teachers* (1929), referred to in H.M. Burton, *The Education of the Countryman* (London, 1944), 148.

13 Board of Education, Education Pamphlets, No. 46, *Rural Education* (London, HMSO, 1926), 6–7.

14 Consultative Committee, *Primary School*, 80.

15 C.L. Mowat, *Britain Between the Wars 1918–1940* (London, 1959), 257.

16 Ibid., 253.

17 J. Saville, *Rural Depopulation in England and Wales 1851–1951* (London, 1957), 61–2.

18 Board of Education, *Rural Education*, Circular 1365, 54.

19 Board of Education, Circular 1365, 54.

20 Ibid., 54–5.

21 Board of Education, Educational Pamphlets No. 60, *The New Prospect in Education* (London, HMSO, 1928).

22 PRO ED 10/148 1926–1929, 1931 The Primary School Committee Papers 'S', Paper S.90, Memorandum by the National Council of the Evangelical Free Churches written by Rev J. Scott Lidgett, 25 Sept. 1929, 1.

23 PRO ED 10/148 S.41 Memorandum by Mr E.G. Davies, Head Teacher of Lavenham Council School, Suffolk, 5.

24 PRO ED 10/148 S.40 Memorandum by Mr H.H. Sterne, Head Teacher of Elmswell Council School, West Suffolk, 2.

25 M. Parkinson, *The Labour Party and the Organisation of Secondary Education 1918–1965* (London, 1970), 15.

26 The great majority of those involved in education believed that different types of post-primary education were necessary to meet the differing needs of pupils.

27 M. Parkinson, op. cit., 22.

28 P. Gordon and D. Lawton, *Curriculum Change in the Nineteenth and Twentieth Centuries* (London, 1978), 155–6.

29 PRO ED 24/1226 'The Primary School (A Review of the Report of the Consultative Committee of the Board of Education, 1931)', Article reprinted from *Education* (anon., n.d.), 5.

30 Consultative Committee, *Primary School*, 91.

31 Board of Education, *New Prospect*, 2.

32 Apart from prestige, there was an important distinction between free places and scholarships. The former were 'free of tuition and entrance fees' and most carried extra allowances for books or travel. However, the important maintenance allowances were, more often than not, confined to scholarship holders, although there were considerable regional variations. In 1913–14, when there were over 1,000 grant maintained secondary schools, only six charged no fees. Between 1929 and 1938, the number of free places in secondary schools in England rose from 139,016 to 185,1992, corresponding respectively to 40.5 and 43.8 per cent respectively of the percentage of all secondary school pupils (Board of Education, *Annual Reports and Statistics*). The percentage of free places in Wales was higher throughout, increasing in the same period from 59.5 to 64.2 per cent.

33 L.G.E. Jones, *The Training of Teachers in England and Wales. A Critical Survey* (London, 1924), 21.

34 B. Simon, *Education and the Labour Movement 1870–1920* (London, 1965), 116.

35 Selleck claims that the progressive movement gained momentum through the support of Holmes, who had come from the educational establishment. R.J.W. Selleck, *English Primary Education and the Progressives, 1914–1939* (London, 1972), 23, 26.

36 E. Holmes, *What is and What Might Be* (London, 1911); G.A.N. Lowndes, *Silent Social Revolution* (London, 1955), 143.

37 B. Simon, op. cit., 116 (fn.).
38 G.A.N. Lowndes, op. cit., 159.
39 Even as late as 1954, out of a total of six million, three-quarters of a million children were in schools built before 1870 and a further two million in schools built before 1903. A. Part, *The Making of a Mandarin* (London, 1990), 69.
40 PRO ED 10/148 Paper S.83 Summary of Important Points Which Have Emerged from the Oral Evidence and from the Memoranda, continued, 4.
41 Consultative Committee, *The Primary School*, 116.
42 Ibid., 116.
43 B. Simon, *The Politics of Educational Reform, 1920–1940* (London, 1974), 191.
44 R.J.W. Selleck, *English Primary Education and the Progressives, 1914–1939* (London, 1972), 25–6.
45 Ibid., 46–7.
46 Summaries of this evidence to the Consultative Committee are held at the Public Record Office, Kew, under ED 10/148. However, the records are far from complete; the evidence of many witnesses is missing.
47 Consultative Committee, *The Primary School*, 138.
48 Ibid., 92.
49 Ibid., 93.
50 Ibid., 139. This view was restated in relation to infant and nursery education. Consultative Committee, *Infant and Nursery Education* (London, HMSO), 183.
51 Consultative Committee, *The Primary School*, 153.
52 PRO ED 10/148 S.51 Memorandum on Rural Education Submitted by The National Union of Agricultural Workers, 5.
53 PRO ED 10/148 Paper S.51 National Union of Agricultural Workers, 5.
54 PRO ED 10/148 Paper S.50. Memorandum submitted by the Joint Committee of the Welsh Branches of the Incorporated Association of Assistant Masters in Secondary Schools, 7.
55 PRO ED 10/148 S.67 Notes by Miss Ellen Healey on some of the essentials of any adequate scheme of education, 6.
56 PRO ED 10/148 S.75 Memorandum submitted by Miss E.J. Cook, Head Teacher of St. Martin's Girl's School, Dover, 5.
57 Consultative Committee, *The Primary School*, xvi.
58 Consultative Committee, *Education of the Adolescent*, 83.
59 Ibid., 140.
60 PRO ED 10/148 Paper S.12(11) Summary of Evidence Given on Behalf of the National Union of Women Teachers, 7.
61 PRO ED 10/148 Paper S.12(27) Summary of Evidence Given on Behalf of the NUT, 22.
62 PRO ED 10/148 Paper S.12(25) Summary of Evidence Given on Behalf of the TUC General Council, 5.
63 PRO ED 10/148 Paper S.44 Excerpts from a Memorandum submitted by Mr A.B. Neal, Head Teacher of the Sir Henry Fermer's School, Crowborough, Sussex, 21.
64 PRO ED 24/1226 'The Primary School', 6.
65 E.J. Cook, see n. 56.
66 PRO ED 10/148 Paper S.97 Memorandum by Mr T. Caden, Head Teacher of the Towneley Memorial Intermediate R.C. School, Stanley, Co. Durham, 3.
67 PRO ED 10/148 Paper S.27 Extracts from a Report of the Commission on Education appointed by the Bradford ILP, Part III, Ages 7–11.
68 Consultative Committee, *The Primary School*, 140.
69 PRO ED 10/148 Paper S.39 Education Section of the British Psychological Society, 5; Paper S.38 Memorandum Submitted by the WEA, 2.
70 R.J.W. Selleck, *English Education and the Progressives*, 41–2.
71 PRO ED 10/148 Paper S.27 Bradford ILP, 5–6.

72 R.J.W. Selleck, *English Education and the Progressives*, 40–41.
73 PRO ED 10/148 Paper S.48 Memorandum by the Auto-Education Institute, 1; Paper S.37, Memorandum by Miss H.E. Wix, HMI, on Auto-Individual Methods in Infant Classes (ages 4¾/5–11), 1.
74 PRO ED 10/148 Paper S.93, Memorandum of Courses of Study Available for Children (Other Than in Infants' Departments) Up to the Age of 11, Who are in Attendance at Elementary Schools in Rural Areas, by the Principal, Miss A.E. Varley and Members of Staff of Saffron Waldon Training College, 3. This method was advocated by various witnesses, including the Bradford ILP which advocated experimenting with a method such as the American 'Project' or the Soviet 'Complex' system. Paper S.12(48) Summary of Evidence Given on Behalf of the Education Commission Appointed by the Bradford ILP by Mr Fran Belts (Chairman) and Mr Walter Hyman (Secretary). 3; Miss E.E. Kenwrick of the Maria Grey Training College, PRO ED 10/148 Paper S.84 1; and in Paper S.12(38) Summary of Evidence given on Behalf of the Training College Association and the Council of Principals of Training Colleges, 4.
75 Consultative Committee, *The Primary School*, 104.
76 PRO ED 10/148 Paper S.10 Memorandum on the Curriculum of the Junior School by Miss M. Storr, Goldsmith's College, University of London, 4.
77 Consultative Committee, *The Primary School*, 104.
78 Ibid., 154–203.
79 Ibid., 186.
80 Ibid., 183.
81 Ibid., 186.
82 C. Burt, 'Memorandum on the Mental Characteristics of Children Between the Ages of Seven and Eleven', Appendix III of Consultative Committee, *The Primary School*, 257.
83 Ibid., 258.
84 Ibid., 258.
85 Ibid., 77.
86 Ibid., 77–8
87 M. Galton, B. Simon and P. Croll, *Inside the Primary Classroom* (London, 1980), 37.
88 Ibid., 37.
89 However, when the Plowden Report was published in 1967, it recommended the abolition of streaming, precisely because of its belief in the individuality of children and their educational needs. It advocated a more flexible approach, whereby children would not be lumped together in groups. B. Simon, *Education and the Social Order 1940–1990* (London, 1991), 367.
90 P.B. Ballard, *Groups Tests of Intelligence* (London, 1923), 232–3.
91 Consultative Committee, *The Primary School*, 124.
92 PRO ED 10/148 Paper S.11 Memorandum by Mr T.H. Kirkham, Headmaster of Westhill Junior Mixed School, Torquay, 22–3.
93 PRO ED 10/148, Paper S.100 Memorandum by Miss M. A. Braybrooke, lecturer at the Diocesan Training College, Derby, 2.
94 PRO ED 10/148 Paper S.12(2) Summary of Evidence given by Miss Grace Owen, Hon. Secretary of the Nursery School Association, 1.
95 PRO ED 10/148 Paper S.47 Statement submitted to the Consultative Committee by the Women's Co-operative Guild with regard to a School Curriculum for Elementary School Children up to 11 Years of Age, 15.
96 PRO ED 10/148 Paper S.2 Report on the Aims of the Junior School by a Committee of the Board's Inspectors in one of the inspectorial divisions of England, 17.
97 PRO ED 10/148 Paper S.12(28) Summary of Evidence given on behalf of the Froebel Society and Junior Schools Association, 2.

98 PRO ED 10/148 Paper S.44 Neal, 4; Paper S.12(25) Summary of Evidence Given on Behalf of the TUC General Council, 8.
99 PRO ED 10/148 Paper S.44 Neal, 5.
100 PRO ED 10/148, Paper S.64 Memorandum on the Free Place Examination and the Junior School by Mr C.A. Richardson, HMI, 4.
101 PRO ED 10/148 Paper S.12(2) Owen, 1.
102 PRO ED 10/148 S.42 Memorandum by Mr F.E. Amos, Head Teacher of Badsey Council School, Worcestershire, 7.
103 There was general agreement among witnesses that different types of post-primary education should exist to match children's differing needs, and thus some method of differentiating children was necessary.
104 Consultative Committee, *The Primary School*, 126–9.
105 Board of Education's *The Departmental Committee on Scholarships and Free Places* (HMSO, 1920) and in *Examinations in Public Elementary Schools*, The Report of an Enquiry undertaken by the Joint Advisory Committee of the Association of Education Committee and the National Union of Teachers into Examinations for Pupils in Public Elementary Schools (London, 1930).
106 Consultative Committee, *The Primary School*, 78.
107 Ibid., 123.
108 The 1931 Hadow Report notes that some education authorities tested in History, Geography, and in a few instances, even Nature Study. Consultative Committee, *The Primary School*, 126.
109 AEC/NUT's *Examinations in Public Elementary Schools*, 144. The Board of Education opposed the inclusion of subjects other than English and arithmetic.
110 Board of Education, Educational Pamphlets, No. 63, *Memorandum on Examinations for Scholarships and Free Places in Secondary Schools* (London, HMSO, 1936 edition, first published in 1928), 26.
111 PRO ED 10/148 S.60 Digest of Memoranda from Head Masters and Head Mistresses of Secondary Schools, 9–10.
112 C. Burt, 'Memorandum on the Mental Characteristics of Children Between the Ages of Seven and Eleven', Appendix III of Consultative Committee, *The Primary School*, 258.
113 P.B. Ballard, *Mental Tests* (London, 1920), 25.
114 Consultative Committee, *The Primary School*, 127.
115 M. Galton, B. Simon and P. Croll, op. cit., 36.
116 Consultative Committee, *The Primary School*, 92.
117 K. J. Brehony, 'What's Left in Progressive Education?' in A. Rattansi and D. Reeder (eds), *Rethinking Radical Education: Essays in Honour of Brian Simon* (London, 1992), 209.
118 Ibid., 209.
119 M. Parkinson, op. cit., 29.

3

Nature study: science or sentimentalism?

In 1904, the *Code of Regulations* governing the work of public elementary schools in England and Wales prescribed the scientific education of pupils in terms of 'knowledge of the common phenomena of the external world'. In the following year, this prescription was amended to require 'Observation Lessons and Nature Study', taught with particular reference to the surroundings and in a manner 'suitable to the age, circumstances and capacities' of those scholars who took it.[1] The requirement was amplified in the Board of Education's *Suggestions for the Consideration of Teachers* published in the same year. Object lessons, teachers were advised, were intended to 'cultivate exact observation' and were particularly appropriate for younger children. With older pupils, this 'power of exact observation' could be presupposed, so that the main purpose of the lesson was to

> exercise the scholars in reflecting and reasoning upon the results of their own direct observations. Lessons of this kind are now commonly described as nature study.[2]

Writing about the history of elementary education in England and Wales, Birchenough claimed[3] that the 'Nature Movement may be said to have begun' with an exhibition of school nature study activities held in the gardens of the Royal Botanic Society in Regent's Park, London, between 23 July and 5 August 1902. This exhibition, the first of its kind in Britain, was associated with five conferences devoted to the aims and scope of nature study and it set a pattern of competition and display which was quickly and widely adopted elsewhere, for example at Cambridge, Liverpool, Aylesbury, Beverley, Dulwich and Manchester. Drawing upon their experience of the exhibits, the judges of the 1902 exhibition publicised guidelines for the teaching of nature study and established that geographical, geological, biological, meteorological and astronomical work all fell within its scope.[4]

The overwhelming majority of practising teachers had no formal training in the teaching of nature study and a number of organisations were established in the early years of the century to provide them with assistance. The most notable and enduring of these was the School Nature Study Union (SNSU), set up in 1903[5] to bring together 'for mutual help and advice, those interested in Nature Study in general, and its place in education in particular'.[6] The Union sought principally to assist those who wished to teach nature study, but lacked the necessary competence and/or confidence to do so.[7] Initially, the intention was simply to provide nature-study materials, a reference library and museums, but the Union soon decided to focus its attention on helping teachers more directly to teach nature study in the schools.[8] In the early years, this help took the form of conferences, exhibitions and Saturday excursions and rambles into the countryside. The SNSU also encouraged school gardens, published lists of suppliers of specimens which could be delivered to schools to correspond on a weekly basis with the schemes of work which the Union outlined in its journal, and introduced a scheme to lend plant and animal specimens to schools in return for a small charge. The nature study topics covered in the Union's journal, *School Nature Study*, were drawn from biology, botany, zoology, geography, geology and astronomy, but the strong overall emphasis was on natural history.

The School Journey Association, established in 1911, also promoted aspects of nature study. Its chairman, G.G. Lewis, had been a founder member of the School Nature Study Union. Since the code of 1896, it had been possible for visits to 'institutions of educational value' to count as school attendance[9] and the teaching of elementary school lessons outdoors was first permitted in the Code of Regulations for 1906, with week-long excursions being allowed two years later.[10] Lewis was well aware of the potential which school journeys and excursions offered for the study of plants and animals in their natural environment. In 1913, the Association helped to send nearly one hundred children to the sea-side, forest or mountain, for anything from four days to two weeks. Not all of this time was, of course, devoted to nature study, but the School Journey Association and the SNSU worked closely together, Lewis describing the former as a sister movement to the latter.[11] The nature study movement received further encouragement and, occasionally, support from a variety of local natural history organisations and from the Council for the Promotion of Field Studies.

From the outset, however, the movement was beset by different and sometimes conflicting prescriptions of what nature study involved. It was to be different for urban and rural scholars, different for older and younger children, and different for boys and girls. The Board of

Education *Suggestions* issued in 1905 offered the following, not entirely helpful, definition.

> The term 'Nature Study' is here used in default of a better one for that class of elementary instruction which deals with the out-door world, with the life of animals and plants, with the clouds and the seasons, the rocks and the soil, in fact with any side of the changing panorama we call Nature.
>
> ... in addition to observation it demands some touch of the method of scientific enquiry; on the other hand, it cannot be confined within the limits of a particular 'Science,' for it may deal with many branches of science and with their applications to such crafts as agriculture or gardening.[12]

As noted in the previous chapter, the need to provide different schemes of work in nature study for children attending schools in rural and urban areas was emphasised by the Hadow report of 1931, which also claimed that work of this kind had 'an additional significance in the mental development of the country child'.[13] This additional significance which the Hadow Committee had in mind seems to have been the development of a 'breadth of outlook and grasp of essentials which raises the value and increases the dignity of rural occupations'. This concern to improve the standing of rural occupations was, in reality, directed at stemming increasing urbanisation and its attendant problems and, as noted in Chapter 2, was a recurrent aspect of government policy for elementary education during the first half of the twentieth century. As early as 1901, the Board of Education had published *Specimen Courses of Object Lesson on Common Things connected with Rural Life and Industries of all Classes in Rural Schools*, intended to help elementary school teachers promote in their pupils 'an intelligent interest in the pursuits and occupations which are open to those whose lives and homes are in the country'.[14] By the time of the Hadow report, responsibility for this promotion lay with nature study.

> The child who has been taught to find joy and interest in Nature is less likely in after years to exhibit the craving for unhealthy excitement that is so characteristic of urban life.[15]

Not for the first time, schools, and nature study in particular, were to be given responsibilities that realistically they could not hope to meet. The need to ensure that the work encompassed by nature study made use of the environment of the pupils was, however, of paramount importance.

> It will use one sort of material in a colliery or textile district, and another in an agricultural village, where nature supplies living specimens for children to observe, where plants, birds and animals, the configuration of the country and its geological characteristics, can be studied at first hand, where the weather is not merely an unavoidable convenience but a significant phenomenon, and where gardening and the keeping of animals can be carried on without difficulty.[16]

The extent to which nature study might properly be regarded as providing an elementary education in some aspects of science was somewhat undermined by the range of topics offered by the Board of Education in its *Suggestions*, since these included the police force and the posting of letters.[17] Some commentators were clear that nature study could, and should, be sharply distinguished from science.

> 'nature study' is not synonymous with the 'study of nature' or with 'science', much less with any particular branch of the latter. True it is that the materials for nature-study are the sun and the earth, plants and animals, even the weather, but these may be taken almost at random, and the informality of the pursuit is a pillar of its strength.[18]

There was debate, too, about whether nature study might be regarded as a subject and, if so, where its boundaries might be drawn and how it might be schooled. For many, nature study was not a subject, if this implied an organised body of knowledge to be taught to pupils. Rather, it was to be conceived as an approach or a method. For the Board of Education in 1905, 'the method by which the instruction is given counts for everything, the information imparted for very little'.[19] For M.D. Hill and W.M. Webb, authors of *Eton Nature-Study and Observation Lessons*, 'nature study meant dealing with a method not a subject',[20] an opinion supported by many of their contemporaries.[21]

Prominent among these was the energetic and enthusiastic Clothilde von Wyss, who played a key role in the establishment of *School Nature Study*, the journal of the School Nature Study Union, and served as its founder editor for 30 years. Born in 1871, Clothilde von Wyss trained as a teacher at Maria Grey College and taught in schools and colleges before settling at the London Day Training College in 1903 where she remained for the rest of her career. During the late 1890s, she taught in Edinburgh where she was much influenced by the ideas of J. Arthur Thomson, and became greatly interested in nature study and natural history. A founder member of the School Nature Study Union, Miss von Wyss was clear that nature study was 'essentially a particular attitude of mind, which generates a particular method of approach'. She was equally clear about the consequences of this position, namely that nature study was 'absolutely unrestricted in its choice of material for study'.[22] Attempts at 'general and systematic treatment' were to be avoided.[23] For her, nature study was about developing in children 'boundless delight in discovery and first-hand observation' and making their minds 'so plastic and receptive that they become susceptible to all the influences of the natural environment'.[24] When nature study became 'too bookish or too much of a "lesson"', it had 'gone wrong'.[25] Central to the successful teaching of nature study, therefore, was a love of nature and a willingness to break 'away from the old didactic methods of imparting information'.[26]

Claims such as these make clear that nature study was a curriculum embodiment of the so-called 'naturalist' approach to education. Although late nineteenth and early twentieth century disciples of Pestalozzi and Froebel, such as Maria Montessori, Homer Lane and John Dewey were far from unanimous in their views, they all shared the belief that the prime aim of education was to develop the latent powers of each pupil 'in accordance with nature's laws'. The naturalists thus placed their emphasis on freedom and self-expression and on self-development rather than faculty training, thereby helping to generate a 'new spirit' in education, the essentials of which were 'reverence for the pupil's individuality and a belief that individuality grows best in an atmosphere of freedom'.[27] As the Board of Education observed in 1925, 'The leading principle which determines the methods of education suitable to early childhood is the recognition of the spontaneous activities of the children'.[28]

Clothilde von Wyss attempted to impose some intellectual order upon these spontaneous activities by relating them to the age of the children. She argued that children's learning was marked by three different stages, each with distinctive characteristics. A stage of wonder and curiosity, up to the age of seven, was followed by a second stage marked by intense physical energy, which lasted until about the age of ten. The third stage, up to about 12 years old, was said to be characterised by the desire to investigate, understand and systematise the natural world.[29] The notion of relatively distinct stages in children's intellectual development had many supporters in the early twentieth century, and it is likely that von Wyss's views were strongly influenced by those of T.P. Nunn who, as Vice-Principal of the London Day Training College in 1905, had elaborated the view that the interest of children in science exhibited a rhythm corresponding to the rhythm of its history. Nunn detected in the history of science, as in the minds of children, three 'motives', of 'wonder, utility and systematisation'.[30] His ideas, which constituted a new 'learning theory', commanded significant support, not least from A.N. Whitehead,[31] and they were to prove of seminal importance. The Spens Committee accepted Nunn's ideas in its discussion of the principles of the curriculum,[32] and they are evident in many of the books about pedagogy published in the first half of the twentieth century. Poulton, for example, writing in 1924 about the teaching of biology in schools and training colleges, was particularly interested in how children's interest in their environment progressed as they matured. She claimed that very young children show an interest in their environment, and that this should be reflected in the form and content of nature study lessons. Children progress from observation, through touching, to imitation, which, in turn, develops into a desire to investigate and analyse, and eventually, to experiment.[33] For the teacher of nature study, this meant that

> In selecting material and in devising methods of teaching, it is necessary to bear in mind that interest in the world of Nature is changeful, different aspects being found attractive at different periods of development. Practical and aesthetic interest precede the more intellectual and abstract features.[34]

For young children, therefore, the teacher 'must supply the opportunity for thus widening the interest and experience of the child, and for the enjoyment of the beauty of natural objects.'[35] She stressed that 'In future, the courses of Nature study and their modes of treatment will harmonize more completely with the different phases of the child's mental development.'[36]

Given the pedagogical importance attached by most advocates of nature study to investigation and enquiry, it might be expected that the nature study movement would have attracted the support of H.E. Armstrong whose heuristic approach to teaching science, with its emphasis on the development of scientific method, was much in vogue in the early years of the twentieth century.[37] There were some, perhaps mindful that nature study could readily become 'easy-going and lacking in serious purpose', who claimed that the teaching of nature study should be heuristic, as well as practical and dynamic.[38] For von Wyss, however, the heuristic method was to be used only 'in moderation' when teaching nature study,[39] perhaps because she judged that Armstrong's insistence on precise measurement as the basis of all true science did not readily accommodate the flexible and less instrumental approach to the natural world which many advocates of nature study sought to promote. As for Armstrong himself, he had formed his own opinion of the nature study movement and, in 1913, he expressed it in characteristically forthright language.

> Admirable as were the professed objects of the promoters of the cult, the declared intention of the faddists who were its early advocates to have nothing to do with science put them out of court from the beginning and showed that they were unfit to act as leaders – the verdict must be, I believe, that they have failed.[40]

Among those seeking a place for a new component of the school curriculum, disagreements and tensions are, of course, inevitable. As Goodson has acknowledged, even established subjects within the school curriculum 'are not monolithic entities but shifting amalgamations of sub-groups and traditions.'[41] Stanley Coulter, at the first meeting of the American Nature Study Society in 1908 described nature study as 'hampered by definition, ... obstructed by material, ... deflected by sentimentalism'.[42] The Board of Education's *Report for the Year 1909–10*, described nature study as a 'conveniently elastic term', which covered work 'of the most various kinds'.[43] The nature of the diversity was indicated in 1914 when the Board offered a description of the work of a 'Good Elementary School'.

> Elementary Science and Nature Study are so varied in their details in schools in towns and country that it is difficult to describe a typical course; but in the good country school it will be closely associated with practical Gardening and at its best in a town school will involve some simple knowledge of animals, birds and flowers, and with older boys often a simple course of experimental physics.[44]

Much of the nature study work undertaken in public elementary schools was organised on a seasonal basis, with the arguments for doing so sometimes verging on the religious. J.A. Thomson, for example, pointed out that 'Our life is rhythmic and it is punctuated by the seasons'[45] and Clothilde von Wyss claimed that 'our own mental and physical conditions vary with the seasons and we are naturally more sympathetically inclined towards things that sound the same elemental note'.[46] There was, however, the more practical reason that if pupils were to work with fresh or living organisms in their natural environment, and to study life or other natural cycles, a seasonal approach was unavoidable. It was thus very common for classes to keep nature calendars. These recorded the dates, times and places of appropriate observations and occasionally incorporated suitable sketches or cuttings. Sometimes a class was divided into groups concerned with specific types of animals (birds, fish, insects, and so on) or plants (trees, shrubs, flowering plants), each group producing a display to illustrate the significant aspects of the life-cycles of the organisms concerned. In this way, tree and floral calendars were produced in abundance, each typically emphasising such features as the arrangement of leaves and branches on a stem or trunk, the doubling and sporting of wild flowers, the dates of fruiting and the mechanisms of seed dispersal. Aquaria were introduced into classrooms to enable pupils to study aquatic organisms such as water snails, sticklebacks, freshwater shrimps and algae, or to investigate such phenomena as the respiratory, locomotor and nutritional habits of the larval gnat, the changes in the size, respiration and external form of the maturing tadpole, and the adaptive features and carnivorous habits of water-beetles. Bulbs, corms and cuttings were planted and seeds sown in pots, window-boxes and garden plots, and space was created within classrooms to allow pupils to observe and rear caterpillars, silk-worm moths, butterflies, cockroaches, snails and slugs.[47]

In some elementary schools, nature study was allied with school gardening, an activity which had first become eligible for government grant in 1895. The 1905 *Suggestions* indicate the view of the Board of Education.

> The school garden will, in the first place, be of great service in illustrating object lessons and elementary science lessons, whether given to scholars who are taught gardening or to others: instruction in the rudiments of the gardener's craft will have some value as manual instruction; and the boys (*sic*) will find opportunities for making a definite practical application of the elementary science they are taught.[48]

School gardens were sometimes entered for competition in nature study exhibitions and a few of them reflected an attempt to teach taxonomic botany[49] rather than simply to grow vegetables or flowers. The School Nature Study Union responded in 1914 to this aspect of the schools' work by establishing a gardening section. Although this was relatively short-lived, it was of some significance. The section facilitated the exchange of surplus plants, published articles and leaflets, organised visits to school gardens, parks and nurseries, and held a number of demonstrations, lectures and exhibitions. The outbreak of war in 1914 prompted vigorous activity among the members of this section. Several articles about gardening were published in the Union's journal and the importance of gardening to the war effort emphasised. In a contribution entitled 'The Social Value of Gardening', the author linked school gardening with the need for more allotments, claiming, rather grandly, that

> Every cabbage that is grown, every crop of potatoes that is gathered, every fruit tree that is planted, adds to the actual material wealth of the nation.[50]

The gardening section of the School Nature Study Union sent a resolution to the Board of Education and to the Board of Agriculture urging the official encouragement of 'schools throughout the country to utilise vacant land in their vicinity for the cultivation of vegetables'.[51] An editorial in the SNSU journal in 1917 commented that 'Subjects related to gardening have received special attention, inasmuch as they loom large, when the difficulties of food production and supply exercise the minds of all thinking citizens'.[52] That supply was particularly affected by German submarine warfare from 1916 and Bramwell, reviewing elementary school work in the first quarter of the twentieth century, claimed that this led to an increase in the number of school gardens.[53] While the usefulness of the gardening section of the School Nature Study Union was not questioned during the war, the ending of hostilities brought a reassessment of its role by the Union. In 1920, the SNSU expressed the view that 'nature study has no direct connection with food production and patriotism, and there may have been a tendency in some quarters to lose sight of its great value as an educational factor'.[54] Although the gardening section became affiliated to the Royal Horticultural Society in 1917, it did not survive beyond 1925. Predictably, the Union's interest in school gardens revived during the Second World War, articles appearing more frequently in the journal alongside other contributions related to the war effort, for example, the promotion of parsley[55] as a source of vitamin C, the collection of leaves for medicinal purposes,[56] and advice on sources for obtaining rubber.

When nature study was allied with gardening, the emphasis was placed on the practical and economic aspects of horticulture such as sowing seeds, harvesting and storing crops, pest control, the cultivation of trees and shrubs, and the pickling, bottling and preservation of fruit, although there were obviously also opportunities for pupils to study the variety and properties of soils and the effects of different ways of treating them. Ideally, the work in the garden and the work in the classroom were closely interrelated. The plants whose life-histories were to be studied were grown in the garden and the habits of caterpillars and other pests were illustrated by reference to the damage they did in the pupils' plots. The calculation of the areas of these plots, the estimation of quantities of seeds and crops and the construction of charts showing the rates of growth under different conditions provided a basis for some lessons in mathematics, and studies of pollination and seed-dispersal were of immediate and obvious relevance. In practice, the nature study associated with school gardening varied greatly in quality. At its best, the opportunities provided by a school garden for the systematic and long-term study of part of the natural world were exploited to the full. At its worst, the school garden was cultivated solely to discover who could grow the biggest turnip or produce the finest bloom or, in a few instances, to meet the culinary needs of the headteacher.

An activity common to perhaps all schemes of work in nature study was the collection of specimens of plant or animal life or of natural 'curiosities'. Pupils were encouraged to make collections of stones, shells, insects, ferns, flowers and crystals, and the better specimens were often given pride of place in a school museum or a nature cabinet. Sometimes, the collection of specimens was the principal purpose of a nature study ramble, or of a pond-dipping expedition to find and collect the spawn of a frog or newt, caddis and dragonfly larvae, water-scorpions and water-beetles. In other instances, classes undertook school journeys of a day, weekend or even a week's duration, in which the educational purposes usually widened the scope of nature study to include aspects of geology and geography and sometimes went beyond this to encourage the development of such personal qualities as thrift, self-reliance and initiative.[57] Out-of-school excursions were particularly popular between 1900 and 1910 and there are several accounts of the work done, some of which were published by the Office of Special Enquiries and Reports of the Board of Education.[58] Like the School Journey Association, the Children's Country Holiday Association also provided pupils with experience of the countryside and it established a nature study section, awarding prizes and certificates for the best nature records.[59] Notwithstanding the activities of these two Associations and the encouragement of the Board of Education, school journeys in England and Wales were never conducted on the scale common in continental Europe, especially in Germany, where *Heimatskunde* was well-established by the early 1880s and the school journey, lasting up to 14 days, sometimes for pupils as young as eight, became an important and regular event.[60]

In England and Wales, it was generally held to be more difficult for city schools than for their rural counterparts to find adequate resources for the nature study work. School journeys, where these were organised, were, at best, only a partial solution of this difficulty and many teachers preferred to make frequent use of more convenient local resources such as parks and municipal museums. Although there were restrictions on the number and types of visits of this kind that could be made in a school year, they were a well-established feature of the work of public elementary schools in many parts of the country by the beginning of the present century. However, many teachers appear to have felt that the teaching of their pupils in a museum was primarily the responsibility of the curator and his staff, principally because they were thoroughly familiar with the exhibits. Since museums were often inadequately staffed and such staff as were available rarely had the time, experience, or perhaps the inclination to be competent teachers of large classes of pupils, some compromise was usually necessary. The nature of this compromise varied from one locality to another,[61] depending upon the resources available and the commitment of the local authority to the development of museums, upon which they were empowered to spend the product of a halfpenny rate under the Museums and Gymnasiums Act of 1891. At Leeds and Sheffield, the curators gave lectures to teachers who, in turn, prepared the children for their subsequent visits to the museum. In 1928, the programme in Leeds was still thriving and the curator, H. Crowther, informed[62] the Museums Association that 'nearly 20,000 children' came yearly and that, since its inception in 1901, '520,000 scholars and 12,000 teachers' had been to the museum. At Manchester, the museum appointed a teacher to work with pupils between the ages of 10 and 14 and some classes were held at the Zoological Gardens at Belle Vue.[63] Jonathan Hutchinson's Haslemere museum, founded in 1889 and moved to another site in 1895, was notable not only for its emphasis on the use of living organisms but also for its 'museum examinations'. All the questions in the examination were printed as a 10-page pamphlet, with 20 questions per page, and made available before the test took place. When a candidate felt confident of answering all 200 questions, he or she presented for examination and was then tested on one of the pages selected at random.[64] At Liverpool, a travelling museum was introduced in 1884, serving 64 schools, and, by 1890, the collection consisted of 19 cabinets containing specimens of metals, rocks, corals, sponges, shells, crustacea, insects and starfish.[65] W.M. Webb, a member of the Executive Committee of the Nature Study Exhibition of 1902, developed a travelling museum based upon nature study ideas for the Nottinghamshire

County Council in 1901.[66] In addition, or as an alternative to these travelling museums, many local education authorities, including Leeds, Sheffield, Newport, Reading and Salford, developed loan services whereby cabinets of specimens were simply lent to schools for a specific period. Although local museums were not concerned exclusively or even principally with nature study, the collections they housed and the expertise they offered were such that they constituted an obvious and important resource for teachers constructing schemes of work which placed a substantial emphasis on the observation, identification and classification of specimens drawn from the natural world.

The ready adoption of nature study by many elementary schools at the beginning of the twentieth century and the diversity of the work undertaken undoubtedly owes much to the fact that many schemes of work were derived directly from the sequence of object lessons with which teachers were already familiar.[67] There were, of course, important differences between object teaching and nature study, particularly in their objectives and in the manner in which topics were arranged and presented, but the relationship between them was such that transformation was often readily possible. Thus, Webb, reviewing the 'progress and interpretation of nature knowledge' in 1902, denied that much of the teaching carried on in the name of object lessons was necessarily bad and claimed that, providing the method of eliciting information and encouraging observation was carried on with 'real things in children's hands', much actual nature study could be done.[68]

The transformation of the effete object lesson into the more coherent and stimulating nature study was encouraged by the enthusiasm with which the later Victorians and Edwardians of all ages and classes embraced natural history,[69] and by the vitalist philosophy which provided an impetus for so much of the social and educational reform at the turn of the century. It is significant that two of the influential advocates of nature study, Patrick Geddes[70] and J. Arthur Thomson,[71] were both inspired by this philosophy which, despite pre-Darwinian origins, was born of the collapse of orthodox religious belief when confronted with the theory of evolution. The vitalists replaced the emphasis on the struggle for survival which characterised this theory with a reference to a vital quality of 'insurgence', inherent in each particle of life. They thereby substituted a more encouraging and co-operative view of the natural world and of man's place within it for the sterile, competitive and remorseless mechanism demanded by the doctrine of the survival of the fittest. Particular importance was thus attached to the preservation of life in all its forms, rather than its wanton destruction, and to the development and maintenance of harmonious relationships between man and nature.

The arid teaching of object lessons with its emphasis on dead and preserved specimens was obviously vulnerable to vitalist ideas. Nature study could awaken sympathy with nature and reverence for life, develop aesthetic, ethical and spiritual sensibilities and lead 'through Nature up to Nature's God'. The 'Nature lesson' could 'deepen the child's wonder, as it step by step (revealed) the marvel and unity of the surrounding world'.[72] It is hardly surprising that nature study was welcomed, at least initially, by the 'new educationists'[73] with their emphasis on the provision of learning experiences suited to the maturing intellect and interests of the child. It was advocated by poets[74] as well as by pedagogues, with the Froebelians, in particular, stressing the educative value of contact with living things which nature study promised to provide.

There were, of course, other and less romantic claims made to support the teaching of nature study. For the 'practical educationists', it also seemed to have much to offer. Nature study incorporated few of the complex scientific ideas which might be difficult for elementary-school pupils to understand and it offered an antidote to that 'weakening of the connection of science with practical affairs'[75] which stemmed from the abstract symbolism associated with the physical sciences. For those concerned with education for citizenship at a time of strong and popular Imperialist sentiments, nature study 'encouraged spontaneity' and the power of acting for oneself under new conditions. When moral instruction[76] became a compulsory component of the curriculum of public elementary schools in 1906, teachers were expected to help their pupils develop a 'respect for beauty in nature' and to do so by basing their teaching upon 'the actual surroundings in town and country'.[77] For this, nature study seemed ideal.

> Nature Study is certainly of great value as an aid towards the culture of aesthetic tastes, and many of our best teachers further recognise in it a powerful aid in moral training ... This appreciation of the beauties and wonders of Nature leads to a sympathy with all living things, thus correcting the natural tendency to destructiveness.[78]

Nature study also offered some hope to those who were alarmed at the ruinous collapse of the agricultural industry and the continuing drift of population from the countryside into the towns. An 'interest in nature', it was claimed, would not only 'make a better worker of the agriculturalist'; it would 'strengthen him morally against, at any rate the lower, attractions of town life'.[79] Finally, there were the examples of nature teaching in other countries, especially Germany and the United States, whose growing economic strength was widely held to be a direct consequence of a greater national commitment to scientific and technical education. Insofar as nature study represented a suitable means of introducing pupils to the more systematic teaching of physics and chemistry, the case for its inclusion in school curricula in the United Kingdom was strengthened by the international comparisons undertaken so frequently by the 'declinists' in the early years of the century.[80] Given such a coalition of supporters, it is hardly surprising that Sir George Kekewich, the Secretary of the Board of Education, felt able to claim in 1902 that there was surely no kind of teaching which conferred upon children 'so many and such varied advantages' as nature study.[81]

These 'many and varied advantages' helped to ensure that nature study survived in some form in elementary and primary education for the larger part of the twentieth century. Despite Clothilde von Wyss's concern[82] in 1915 that the term 'nature study' might soon disappear, the 'lovers of educational fads' having transferred 'their patronage ... to some other unit in the curriculum', nature study was to endure. The 'nature table' found in so many primary classrooms in the 1960s would have been instantly recognisable by the public elementary school teacher of half a century earlier and the rhetoric which linked children's learning to their maturing intellect and interests would have struck a particularly sympathetic chord.

According to Bramwell, the 'pristine brightness of the Nature Study star' had begun to tarnish by 1925. It 'was tending to become a part – though certainly an important part still – of Elementary General Science'. If this was so, then it is likely that this tendency was more marked in the education of the senior pupils attending public elementary schools than in the work of their younger counterparts. For most of the children receiving an elementary education, there is little evidence of the development of programmes of nature study into courses of elementary science, despite attempts by the Board of Education to broaden the scope of the work to include topics drawn from the physical sciences. Indeed, for some elementary school teachers, any association of nature study with the formal study of science was to be resisted. Such formality seemed both to threaten the alleged spontaneity of children's learning and to challenge the child-centred pedagogy which followed from it. Nature study was 'not knowledge ... not facts ... (but) spirit' and was 'concerned with the child's outlook on the world'.[83] Although this notion that the purpose of nature study was to 'put the child in sympathy with nature' was to fade steadily after the First World War, it was never entirely lost. In 1939, two members resigned their membership of the School Nature Study Union because of their belief that the Union's journal was giving too much attention to 'advanced subjects'.[84] In 1960, a commentator upon *Primary Education*, the official advice which replaced the long obsolete *Handbook of Suggestions for Teachers*, mourned the official loss of the term 'nature study' and warned that 'in our desire to produce more scientists we may spoil far too many by trying to force the pace of a process which is one of natural maturation'.[85]

In the interwar years, membership of the School Nature Study Union increased after 1923, following a decline during, and immediately after, the First World War. The Union continued to promote nature study, although it increasingly turned its attention to the teaching of human biology and hygiene in public elementary schools, even at one stage contemplating changing its name to reflect this wider focus of interest.[86] In 1921, when the Secretary of the Labour Party asked the Union for its views on Open Air Education, a joint delegation with representatives of the School Journey Association met with Labour Party members to discuss the issues involved.[87] In 1929, the Board of Education sought the advice of the Union about the teaching of nature study in elementary schools, advice which the Union incorporated in a Memorandum it submitted to the Hadow Committee.[88] At the school level, the Union reprinted large numbers of some of the articles which had appeared in its journal and sold these as leaflets. Income from the sale of these leaflets was a significant source of finance for the Union and one which served to extend its influence beyond London and the Home Counties from where it drew most of its membership.[89]

The interwar years also brought something of a revival in scholarly interest in natural history and ecology, and this, together with the development of radio programmes for schools, helped to reinvigorate school nature study and to assist its gradual transformation into elementary science. The first broadcast given by the BBC specifically for schoolchildren was in 1924 and was devoted to music. Following an experimental scheme involving Kent Local Education Authority, the BBC developed between 1927 and 1939 'a most successful system of schools broadcasting … which soon became the envy of educationists in every other country'. In 1927,

> at a generous estimate, 3,000 schools were listening to the BBC's schools broadcasts in England and Wales, as against 220 in late

> 1924; at the outbreak of war in 1939, the figure had risen to 9,953 (and) thirty-nine programmes a week were being transmitted.[90]

There was, of course, much to learn about how best to exploit the new medium within schools. Some local education authorities were initially suspicious of, even hostile to, school broadcasts, and experience was needed by teachers, programme producers and radio engineers before the potential of school radio could be fully exploited. Elementary science was the responsibility of one of the programme committees appointed by the Central Council for School Broadcasting when this was set up in 1929 under the chairmanship of H.A.L. Fisher, a former President of the Board of Education. Most of the members of these programme committees were teachers who were already using radio programmes in their teaching, and the committees were responsible for drafting the first new schools syllabuses for the school year 1929–30. In that year, 2,356 schools listened on a regular basis to the BBC output and over 560,000 pamphlets were distributed.[91] Elementary science, and nature study within it, was, of course, only a small part of this output.

Successive editions of the Board of Education's *Suggestions* also continued to offer official support to the teaching of nature study in public elementary schools. In doing so, the Board of Education increasingly emphasised the importance of marrying the work done with the developing interests of pupils. In 1927, the Board claimed that, like 'handwork, singing and rhythmic exercises', nature study and elementary science (now coupled together) were 'naturally congenial to children'.[92] A decade later, the revised *Suggestions* explicitly recognised the child-centred approach to the education of young children, the Board acknowledging the 'shift of emphasis from the subject to the child'[93] and stressing that the teaching of nature study and science was to be based on the child's interests and 'natural desire'.

This approach to the teaching of young children survived the reorganisation of public education after 1944 to become a hall-mark of so-called progressive education in the newly-created post-war primary schools. It also became central to the professional expertise of the new generation of primary school teachers which was seen as resting upon an understanding of children's intellectual, personal, social and spiritual development and the ability to teach in ways that were responsive to their presumed individual needs. As the Plowden report observed in 1966, 'the teacher's task is to provide an environment and opportunities which are sufficiently challenging for children and yet not so difficult as to be outside their reach'.[94] It is important, however, not to overlook the evidence, for example from surveys conducted by HM Inspectorate, which suggests that, whatever the rhetoric, the teaching of most young children has remained rather routine and marked by an emphasis on the basic skills associated with reading, writing and arithmetic. As Alexander has commented, the true paradox is not the coexistence of subject-centred and child-centred traditions within primary pedagogy but that, since at least 1945, the progressive rhetoric has been 'apparently espoused across most of the range of primary practice', some of which is 'totally inconsistent' with that rhetoric.[95]

Inevitably, the need to take account of children's age, interests and ability in teaching nature study, allied with the need to retain the 'joy of spontaneity', raised difficulties for those who wished to present and promote schemes of work. These problems were overcome, or at least minimised, by two strategies. The first lay in emphasising repeatedly that published schemes of work could be no more than guides or suggestions for, or even hints at, what might be done in individual classrooms. Thus, von Wyss, occupying an influential position as editor of *School Nature Study*, informed her readers in 1918 that 'the Hints' supplied in the journal were 'not in the nature of indications of the "only way", but mere descriptions of ways and means that have elsewhere been found useful, and which are capable of modification to meet particular needs'.[96] The message was repeated seven years later when G.M. Conacher, author of a scheme of nature study work published in *School Nature Study*, stressed that the scheme was 'not meant ... (to) be blindly followed, (but) merely contained suggestions which might be a help when (teachers) were making their own syllabuses better suited to the neighbourhood in which they were teaching'.[97] When the School Nature Study Union published its own new schemes of work for nature study in 1932, in response to Hadow reorganisation, teachers were yet again advised that they should not adopt 'a ready-made syllabus for their courses of lessons, as such a scheme should be an expression of the opportunities, interests and aspirations of each school'.[98]

The second strategy involved highlighting the importance of nature study as an approach, as a method, rather than as knowledge to be acquired or a subject to be taught. The early characterisation of nature study as 'not knowledge, but spirit, and a particular method of approach' was frequently reasserted. In 1950, a member of the Executive Committee of the School Nature Study Union stressed[99] that all authors drawing up schemes of work in nature study should emphasise 'teaching method rather than subject matter', and two years later a contributor to the Union's journal felt it necessary to emphasise yet again that, in nature study, 'it is the method of investigation that is significant'.[100] The theme was taken up in 1960 (and emphasised by the use of italic script) by the Ministry of Education in its suggestions to teachers for teaching primary science:

> *the learning of facts ... may often be less important than the path to knowledge which is followed and the attitudes that are formed on the way.*[101]

and reasserted in the policy statement adopted by the Association for Science Education in 1963.

> We are more concerned with the development of an enquiring attitude of mind than with the learning of facts.[102]

Sharp contrasts and dichotomies such as child and curriculum, experience and knowledge, and method and content, are, of course, not confined to discussion about the teaching of nature study. They are characteristic of much of the literature of child-centred education, where they are often coupled together to produce statements intended to persuade, rather than illuminate. The Hadow report of 1931 provides perhaps the most succinct and familiar example of writing of this kind.

> The curriculum ... is to be thought of in terms of activity and experience rather than of knowledge to be acquired and facts to be stored.[103]

Nonetheless, the rhetoric associated with the teaching of nature study and, later, of primary science, is particularly rich in examples of what Alexander has referred to as 'knowledge-free child-centredness',[104] a position frequently located by contrasting it with undesirable past practice marked by 'mass teaching, chanting of tables, mechanical reading round the class ... rigid timetables ... the silencing of bells ... (and) the same textbook for every child'.[105]

The transition from nature study to primary science can be dated from the attempts in the 1950s to include more physical science in the primary school curriculum. That curriculum was now largely free from the central government control that had governed the work of the public elementary schools, although tradition and the limited educational background of many teachers remained significant obstacles to reform. It was not until well after the Second World War that the SNSU made any sustained attempt to include elementary physical science in its programme of activities or publications, or to relate nature study to more systematic and advanced work in physics or chemistry. An article[106] in

School Nature Study as early as 1912, suggesting that nature study might be the precursor for work of this kind and offering a scheme of work related to the science of light, significantly failed to prompt the publication of any other programmes based upon the physical sciences.

By the later 1950s, the position that science should occupy in the primary curriculum formed part of a wider debate focused on the need to increase substantially the national supply of qualified scientific and technological personnel. In 1957, B.L. Hampson presented the case for 'primary science' in the following terms.

> Present-day circumstances coupled with the rapid and unparalleled progress of Scientific achievement, demand that Science teaching in the Primary Schools should no longer be restricted to Nature Study.[107]

A conference held at the University of Reading in 1959 gave attention to ways of incorporating aspects of physical science in the primary curriculum 'at a time when the education of scientists is of national and international importance, when the impact and need of a scientific age are compelling teachers to reconsider both *what* is taught, and *how* it is taught'.[108] The title of the conference is of some interest since it referred not to science teaching in the primary school but to scientific exploration, an emphasis which was to be of particular significance for the development of primary science in the 1960s.

In 1957, the editor of *School Nature Study*, J.M. Branson, reminded readers that, although 'work with plants, animals, rocks and weather' had been the basis of the Union's programme for the past 50 years, it was now time for a change. The 'Nature Table', long a feature of elementary and primary schools alike, could give way to the 'Investigation Table' which might display such artefacts as clocks and watches, magnets and compasses as well as the objects more traditionally associated with nature study. In addition, simple experiments involving sound, electricity and forces could be conducted with young pupils.[109] Wastnedge, the Director of the Nuffield Junior Science Project (see Chapter 4) has documented the shift towards physical science in primary schools in the following terms.

> The object lesson had gone, but the nature table was still common, and here and there individual teachers began to take a broader view of nature, recognising that it had a physical, as well as a biological, component. Physical science became one of the things

> to 'do' in primary schools and by the late 1950s a fair number of teachers were deeply and excitedly involved in this latest development.[110]

The National Union of Teachers added its support to primary science, arguing that it 'should certainly not be confined to what is called "nature study" or elementary biology', and adding that 'the deep interest of our generation in physics and technology must not be excluded from the junior school'.[111]

The growing importance attached at the end of the 1950s to the development of primary science presented the School Nature Study Union with some difficulties. It attempted, with some success, to broaden the scope of the articles published in its journal. In 1963, it changed its name to become the School Natural Science Society and its journal was re-titled *Natural Science in Schools*.[112] The aims of the new society were broader than those of its predecessor. They included a reference to the advancement of 'knowledge in natural science which includes nature study, natural history, biology and the physical sciences' and they extended the Society's sphere of interest beyond primary schools to include 'secondary schools and ... the further stages of education'.[113]

In reality, the initiative for primary science lay elsewhere: with the British Association for the Advancement of Science,[114] with the Nuffield Foundation and the Primary Schools' Science Committee set up by the Association for Science Education in 1963. During the 1960s, three major primary science curriculum projects, the Nuffield Junior Science Project, the Oxford Junior Science project and the Schools Council Science 5–13 Project, generated a wealth of material to support the work of the primary teaching profession which was overwhelmingly female and ill-prepared to teach science (see Chapter 4). The longer-term consequences for the School Natural Science Society of this loss of initiative in primary science education were to prove fatal. Despite several attempts at collaboration with the Association for Science Education which, by the 1980s, was seeking vigorously and successfully to expand its membership among primary teachers,[115] the School Natural Science Society was forced to wind up its affairs in 1994.

As for the pedagogy of primary science, a new learning theory was invoked in the 1960s to justify its commitment to an investigative approach. The faculty psychology that had sustained object teaching was long obsolete and the essentially analogical 'rhythm' theory that had supported nature study gave way to a seemingly more experimentally-grounded psychology derived from the ideas of Jean Piaget.

Although a genetic epistemologist rather than a professional educator, some of Piaget's ideas were pressed into service to emphasise a substantial degree of commonality (and, it seems, for some commentators, a coincidence) between the learning of science by young children and the conduct of scientific research itself. The outcome was a notable exercise of accommodation involving, on the one hand, a psychology of learning which emphasised the importance of experience and discovery, and, on the other, an epistemology of science which, among much else, presented the relationship between observation and explanation as unproblematic. These and related matters are considered further in Chapter 6 but it is important to acknowledge at this point an important outcome of this accommodation, namely the consolidation within primary science education of a view of scientific method, which was naïve and inadequate in its own day and which, within a decade, would be rendered obsolete by the work of sociologists, historians and philosophers of science.

NOTES

1 Board of Education, *Code of Regulations for Public Elementary Schools, 1905* (London, HMSO, 1904).
2 Board of Education, *Suggestions for the Consideration of Teachers and Others Concerned in the Work of Public Elementary Schools* (London, HMSO, 1905), 46.
3 C. Birchenough, *History of Elementary Education in England and Wales from 1800 to the Present Day* (London, 1938), 310.
4 E.J. Thomas, *Views on Science Education 1900–1960 with Particular Reference to the Primary School*, M.Ed. thesis, Chelsea College, London 1978, 12.
5 G.G. Lewis, 'Possibilities of Nature-study in a London Elementary School', *School Nature Study*, 9, 33 (1914), 6.
6 *School Nature Study*, 2, 4 (1907), 15.
7 The shortage of trained science teachers was an enduring problem for elementary education. See E.W. Jenkins, *From Armstrong to Nuffield, Studies in Twentieth Century Science Education in England and Wales* (London, 1979), Chapter 6.
8 G.G. Lewis, op. cit., 7.
9 J. Lawson and H. Silver, *A Social History of Education in England* (London, 1973), 381.
10 Board of Education, *Code of Regulations for Public Elementary Schools*, 1908 (London, HMSO, 1908).
11 G.G. Lewis, op. cit., 10. For the School Journey Association, see *School Nature Study*, 6, 22 (1911), 98.
12 Board of Education, *Suggestions* ... (London, HMSO, 1905), 48.
13 Board of Education, *Report of the Consultative Committee on the Primary School* (London, HMSO, 1931), 182–3. The remit of this report on elementary education up to the age of 11 included the qualification 'with special reference to the needs of children in rural areas'. See Chapter 2.
14 Board of Education, 'Specimen Courses of Object Lessons on Common Things Connected with Rural Life and Industries for all Classes in Rural Schools', (1901),

in *Report of the Board of Education, 1900–01*, Vol. III, Appendix to Report (London, HMSO, 1901), 185.
15 E.M. Poulton, *The Teaching of Biology in Schools and Training Colleges* (Birmingham, 1924), 2–3.
16 Board of Education, *Specimen Courses* ... (n. 14), xxiv
17 Board of Education, *Suggestions* ... (1905), 102.
18 M.D. Hill and W.M. Webb, *Eton Nature-Study and Observation Lessons* (London, 1903), Part 1, vii.
19 Board of Education, *Suggestions* ... (London, HMSO, 1905), 48.
20 M.D. Hill and W.M. Webb, op. cit., Part 1, vii.
21 See, for example, W.S. Furneaux, *A Nature Study Guide* (London, 1912), 2.
22 C. von Wyss, 'The Teaching of Nature Study', in F. Hodson (ed.), *Broad Lines in Science Teaching* (London, 1909), 26.
23 T. Raymont, *The Principles of Education* (London, 1904), 14.
24 C. von Wyss, 'Some Suggestions for Autumn Nature Lessons', *School Nature Study*, 1, 1 (1906), 1.
25 J.A. Thomson, 'Some Suggestions to Teachers for Seasonal Nature Study in Schools' (1908), Appendix B of *Report of the Committee of Council in Scotland with Appendix, 1907–1908, Memorandum on Nature Study and the Teaching of Science in Scottish Schools* (London, HMSO, 1908), 344.
26 M.D. Hill and W.M Webb, op. cit., Part 1, vii.
27 R.J.W Selleck, *The New Education 1870–1914* (London, 1968). Selleck is quoting from the *Report of the Conference of New Ideals in Education*, Aug. 1914.
28 Board of Education, *Suggestions for the Consideration of Teachers* ... (London, HMSO, 1925), 22.
29 C. von Wyss, 'Teaching of Nature Study', in F.H. Hodson (ed.), op. cit., 30–36.
30 British Association for the Advancement of Science, *Report* (1917), 135–6. Nunn was appointed Vice-Principal of the London Day Training College in 1905 and from 1922 to 1936, he was Director of the London Institute of Education. His most famous work, *Education: Its Data and First Principles*, was published in 1920.
31 A.N. Whitehead, *The Rhythm of Education* (London, 1922).
32 Board of Education, *Report of the Consultative Committee on Secondary Education* (London, HMSO, 1938), 163.
33 E.M. Poulton, op. cit., 13–15.
34 Ibid., 19.
35 Idem.
36 Idem.
37 E.W. Jenkins, *From Armstrong to Nuffield* (London, 1979) and W.H. Brock, (ed.), *H.E. Armstrong and the Teaching of Science* (Cambridge, 1973).
38 J.A. Thomson, 'Some Suggestions to Teachers for Seasonal Nature Study in Schools' (1908), Appendix B of *Report of the Committee of Council on Education in Scotland with Appendix 1907–1908, Memorandum on Nature Study and the Teaching of Science in Scottish Schools* (London, HMSO, 1908), 360.
39 C. von Wyss, 'Suggestions for Autumn' (n. 24), 15.
40 H.E. Armstrong, 'The Limitations to which Nature Study Must Necessarily be Subject', *School Nature Study*, 8, 29 (1913), 21–2.
41 I. Goodson, *School Subjects and Curriculum Change*, Studies in Curriculum History 20, 1993, Third Edition (First published, London, 1982), 3.
42 Quoted in E.L. Paler, 'Fifty Years of Nature Study and the American Nature Study Society', *Nature Magazine*, 50 (1957), 475.
43 Board of Education, *Report for the Year 1909–10* (London, HMSO, 1910), 75, quoted in E.W. Jenkins, *From Armstrong to Nuffield* (London, 1979), 30.
44 Mr. Ward's Report on the North West Division. *Report of the Board of Education, 1913–14*, in C. Birchenough, op. cit., 341–2.

45 J.A. Thomson, 'The Seasonal Study of Natural History' speaking on 24 July 1902 and reported in the *Official Report of the Nature-Study Exhibition*. See also, 'A Note from the North', *School Nature Study*, 2, 5 (1907), 21.
46 C. von Wyss, 'The Teaching of Nature Study', in F. Hodson (ed.), *Broad Lines in Science Teaching* (London, 1909), 28.
47 *The Official Report of the Nature Study Exhibition and Conferences* (Glasgow, 1903) and *The Record of Secondary and Technical Education*, XI (1902), 48 and XIV (1905), 58.
48 Board of Education, *Suggestions* ... (London, HMSO, 1905), 82.
49 See, for example, the illustration in E.W. Jenkins, op. cit., 115.
50 G.H. Ellis, 'The Social Value of Gardening', *School Nature Study*, 1, 43 (1916), 35.
51 SNSU, Executive Committee Meeting held on 9 July 1915. *Minute Book*, 2, 31.
52 Editorial in *School Nature Study*, 12, 47 (1917), 17.
53 R.D. Bramwell, *Elementary School Work 1900–1925* (Institute of Education, University of Durham, 1961), 61.
54 Seventeenth Annual Report, *School Nature Study*, 15, 59 (1920), 31.
55 E.J. Morgan, 'The Richness of Parsley in Vitamin C (Ascorbic Acid)', *School Nature Study*, 37, 149 (1942), 60. In much the same vein was F.W. Howes, 'Rubber: Past and Present Sources', ibid., 37, 148, (1942), 33.
56 'The Schools in Wartime', ibid., 36, 144, (1941), 111.
57 See, for example, Board of Education, *A School Week in the Country* (London, HMSO, 1910).
58 For example, J.H. Cowham, 'The School Journey (London to Caterham etc.) Made by Students at the Westminster Training College', in Board of Education, *Special Reports on Educational Subjects*, 8 Cd. 835 (London, HMSO, 1902); J.M. England *et al.*, 'Three School Journeys in Yorkshire', ibid., 21 (1907).
59 D. Wilson, The Nature Study Section of the Children's Holiday Fund', *School Nature Study*, 3, 7 (1908), 3.
60 C.I. Dodd, 'A School Journey in Germany', *The National Review*, XXX (1897–98), 445–52. See also, G.H. Thomson and K. Haehnel, 'Wandervogel, A German Society for the Promotion of School Excursions', *The Geographical Teacher*, V (1909–10), 30–32.
61 G.I. McGabe, *Museums in Education: the educational role of museums in the United Kingdom*, Unpublished MA thesis, University of Sheffield, 1975.
62 H. Crowther, 'Discussions on Sir Henry Miers' Report', *Museums Journal*, XXVIII (1928–9), 224.
63 B. Hindshaw, 'The Young Visitor', ibid., XXIX (1929–30), 227–8.
64 J. Hutchinson, 'Museum Examinations', *The Nineteenth Century*, LXII (1907), 248–53.
65 J. Chard, 'On Circulating Museum Cabinets for Schools and Other Educational Purposes', *Proceedings of the Museums Association* (1890), 57–63.
66 W.M. Webb, 'Nature-Knowledge: its progress and interpretation', *The Record of Secondary and Technical Education*, XI (1902), 413.
67 J.W. Bainbridge, 'Origins of the Nature Study Movement', *Natural Science in Schools*, 16, 1 (1978), 11–14.
68 W.M. Webb, op. cit., 413.
69 D.E. Allen, *The Naturalist in Britain, A Social History* (London, 1976).
70 For Geddes's views on nature study, see the *Official Report of the Nature Study Exhibition*, op. cit., 111–24.
71 For a brief survey of Thomson's work, see his obituary in *The Aberdeen University Review*, XX, 59 (1933), 97–9. He was the co-author with Geddes of *Life: Outlines of General Biology*, published in two volumes in 1931.
72 H.T. Mark, *Modern Views on Education* (London, 1914), 114.
73 The term is taken from R.J.W. Selleck, *The New Education, 1870–1914* (London, 1968).

74 Edward Thomas, 'The Scope of Nature Study', in F. Hodson, (ed.), *Broad Lines in Science Teaching* (London, 1909), 16–22.
75 D. Layton, *Science for the People* (London, 1973), 170.
76 F.H. Hilliard, 'The Moral Instruction League 1897–1919', *Durham Research Review*, III, 12 (1961), 53–63.
77 Board of Education, *Code of Regulations for Public Elementary Schools 1906* (London, HMSO, 1906), vii.
78 W.D. Furneaux, *A Nature Study Guide* (London, 1912), 3.
79 F. Ware, *Educational Reform* (London, 1900), 62.
80 See, for example, Sir W. Huggins, *The Royal Society in the State and in the Schools* (London, 1906).
81 Sir G. Kekewich, *Official Report of the Nature Study Exhibition*, op. cit., 1903, 215.
82 C. von Wyss, 'The School Nature Study Union: Looking Backward and Forward', *School Nature Study*, 10, 38 (1915), 3.
83 L.H. Bailey, *The Nature Study Idea, Being an Interpretation of the New School Movement to Put the Child in Sympathy with Nature* (London, 1903), 4, 5.
84 SNSU, Executive Committee Meeting held on 10 February 1939, *Minute Book*, 4, 82–3.
85 Editorial in *School Nature Study*, 55, 219 (1960), 1.
86 E.W. Jenkins and B.J. Swinnerton, 'The School Nature Study Union 1903–94', *History of Education*, 25, 2 (1996), 191.
87 School Nature Study Union, Executive Committee Meetings held on 9 September 1921 (*Minute Book*, 2, 123) and 11 November 1921 (*Minute Book*, 2, 128).
88 School Nature Study Union, Executive Committee Meeting held on 8 February 1929, *Minute Book*, 3, 31; PRO, ED/10/148, Paper S36, *Memorandum by the School Nature Study Union*, 1; Board of Education, Consultative Committee, *The Primary School* (London, HMSO, 1931), 182–3.
89 The Union did attempt at various times to set up branches but without much enthusiasm. E.W. Jenkins and B.J. Swinnerton, op. cit., 183. The 1930s, and again after 1947, were periods of rapid growth in the membership of the SNSU, when the number of members just exceeded 2,000. Throughout its history, therefore, the membership of the SNSU accommodated only a very small proportion of those teaching in public elementary schools.
90 A. Briggs, *The Golden Age of Wireless* (Oxford, 1965), 189.
91 Ibid., 197.
92 Board of Education, *Handbook of Suggestions for the Consideration of Teachers and Others Concerned in the Work of Public Elementary Schools* (London, HMSO, 1927), 15.
93 Board of Education, *Handbook of Suggestions* ... (London, HMSO, 1937), reprinted 1947, 135.
94 DES, *Children and their Primary Schools*, Vol. 1, *Report* (London, HMSO, 1966), para. 533.
95 R.J. Alexander, *Primary Teaching* (London, 1984), 14.
96 C. von Wyss, 'Wild Life Held Captive', *School Nature Study*, 13, 51 (1918), 25.
97 G.M. Conacher, 'Suggestions as to Scheme of Work in Nature Study', *School Nature Study*, 20, 81 (1925), 81.
98 'Schemes of Nature Study', *School Nature Study*, 27, 109 (1932), 116.
99 SNSU, Executive Committee Meeting held on 12 May, 1950, *Minute Book*, 5, 80.
100 T. Morris, 'A Critique of School Nature Study; A View from the Antipodes', *School Nature Study*, 47, 189 (1953), 58.
101 Ministry of Education, *Primary Education, Suggestions for the Consideration of Teachers and Others Concerned with the Work of Primary Schools* (London, HMSO 1959), 292.
102 Association for Science Education Primary Schools' Science Committee, 'Policy Statement', *ASE Bulletin*, Nov. 1963, 19.

103 Board of Education, *Report of the Consultative Committee on the Primary School* (London, HMSO, 1931). For a discussion of the role of ideology in primary education, see R.J. Alexander, op. cit., Chapter 1.

104 R.J. Alexander, op. cit., 17.

105 N. Kirby, *Personal Values in Education* (London, 1981), 11 quoted in ibid., 17.

106 J. Riley, 'Nature-study Introductory to the Science of Light', *School Nature Study*, 7, 25 (1912), 50. Riley presented his ideas using the fashionable 'stage theory' of children's development, an observational approach based on the younger child's sense of 'wonder' gradually giving way to more complex and experimental strategies to appeal to the older pupil's presumed concern to impose order and systematise knowledge.

107 B.L. Hampson, 'Science from the beginning for the Primary School', *School Nature Study*, 52, 209 (Oct. 1957), 66.

108 Underlining in the Original. Weekend Conference on 'Scientific Exploration in the Primary School', held at the University of Reading, 24–25 April 1959.

109 J.M. Branson, 'Tea Discussion: College of Preceptors', *School Nature Study*, 52, 206 (1957), 9.

110 Ron Wastnedge, 'Nuffield Junior Science: The End of a Beginning', in D. Holford and C. Richards (eds), *The Teaching of Primary Science: policy and practice* (London, 1983), 139.

111 National Union of Teachers, *The Curriculum of the Junior School* (London, 1948), 136–7.

112 *Natural Science in Schools* (1963), 1, 1.

113 School Natural Science Society, Executive Committee Meeting held on 21 June 1963, *Minute Book*, 8, 65.

114 The British Association organised an influential conference on 'Approaches to Science in the Primary School' in Sept. 1961.

115 E.W. Jenkins and B.J. Swinnerton, op. cit., 196.

4

Primary science curriculum development

The Education Act of 1944 formally established primary schools as the first stage of compulsory schooling and linked them to a tripartite system newly-created to provide a free secondary education for each pupil in accordance with his or her age, ability and aptitude. The effective implementation of the legislation, however, was constrained by several factors. A rapid post-war rise in the birthrate and the destruction or damage of about 5,000 schools during the war led to a severe shortage both of accommodation and of teachers, although the latter had a more marked effect on secondary, rather than primary, schools. The estimate that at least 2¼ million new school places would be needed by 1961 soon proved seriously inadequate and by 1959 the stock of school places had been increased by 3 million.[1] Most of the primary schools built immediately after 1945 were 'not dissimilar to pre-war schools'[2] but by the early 1950s, pressure on building costs allied with architectural responses to developing ideas about how young children should be taught (see Chapter 7) led to significant initiatives in primary school design. These initiatives, however, did not include specialised accommodation for the teaching of primary science which, as in the pre-war years, remained largely confined to nature study.

Although any form of specialised accommodation for science was to remain quite exceptional in primary schools, not least because of cost and the challenge it offered to an educational philosophy that was suspicious of subject teaching and emphasised an 'integrated day' and 'a seamless curriculum', the position of science within primary schooling received greatly increased attention during the later 1950s. To some extent, this was part of a wider scrutiny of scientific and technological education which, fuelled by political concern at an enduring shortage of qualified scientific personnel and the consequent implications for both defence and economic competitiveness, was to lead among much else to the establishment of Colleges of Advanced Technology and the appointment of the country's first Minister for Science. Schools, in particular the grammar schools, were seen as the source of the new 'technocrats', the scientifically literate captains of industry and the civil servants fit for a society which Harold Wilson, in the 1960s, was to claim would be forged in the white heat of technological revolution. For some, education in the future was to be based not upon science as technique, but as culture, as had been the case with classics in the previous century. Although this was arguably less a vigorous new social movement than a distant and ironic echo of a public school ideology that had reached its zenith towards the end of the nineteenth century, it was unquestionably a beguiling and powerful vision which appealed to industrialists, scientists, the public and, inevitably, the science teaching profession.

At the secondary level, this vision, underpinned by important initiatives taken by the Science Masters' Association to reform grammar school science teaching in the late 1950s, eventually made it possible for the Minister of Education, Sir David Eccles, to announce to the House of Commons on 4 April 1962, that the Nuffield Foundation had

> decided to make available £250,000 towards the cost of a long-term development programme to improve teaching in (science and mathematics).

The events leading up to this announcement and the subsequent programme of science curriculum reform have been described by a number of authors, notably by Layton[3] and Waring.[4] It will be enough in the present context, therefore, to note three points. First, the earliest of the Nuffield Projects were concerned with the reform of science teaching at the Ordinary level of the GCE in physics, chemistry and biology, a decision that reflected both the historical origins of the two secondary science teaching Associations[5] and the importance attached to the education of greater numbers of qualified scientists and, therefore, in 1961, to science education within the grammar schools. Second, the mechanism for effecting change in the practice of school science teaching was that of 'centre–periphery' curriculum reform. In accordance with this model, the new ideas and practices devised by a 'central' curriculum development team were trialled in schools before a final version was published for use by the profession as a whole. Finally, although science curriculum developments in the United Kingdom had their own distinctive characteristics, they were part of a commitment to curriculum reform which was global in scale, extended beyond science and mathematics to embrace most of the secondary curriculum and served to justify the description of the 1960s and the first half of the 1970s as the 'curriculum development era'.

THE NUFFIELD JUNIOR SCIENCE PROJECT

Until the late 1950s, neither of the two school science teaching organisations, the Science Masters' Association and the Association of Women Science Teachers, was particularly active in promoting primary science, although the position changed rapidly after the two organisations merged in 1963 to form the Association for Science Education (ASE). Their membership was drawn principally from grammar and public schools and, as noted above, the earliest of the many Nuffield curriculum initiatives were directed at pupils being prepared for science examinations at the Ordinary level of the GCE. In addition, as noted in Chapter 3, the School Nature Study Union had a relatively small membership which was divided over the issues of whether, and if so, in what ways, the primary curriculum might give more attention to the teaching of science, especially physical science. In these circumstances, responsibility for promoting primary school science fell upon a number of other organisations and individuals. In September 1961, the British Association for the Advancement of Science organised a conference on primary science because of its deep concern with the 'the problems of what can be done about science in the primary school'.[6] A one-day conference on the teaching of science in the junior school held at the University of Leicester in April 1959 was followed immediately by a weekend conference on 'Scientific Exploration in the Primary School' at the University of Reading Institute of Education. The University of Leicester continued its commitment by offering a series of lectures on 'Natural Science in Primary Schools' throughout the summer and autumn of 1961, and similar initiatives were taken by universities and colleges in other parts of the country. Advocacy of primary science also began to sustain a small publishing industry. The Association of Teachers in Colleges and Departments of Education (ATCDE), the Association of Women Science Teachers, the London Association of Science Teachers and the Science Masters' Association collaborated to produce *Science in the Primary School*, published in 1959. The Ministry of Education issued a pamphlet, *Science in Primary Schools*, in 1961 which offered important insights into official thinking[7] and the National Froebel Society, sponsored by the British Association for the Advancement of Science, initiated a 'Finding Out' Project. Directed by Nathan Isaacs, the Project studied the work of 30 primary school teachers who had carried out scientific investigations derived from their pupils' interests and questions. The results of the study were eventually published in 1966 with the significant title *Children Learning through Scientific Interests*, and they offered important insights into such matters as the role of the teacher and the keeping of records of pupils' progress. As soon as the Association for Science Education was formed in January 1963, its Science and Education Committee recommended an extension of the Association's remit to include the teaching of science in schools of all types, and a primary school sub-committee was established under the chairmanship of D.H.J. Marchant of Kesteven Training College. By November 1963 the Association had produced a Policy Statement on *Primary School Science* which commended a discovery approach, based upon 'finding-out activities'.[8] When, in 1965, the ASE published its more general policy statement, *School Science and General Education*, attention was given for the first time to 'Primary Stage Science Education'. However, despite the appointment of a new sub-committee and, later, of a working party, to 'look into the matter of publicity for the ASE in primary schools', little progress was made in recruiting primary teachers into membership until the 1980s, when a reduced subscription rate, programmes of activities that gave greater attention to primary teachers' needs, and a substantial publicity campaign that included the publication of a termly news-sheet, *ASE Primary Science*, brought greater success.[9]

By the early 1960s, therefore, there was substantial and growing agreement about a number of issues relating to the development of science teaching within primary education. The rationale seemed secure. When, in 1961, Nathan Isaacs claimed[10] that 'In this scientific age of ours, there is a strong case for bringing science, at least in some measure, into the education of all of us', he was doing no more than reasserting a theme that had by then become something of a commonplace. For example, *The Guardian*, some months earlier had commented that

> ... the process by which scientific discovery has enlarged the limits of the physical universe in which we live has also created a need for much greater familiarity with concepts which may often, until recently, have been the prerogative of scientists. In a world of iron ships, even children should have some feeling for why they float.[11]

These essentially educational claims were, of course, reflective of wider concerns about economic prosperity, national prestige and, at the height of the Cold War, advantage in offensive and defensive technology. As Gordon has observed,

> *Technological and economic* factors are responsible for curriculum change. Fears raised by continental competition in the mid-

> nineteenth century led eventually to a wider definition of the nature of elementary education. Similarly, inter-nation rivalry in the space programmes of the 1950s was a stimulus to the proliferation of new mathematics and science projects in Britain and the USA.[12]

There was agreement, too, about how science should be taught, at least in general terms, to children of primary school age. Science, regarded less as a body of knowledge than as a method of inquiry and investigation, seemed to have much to offer the progressives within primary education. Its emphasis upon direct interrogation of the natural world by processes of active inquiry had an obvious, although beguiling, appeal to those for whom first-hand experience of phenomena and 'discovery learning' were the *sine qua non* of primary education. Young children, therefore, were to be taught science by 'investigative methods' that promoted outcomes that eventually came to be identified by a variety of labels, including investigative or inquiry skills, scientific processes, and even thinking skills. At the British Association Conference on the Place of Science in Primary Education held in September 1961, both Nathan Isaacs and J.F. Kerr used their speeches to advocate 'finding-out' methods, a stance which was reflected strongly in the *Policy Statement* produced by the Association for Science Education in 1963.

> At this level, we are concerned more with the developing of an enquiring attitude of mind than with the learning of facts. Of course we cannot deter children (nor do we wish to) from collecting scientific information, but our aim should be to give significance to the facts which children will inevitably acquire; at no time is the imparting of factual knowledge to be regarded as an end in itself.
>
> The kind of approach we recommend is discovery and 'finding-out' activities.[13]

Another advantage of prioritising scientific ways of investigation over science as a body of knowledge in the scientific education of young children was that it offered to mitigate the problem of the lack of scientific knowledge among primary school teachers. In 1964, 76 per cent of teachers in maintained primary schools in England were female[14] and, like their male colleagues, few of these had any formal education in physical science as part of their higher education and professional training. A survey of a representative sample of teacher training colleges in 1961 revealed[15] that 95 per cent were in general agreement with the idea that the scope of nature study should be extended to include physical science, although ten colleges had reservations and two were opposed to such a development. In 45 per cent of the colleges sampled, the training of students to teach primary science accounted for less than 30 hours during the entire three-year course, with only two colleges providing more than 100 hours, and only 40 per cent of the sample required all their students to have at least some training in science. Another survey[16] of eight training colleges in 1962 found that the relevant component of the teaching practice experience of the college students was restricted almost entirely to nature study, with only five per cent being devoted to any significant teaching of the physical sciences. The problem, therefore, was widely recognised and seen as a major obstacle to any extension of science within the primary curriculum.

> As science and technology increasingly dominate our culture, the training colleges are faced with the responsibility of producing teachers who will be able to play a major role in raising the level of the scientific literacy of the people.[17]

Responses to the problem, however, took a variety of forms. For some, the need was to train primary teachers, including those already in service, to teach 'for learning through scientific investigations', that is, to teach science in ways that were consonant with the ideals of progressive primary education. For others, in contrast, teaching children to investigate natural phenomena presented at best only a modest challenge, since children were 'naturally curious' about the world around them and a skilled, if scientifically unknowledgeable teacher, could engage collaboratively with his or her pupils in investigative activities. In such cases, it was the activities and the experiences which mattered rather than the scientific concepts that might have been acquired. For no less an authority than the Ministry of Education,

> the pursuit of science ... is no more than a natural extension of a process already developed in environmental studies and is in keeping with children's interests, sometimes their dominating interests ... It can knit well with the child's whole education.[18]

From this, it is but a short step to the belief that young children are naturally imbued with the 'scientific way of working'. It was this belief, together with the claim that 'science presents the teacher with a constant challenge to learn and discover for himself' (*sic*), which underpinned the work of the Nuffield Junior Science Project[19] and which allowed Waring subsequently to claim that its proposals 'rested squarely on a set of assumptions, each of which was part of the then largely accepted English social, political and educational way of life'.[20] Any challenge to the approach eventually adopted by the project was, therefore, easily rebutted by reference to an array of contemporary authoritative opinion. For example, criticism from Irene Finch HMI prompted the response that the Project philosophy was

> completely acceptable to the Primary Schools Committee of the ASE, to the Froebel Institute, the Froebel Foundation, Nathan Isaacs, to many training college lecturers, to a number of psychologists including Jerome Bruner, and perhaps most important of all to a great many teachers who already use this approach (and who are generally regarded as progressive). One of the criticisms raised so far by HMI is that we have not offered enough to the progressive teachers who are saying, 'We are doing this already, what else do you want us to do?'[21]

A primary science project to complement those already initiated at Ordinary level formed part of the original commitment[22] of the Nuffield Foundation in 1961 to improve the teaching of science in schools. During 1962, discussion about the way to proceed was underway both within and beyond the Nuffield Foundation. A Primary School Science Study Group, set up by the (then) Royal Institute of Chemistry had met during 1961 and 1962 before preparing a report which was sent both to the Nuffield Foundation and the Ministry of Education. Its essential recommendation was that a national programme of primary science curriculum development be undertaken. There were, according to J.F. Kerr, good grounds for optimism that the Foundation would soon fund a primary initiative as it was already doing at the secondary level.[23] Kerr's judgement was sound and a decision to take matters forward was made at a meeting of the Trustees of the Foundation held on 26 April 1963 at Nuffield Lodge after the presentation of a policy document outlining the aims and expected organisation of a primary science Project.[24] The Project, funded with a grant of £75,000, received formal approval later that year.[25] E.R. Wastnedge was appointed the Organiser of the Nuffield Junior Science Project and he came to be supported by eight Team Leaders and a Consultative Committee of 11 which included three members of Her Majesty's Inspectorate of Schools. The commitment of the Organiser to a child-centred philosophy was widely shared among the Team Leaders and the Consultative Committee and it was one which the Nuffield Foundation did not seek to challenge. In addition, at a meeting in the middle of 1963 with, among others, two HMI and Tony Becher of the Nuffield Foundation, Wastnedge successfully challenged views expressed in papers about primary science prepared by the

Organisers of the Ordinary level Projects in physics, chemistry and biology. In Wastnedge's view, the papers were to be discarded because they were 'about what the secondary schools wanted, not what's right for primary schools'.[26] There was, however, an important issue at stake here, namely that of continuity between primary and secondary science education. While Wastnedge was undoubtedly wise to press for what was 'right for primary schools', it was obviously important for him and his Team leaders, not least in wider political terms, to see

> Science not only as a valuable aspect of the well-integrated study in the less formal school, but also as a subject in the timetable in the very formal school. In this way, we should antagonise no one.[27]

In practice, the Organisers of the three Ordinary level projects were consulted before the Junior science project began its work in earnest and Frank Halliwell, the Organiser of the Chemistry project, was brought onto the Consultative Committee.[28] In addition, the press announcement of the setting up of the Junior Science project indicated that particular attention would be paid to the question of continuity between the primary and secondary stages of schooling.[29] This desire to try and provide for continuity was, in part, why the work of the Junior Science Project formally involved pupils up to the age of 13, rather than 11 when primary schooling commonly ended.[30] Wastnedge also claimed that the informal methods associated with primary education had no less value for somewhat older pupils.

> We believe that the majority of children when they are transferred to secondary schools have not matured sufficiently to accept the approach (of a subject-based timetable). In other words, they will still need to solve practical problems, many of them will still transcend subject boundaries.[31]

The Primary Schools' Science Committee of the Association for Science Education expressed the issue rather more bluntly and emphatically.

> **We do not consider that children at 11 can be regarded as undergoing a strange metamorphosis that makes possible the immediate adoption of the formal methods which are most appropriate at a later stage.**[32]

However, as the Junior Science Project developed, a lack of time and resources ensured that the 11–13 age range received relatively little attention with initially only one, and then two, people being responsible for the necessary work in the lower years of secondary schooling.[33] The focus of the project, therefore, was firmly[34] on the teaching of science in the primary school and, more specifically, on the age range 8–11.

* * *

The task of the Project Team was initially perceived as that of producing materials which would help teachers to include and exploit science in their teaching programmes. However, Wastnedge, writing in 1983, commented that

> As things turned out, the major contribution of the project was made at a more fundamental level and concerned the nature and role – if any – of science in primary education ... We knew that we needed to know much more about children's responses to scientific problems and we were also very conscious of the exciting trends in primary education.[35]

In finding out more about 'children's responses to scientific problems', the Junior Science Project drew upon the writings of those, notably Pestalozzi, Froebel, Susan and Nathan Isaacs, and Jean Piaget, whose ideas were used to support progressive ideas within primary education more generally. The influence of these 'learning theorists' upon the work of the Project is discussed in Chapter 7 and it will be sufficient here to anticipate two points. The first is to acknowledge the contribution of Nathan Isaacs to the thinking underpinning the Junior Science Project and, in particular, the emphasis which he placed upon listening and responding to children's own questions as the basis of classroom practice. Isaacs, as early as 1927, had argued that science teaching should begin with

> that which emanates from the child itself, spontaneously and usually actively. Most normal children of, let us say, 4–5 years of age show a lively, inquiring curiosity in the world around them and want to know how things work, what they are, how they are made. Their curiosity seeks knowledge and takes pleasure in finding it. We should be endeavouring so to guide, reinforce, and develop this curiosity of the normal child in the world around him that it could pass continuously by its own activity into the same interest, informed and organized, in the world – not different but greater – of science.[36]

The second is that, although the Teacher's Guide eventually published by the Project included an Appendix briefly summarising Piagetian ideas about cognitive development, Piagetian stage theory was not a strong operational influence upon the direction taken by Wastnedge and his team. It seems to have served principally to legitimise the emphasis to be placed upon the kinds of experience and activities associated with progressivism in primary education. The implications of a stage theory of cognitive development for the sequencing of a science component within a primary curriculum received scant attention and teachers were advised that

> The evidence suggests that it is not possible to hasten the forming of concepts, but that schools can make it easier by providing suitable materials and situations.[37]

In more practical terms, finding out more about 'children's responses to scientific problems' meant finding out more about 'their ability to experiment, to observe, to generalise or find patterns, and to predict', and establishing whether 'science could fit easily and naturally into the most advanced primary education of the day'.[38] The Project team began to address these issues by studying the science work done in primary schools in a number of 'pre-pilot' areas of the United Kingdom. Reports drawn from this work, which constituted Phase 1 of the Project, were eventually published as Volume 2 of the Teacher's Guide but their immediate purpose was to provide a basis for writing materials which could be tried out in the schools drawn from a range of Local Education Authorities and (in Northern Ireland) Education and Library Boards. These trials constituted the second phase of the Project. The final, third phase of the Project was devoted to revising these materials in the light of teachers' comments upon, and experience of using, them and thus preparing them for publication.

In the first phase of the three-year Project, Wastnedge and his team worked collaboratively with primary teachers to explore what could be achieved within primary science education. Given that the starting points for the work derived from children's own natural curiosity about the world around them, the range of topics covered was wide. It included, for example, colours and sound, rats, central heating, angling, electricity, bones and day-old chicks. The following, derived from an account of a class of 35 boys and girls, aged 6–7 years, studying electricity, illustrates the kind of observations made and data collected.

> One of the articles on the discovery table ... was a small torch ... One day, Raymond announced that he had made a torch at home ... it consisted of a small battery, a bulb, and a short piece of wire.

> Because Raymond was concerned about the life of the battery, he refused to let his classmates use it, so the teacher supplied (the necessary materials).
>
> ... After much discussion, several children became involved, until, about two-thirds of the class could produce a light using the 3V and 4.5V batteries ...
>
> By now, many children were working on individual problems concerned with the electricity materials ... Much of the exploration did not produce positive results ... One girl lit her bulb and then twisted it round and round. This was a lighthouse.
>
> Benny announced loudly that his bulb would not light, and immediately received advice from half the class. First they tried to prove that his experimental technique was unsound but it soon became clear that there really was something wrong with the bulb. There were many reasons suggested.
>
> 'Someone's dropped it.'
>
> 'Too much got in.'
>
> 'The wire was too hot.'

The teacher of this class kept notes on the progress of this work and commented as follows.

> ... during group and individual discussions it becomes obvious that they do not yet understand some of the ideas which seemed to me to be very simple.
>
> 1 Martin used a cylindrical battery upside down and *all* were staggered that it worked in exactly the same way ...
> 2 Many children believe that all the different bulbs give the same brightness.
> 3 They are sure that the wire they happen to have used is probably the only one that will produce the result.

The approach adopted in this 'pre-trial' phase of the Project did more than explore ways in which the professional practice of primary teachers might be developed to include scientific topics not hitherto taught to young children. It offered important insights into the nature and quality of children's thinking in ways that reveal clearly the influence of Nathan Isaacs. For example, two separate accounts were eventually provided of work by children of different ages studying aspects of sound. The interest of six- to seven-year-old pupils in this topic led them to investigate the relationship between the sound produced by xylophone bars of different length, weight and shape, and subsequently to a study of vibration. With older children of nine to ten years in a different class, an interest in sound led to the study of sound production, pitch, amplification, transmission and insulation, and acuteness of hearing.[39] The 'pre-pilot' phase also held out at least the possibility that the Project team might be able to identify areas of interest that were common to at least most young children. Blackwell, a Team Leader responsible for seven primary schools in the Kent area, had no doubt 'about the universality of appeal of certain topics', adding that such appeal sprang from 'the dual sources of the basically stimulating effect of the material, topic or situation and the fact that it seems to serve as a natural focus for the attention of the child at a particular point in its development'.[40] Finally, this first phase also exposed many of the problems which teachers encountered in organising the science work, accommodating it within the school timetable and managing a class of perhaps more than thirty pupils engaged in investigative activities. These problems were noted and advice eventually offered to teachers in the first volume of the Teacher's Guide.

The testing of the interim materials generated from the first phase of the Project began in September 1965. The trials were organised in conjunction with the newly-established (1964) Schools Council which organised a preliminary meeting in January 1995 of representatives of the Local Education Authorities responsible for the pilot schools. These schools and Authorities were chosen so as to give 'a good cross section of social background, types of buildings, rural and heavy industrial regions, size of school, age and ability ranges of child and teacher', although other criteria were also invoked, notably the availability of good in-service training or the proximity of a Team Leader.[41] In the event, rather too many Local Education Authorities wished to become involved in the trials and it was not possible to take advantage of all the offers of collaboration. Sheffield, Nottingham, Devonshire and Lincolnshire, for example, provided no trial schools because the teaching in the primary schools in these Authorities was thought to be so progressive as to be 'unrepresentative',[42] although the Authorities were drawn into the work of the Project as 'Consultative Areas'. This allowed primary teachers working in these Authorities and in the vanguard of primary science education to comment upon the materials that were being tried out in the formally designated pilot schools[43] which, by May 1965, numbered 75. By the end of that year, however, there remained 100 Local Education Authorities that were not involved in any way with the trials, although access to the Project materials was not normally denied.[44] A further 12 areas joined the trials in September 1966.[45]

Of particular importance in this second phase of the Project were the arrangements made to develop the professional competence and confidence of primary school teachers to undertake investigative work in science with their pupils. Teachers and administrators from pilot areas attended national courses, presented principally by Project staff and members of Her Majesty's Inspectorate, which introduced them to the Project materials and their underlying philosophy. The teachers introduced to the materials in this way were then asked to organise similar courses for their colleagues within their own Local Authorities. The Authorities themselves were strongly encouraged to set up Teachers' Centres which could be used for meetings, courses, lectures and the display of resources, and so on, and by June 1966 there were 45 such Centres in existence, although a few, for example, those at Birmingham and Carlisle, pre-dated the Project. Using Folkestone as an example to illustrate the pattern and scale of training associated with the Project, 14 primary schools and seven secondary schools (four modern, three selective) participated in the junior science and/or mathematics curriculum initiatives associated with the Nuffield Foundation. Initially, two members of the Inspectorate/Advisory staff of the Kent LEA and four primary school headteachers attended two 'leader courses'. The training they subsequently organised for their colleagues between February and June 1965 involved a number of talks and lectures, including one on 'Using the Environment', and seven sessions devoted to the education of infant school pupils. Seventeen teachers visited a junior school where work of interest to both the Nuffield Science and Mathematics Projects was taking place. Appropriate courses were attended by 14 primary and two secondary teachers, the involvement of the latter justified not only by the 5–13 remit of the Project but by their eventual accommodation of pupils who would leave the feeder primary schools involved in the trials.[46] The Schools Council arranged further courses for the pilot schools between December 1965 and the summer of 1966.[47]

The longer-term professional development of the teachers was seen as an important role for the various Teachers' Centres referred to above, the precise organisation of which differed from one part of the country to another, not least in the extent to which they collaborated with Institutes of Education working as part of the Area Training Organisations, set up in 1948 after the McNair report, or other agencies within higher education (see Chapter 5). The development of Teachers' Centres was strongly encouraged by the Plowden report and by 1970 more than 280 had been established, with the number rising to over 600 in the following few years. Wastnedge attached particular importance to the work of the Teachers' Centres which the Junior Science Project had done so much to bring about, judging in 1983 that they had developed into 'essential components of all local education services'.[48]

Not all aspects of the organisation of the project proceeded as smoothly as the Project Team would have wished. For example, at a course for Leaders held in Cardiff in April 1965, it became clear that some LEAs, including Liverpool, Cardiff and the London County Council, had not informed their schools and teachers about the nature of the pilot trials to be undertaken. In addition, some LEAs had chosen the schools and teachers to be involved in the Project without any regard for the concern on the part of the Project Team to ensure a good cross section of schools and catchment areas of different types.[49]

During the final year of the Nuffield Junior Science Project, the experience gained by the teachers in the pilot schools was used to revise the interim materials in preparation for commercial publication. The first of the two Teacher's Guides set out the general educational philosophy of the Project and attempted to illustrate this in terms of practical, classroom activities offered to teachers as suggestions of what might be done. This same volume, as noted above, also addressed many of the difficulties and concerns that teachers had experienced during the course of their involvement with the trial and development of the Project materials. The second Teacher's Guide reported upon work done in pre-pilot and pilot schools and attempted to 'extract general information on what kinds of topics have been covered, what limitations appear to exist, and so on'.[50] Two further volumes were also published. *Apparatus: a Source Book of Information and Ideas* was intended to assist primary school teachers who had little experience of constructing their own apparatus for teaching science to young children. In a similar manner, *Animals and Plants: a Source Book of Information and Ideas*, offered advice about issues suggested by its title, including the keeping of live animals within primary classrooms. The publication programme was completed by three background booklets for teachers, *Autumn into Winter*, *Science and History*, and *Mammals in Classrooms*.

The apparatus source book was based on work undertaken principally by F.F. Blackwell who was largely responsible for this aspect of the Project's work. After the first phase, the Kent area, where Blackwell was the Team leader in 1964, was used specifically for testing apparatus and audio-visual equipment that might be used to support the work of the Project.[51] Blackwell examined the various commercially-available kits of apparatus to ascertain whether the items within them could be made, rather than bought,[52] and the volume which was eventually published offered teachers ideas of how they and their pupils could make simple apparatus rather than purchase expensive, ready-made equipment. The purpose here was not simply economy. In Blackwell's view, commercially-available kits of apparatus were also a restriction upon the work that might be done since 'their very completeness destroys any need for the child to enter with initiative into the situation (and) its creative participation is kept to the minimum'.[53] The Consultative Committee to the Project shared this view, endorsing the 'general feeling of the team' that it was

> desirable at this stage for children to improvise apparatus from everyday materials. This enables them to solve more problems, encourages them to do scientific work at home, and helps to dispel the idea of science as a mystique, comprehensible only to special people, wearing special clothes and working in special rooms.[54]

It was also desirable that children of primary school age and their teachers should see science as a whole and not, as within the secondary school, as composed of separate subjects. Making connections between the various scientific disciplines and between science and the remainder of the primary curriculum was seen as important because children viewed the world as a whole. In Blackwell's view, 'Children look on the world with this unity of vision and it is both in the interest of their education and that of Science to preserve this'.[55]

The Project was evaluated both internally and externally. Area leaders involved in the pilot trials of the Project materials sent back reports on a regular basis to the central Project team. These reports were based upon questionnaires devised by the team and addressed issues relating to the usefulness to teachers of the trial materials. The reports seem to have presented a fairly consistent and generally positive response, with particular praise for the case histories, although there were, perhaps inevitably, difficulties and problems. Some primary teachers involved in the trials found the volume of material difficult to handle and a few suggested an index to improve their access to it. A report from the Liverpool area suggested that the teachers working in that part of the country gained more from the various in-service courses than from the printed materials.[56] They also, its seems, relied less than other areas upon the case histories as a means of generating 'starting points' for the work with their pupils.[57] There was also a general sense that the Project materials were of more help to teachers in junior, rather than infant, schools.[58] In the Chelmsford area, teachers reported difficulties with children flitting from one activity to another, or engaging in more than one activity at the same time. In addition, some children didn't appear to be interested in any activity, perhaps because their teachers were unsure about how much help and direction they should give their pupils. As the report from the Area Leader put it, 'There is a feeling that the Nuffield Scheme frowns on any direction at all.'[59]

The reports from the Area leaders and the various courses provided for the teachers involved with the trials influenced the development of the project in a number of ways. By mid-1965, for example, Wastnedge realised that many teachers were asking for more direct guidance about how to use the Project materials. This presented the Project team with some difficulty since detailed specification of how to exploit the trial materials was inimical to the Project's philosophy and, in particular, to the importance of children's own questions as a basis for developing their scientific education, and its commitment to providing 'resources' and not 'courses'. Wastnedge considered a number of options, including supplying teachers with lists of suppliers of materials and apparatus, advice on how best to make use of the resources of the Teachers' Centres, and the provision of more detail about the teaching of some of the scientific topics in the Teacher's Guides.[60] In the event, a list of 'Sources of Aids for Use in Junior Science' was included in Volume 1 of the published *Teacher's Guide*, much of which was devoted to advice to teachers on such matters as 'Making a Start ' (Chapter 3) and 'Problems in Classroom Organisation'(Chapter 5).

As the Project entered its final phase, the Schools Council commissioned an independent evaluation of its work.[61] Undertaken by R.W. Crossland of the University of Manchester, the necessary study took place between July 1966 and March 1967. It involved visits to schools between July and November 1966 when discussions were held with about one hundred headteachers, assistant teachers and Local Education Authority personnel in eight areas. A further two hundred head and assistant teachers in ten areas responded to postal questionnaires.[62] The study did not involve classroom observation by the evaluator and there was opposition from some of the primary teachers to any approach to evaluation which required the formal measurement of what pupils had learnt as a result of their science-based, investigative activities. As Crossland remarked, such teachers 'feel that testing may destroy creativity, initiative to discover and the interest in scientific phenomena'.[63]

Like the Project itself, Crossland's evaluation was very much a child of its time and it revealed fundamental divisions between primary teachers' attitudes towards the science curriculum reform. Progressive teachers were able to identify examples of how the Project had had a valuable effect on the educational progress of their pupils and were much in sympathy with the pedagogy which the Project sought to promote. In contrast, teachers of a more traditional persuasion expressed their concern about the lack of specified content and found the open-ended approach to following up children's questions difficult to manage. These teachers were unsympathetic to the idea of the teacher as 'an architect ... who with his (*sic*) own knowledge of how the pieces fit together can guide the ultimate shape of the structure as a whole', and they needed more than the Project's attempt to provide a degree of structure by identifying 'starting points' rather than a course or syllabus.[64] Crossland could only conclude that

> It could be held that the children's achievements are closely related to their teacher's sympathy with, and success in practising, informal methods of teaching.[65]

Many of Crossland's findings clustered around teachers' different perceptions of their work and of how children's learning could best be promoted. Compared with their more traditional colleagues, teachers who saw themselves as comfortable with informal teaching methods identified more benefits from their involvement with the Project. These benefits were both 'scientific' and 'non-scientific', although not all were observed with all pupils. The 'non-scientific' benefits were identified as improvements in communication skills, critical thinking, manipulation and measurement skills, curiosity about the environment, and children's confidence, liveliness and initiative. The 'scientific benefits' included the acquisition of scientific facts and concepts, an improved ability to ask pertinent questions and pose problems, an enhanced willingness to investigate, and better classification and identification skills.[66] As was to be the case a generation later, it was the teaching of reading which most sharply divided the teachers. Progressive teachers believed that their pupils' competence at reading was improved, but some of their older and more traditional colleagues suggested that the time spent on science teaching would have been better spent on the teaching of reading.[67]

Members of the Project team were, of course, aware that the teaching approach which they advocated was not one that would come easily to many, perhaps most, primary teachers. The advice to more conservative primary school teachers stressed that informal methods of teaching should be introduced gradually, since 'children need time to adjust to new situations and to respond to new demands'. While there were teachers who had 'made the change in one step ... the process was not always very comfortable', although 'all agreed that the experience was stimulating, provoked thought, and resulted in a completely new and satisfying relationship between teacher and children'.[68] Nonetheless, it is clear, with the benefit of hindsight, that the Junior Science Project asked too much of most primary school teachers in too short a time. The Project involved the teaching of a new component of the primary curriculum and in ways with which most primary teachers were unfamiliar, whatever the rhetoric to the contrary. Writing in 1983, Wastnedge acknowledged that the Project had overestimated the effectiveness of the printed word in effecting the necessary change and that there had been insufficient time for teachers to develop the necessary confidence in using the Nuffield approach

> Like all other projects at the time, we believed that if we collected information and advice from teachers in schools and wrote it down clearly, other teachers would read it and act upon it. How wrong we were.[69]

Jean Conran, in a personal commentary upon primary science spanning the period from 1950 to 1982, judged that

> Nuffield Junior Science represented the ideal of good primary science teaching, but its complex acceptance of an open-ended approach daunted those of us who were inexperienced in the processes of a science, in the physical sciences, and in helping children to devise investigations to answer their own questions. We had not yet learned to ask and answer our own questions.[70]

Despite Crossland's overall conclusion that the Project had achieved much in promoting less formal methods of teaching, the evidence that subsequently became available suggested strongly that any shift in primary teachers' pedagogy, or indeed their commitment to science as a component of the primary curriculum, was modest. The HMI Primary Survey in 1978 reported that serious and effective work in science was achieved in only ten per cent of primary schools. Paul Black, writing in 1980 an article with the significant title 'Why Hasn't It Worked?', recorded that the materials produced by the Nuffield Junior Science Project were studied seriously in only one in five primary schools and were actually used in only seven per cent.[71]

However, if, by the conclusion of the Project in 1966, primary science remained, in Paul Black's words, a 'feeble plant', the outcomes of the Nuffield initiative were by no means insignificant. The Project offered a focus for those seeking to promote science within the primary curriculum and it contributed to a professional and research understanding of the development of children's understanding of scientific concepts.

It helped establish a pattern for professional, in-service development based upon the work of Teacher's Centres, and involving the staff of Local Education Authorities, Training Colleges and Universities. Like other Projects, its relative lack of success eventually revealed much about the complexity of curriculum reform and of effecting change in teachers' professional practice. In 1966, however, what was perhaps most obvious was that much remained to be done to develop the scientific education of primary school pupils. That task fell to the Schools Council Science 5–13 Project.

THE SCHOOLS COUNCIL SCIENCE 5–13 PROJECT

Funded jointly by the Schools Council, the Nuffield Foundation and the Scottish Education Department, the Schools Council Science 5–13 Project was set up in 1967 'to consolidate and extend the work on primary science teaching initiated by the Nuffield Junior Science Project'.[72] Most of the cost was borne by the Schools Council (£180,000), with the Scottish Education Department and the Nuffield Foundation contributing just over £100,000 and £18,000 respectively.[73] It was originally sponsored for three years but subsequent extensions resulted in a curriculum initiative that lasted for eight years and was intended to 'help teachers help children learn about science'.[74] Its formal terms of reference, agreed between the Schools Council and the Nuffield Foundation, referred to

> the identification and development, at appropriate levels, of topics or areas of science related to a framework of concepts appropriate to the age of the pupils.[75]

The Project was also required to give attention to

> the needs of children with varied abilities and environments, to study how to increase primary school teachers' knowledge of science, to advise colleges of education on the science content of curriculum courses and to maintain close liaison with other related projects.[76]

It is pertinent to ask why, given the work of the Nuffield Junior Science Project, a further primary science curriculum initiative was judged necessary. The answer lies principally in the realisation towards the end of the three-year Junior Science Project that most primary school teachers needed further guidance and support if science were to gain a secure place within the primary curriculum. Writing in 1983, the Director of the Junior Science Project judged that

> We had established what kind of science was appropriate in primary schools, that it could be achieved with the brightest and the slowest children, including those in ESN schools, in 'streamed' as well as mixed ability groups, and with boys as well as girls. We had shown that, given support, all teachers could achieve it. But now it was important to produce support materials for teachers.[77]

Interviewed in 1995, he elaborated[78] as follows.

> ... when the Project was coming to an end we had a lot of ... work still to do. There were a lot of questions ... and we said 'There's got to be some continuity' and 'You can't just let this drop' ... Nuffield said ... 'We've already spent £75,000 and we're investing a million in secondary ... we can't do anything about it ... Schools Council ought to do it ...'
>
> So I wrote to the Schools Council and they invited me to talk to their Steering Committee A and Steering Committee B ... I took with me a great sheet of foolscap, closely typed, full of questions ... I appealed to them and said 'Look, all this ... work needs to be done, we've made a start. Don't let it waste, can you fund it?' They took it up with the Nuffield Foundation and between them they funded a project which they called 'The Schools Council Nuffield Continuation Project' and they asked Len Ennever who was then retiring (as an) HMI to take it on ... Len had been a great supporter of ours ... Eventually Nuffield pulled out and it was left with the Schools Council and they called it '5 to 13'.

In essence, notwithstanding the 'series of exemplars' produced by the Junior Science Project to show what could be achieved in primary science education, most primary teachers found it difficult to translate the Project materials into their everyday classroom practice.[79] As Ennever commented to Wastnedge, 'We will have ... to try to somehow give them (i.e. the teachers) some support for the work we want them to do in the classrooms.'[80] As the following paragraphs reveal, an important part of that support was the identification and development of science-based topics or areas within a framework of objectives judged appropriate to children's stages of intellectual development, such stages being derived closely from Piagetian psychology. Sheila Parker-Jelly, a member of the Project team, was later to claim that Science 5–13 was 'the first major project to offer teachers a child-based structure as a framework for the child-centred activity'.[81]

Like the Nuffield Junior Science Project, Science 5–13 was firmly in the progressive mould, advocating an informal, child-centred discovery approach to learning within an undifferentiated, integrated timetable. The Project team, aware that 'discovery methods' was an ambiguous term sensitive to personal interpretation, suggested that it meant

> children being given opportunities, carefully provided by their teacher, to gain first hand experience of living and non-living material around them, being encouraged to ask questions, find problems and seeks answers for themselves, and being free to communicate what they feel and find in an appropriate way.[82]

Roy Richards, a Project Officer and subsequently an HMI, explains further.

> Discovery science with young children is not science in the usual meaning of the word. That is to say, it is not a logical development of observation, classification, hypothesis and experiment. Rather it is the involvement of children through genuine activity in the accumulation of experiences. Structure is important.[83]

For the Science 5–13 Project, the term 'child-centred' also had its own meaning.

> The ethos of Science 5/13 work is that it should be child-based. This does not mean that children learn only what they want to learn and do only what they want to do. They start with something they are interested in and then with the teacher's help they explore and investigate the topic. It is not pretended that such work is easy for teachers. In some ways, it is harder than formal chalk and talk, but many teachers have found that the children benefit. Children work at tasks they are interested in, and those of lesser abilities are not 'put off science' as they are so frequently when dealing with subjects that are either formal or oriented towards O-level.[84]

Support for an integrated timetable was linked to the Project's view that to help children develop a scientific attitude and ways of thinking was more important than the acquisition of scientific facts. For younger pupils in particular, science-based activities had a value that extended beyond the subject itself. In particular, they had

> a vital contribution to make to the 'whole' education of children, a contribution that has very little to do with the acquisition of

> scientific knowledge or with the subject 'science' in the secondary school ... science can mean many things, and in the early years of school at least, 'exploration' would be a more appropriate title.[85]

As a result, it was the view of the Project team that

> We do not intend ...
>
> To advocate that a core of essential scientific knowledge should be built up at this stage. We consider that the development of attitudes is far more important and that patterns of specific knowledge can come later when the child is ready for it.[86]

The following comment, taken from one of the curriculum Units produced by the Project, reminds teachers of this underlying rationale.

> ... it is important to realise that *the Unit has been produced, not because we want children to have a better understanding of wood but rather, to show how working with a familiar material can contribute to their scientific understanding and general personal development*.[87]

This relative lack of emphasis upon the acquisition by pupils of scientific knowledge was, of course, a clear manifestation of a progressive ideology and it was one which drew the Project into a 'process-content' debate that was enlivened, if not enlightened, by the publication of the so-called Black papers.

> I think it's true to say that in the sixties ... process ruled supreme and generally speaking educators would stress that if you gave children the ... processes by which they could investigate and find out for themselves by the time they left the primary school for the secondary school you were doing a jolly good job.
>
> ... No one said content wasn't important but I think what they said was that it didn't matter greatly what content you chose. You had to have content as a vehicle in order to do it, but ... you could choose what content you wanted.[88]

However, the prioritising of procedural over declarative knowledge was also justified by reference to the rapid pace of scientific and technological advance, the Project team claiming that

> in these days when scientific and technical knowledge is doubling every ten years or so, one is faced with the impossible task of training a pupil for a job which does not at present exist but will be based on future discoveries. The development of attitudes of

> mind and behaviour are thought by some to be of greater importance than factual learning. This is not to say that knowledge is unimportant, but only that perhaps we need to look harder at our educational objectives.[89]

The reference in this claim to occupational concerns might be thought to sit rather oddly with the progressive ideology that characterised the 5–13 Project, and it ignores the obvious point that, during a time of rapid change, fundamental scientific ideas assume an added, rather than a diminished, importance.

An integrated timetable was also seen as having value because 'Scientific thinking is not the only type of thinking involved in science nor is science the only subject which involves scientific thinking'.[90] The rather grand claim implied here is that when children are engaged in science-based activities, they can develop experience and skills more commonly associated with other components of the primary curriculum, and that they can also acquire experience and skills relevant to science when engaged in activities that are not science-based. In practical terms, this meant that

> To try to confine problem finding and solving to certain times each week would be to effectively discourage it, since it must mean that at other times in the week problems would have to be ignored or held over to the prescribed time. This means that a questioning, inquiring approach has to be pursued at any time if it is to be pursued at all.[91]

Continuity between the work of the Nuffield Junior Science Project and the Schools Council Science 5–13 Project was enhanced by the involvement of a number of key individuals with both curriculum initiatives. Membership of the Consultative Committee of the 5–13 Project included F.F. Blackwell who had worked for a year as a member of the Junior Science Project team and, thereafter, served on its Consultative Committee (see above). Four other members of the Science 5–13 Consultative Committee had been involved previously with the Nuffield science or mathematics projects, and Len Ennever, the Director of Science 5–13, had previously been a member of the Consultative Committee of the Nuffield Junior Science Project. Wastnedge, the Organiser of this earlier Project, has recalled Ennever saying to him when the Science 5–13 Project was first set up that

> We shall continue to accept your basic tenets, that is, that we shall be looking for children to explore, to work through processes, to

> ... ask their own questions ... for teachers to help them learn in that way.[92]

There were also links with other primary science initiatives. Wynne Harlen, who became the evaluator of the Science 5–13 Project, had carried out work comparing different classes in which materials produced by the Junior Science Project and the Oxford Primary Science Project were being used.[93] In addition, many members of the 5–13 team had close links with the Association for Science Education, an organisation which was clearly of the view that the purpose of the Schools Council project was to 'continue and extend the work already in being'.[94]

Like the Nuffield Junior Science Project, the 5–13 Project was committed to a 'centre–periphery' model of curriculum reform, a strategy frequently followed by Schools Council curriculum initiatives. This strategy, in which 'innovation is accelerated at the centre, and then disseminated to the outposts'[95] by means of materials 'launched ... upon the schools and teachers',[96] eventually came in for much criticism. For one of the more trenchant critics, Lawrence Stenhouse, it implied 'a degree of centralization of ideas which is not acceptable' and which failed 'to take account of local variations and local needs'. For Eggleston, writing in 1976, the centre–periphery approach was incapable of 'successful development aimed at altering styles of teaching as well as content from a far away position remote from the classroom'.[97] For Gibby, it created curriculum 'experts' who 'should act only when called upon to do so by the teachers and not control the initial and, as a consequence, the main course of the direction of the project'.[98] As Skilbeck has pointed out,[99] a central paradox of much of the Schools Council's work was that 'at one and the same time, (it) adopted the large-scale project model, and declared the legitimacy of the school as the principal element in deciding on the curriculum'.

In the mid-1960s, however, much had yet to be learnt about the limitations of the centre–periphery approach to reform. Certainly, the 5–13 Project team was well aware that

> teachers are the best people to help shape classroom material; they are the final arbiters of curriculum development for they are the filters through which innovation reaches the classroom. If the innovation is not filter-passing, it simply does not reach its goal.[100]

Parker-Jelly confirms that

> From the outset the 5–13 team held the view that practising teachers should be actively involved in developing the project and

> ... very many teachers helped to shape the nature of trial materials, the way the trials were carried out and the revisions necessary to produce final publications.[101]

There is no doubt that the involvement of practising teachers in the work of the Project was very important. Harlen has identified the importance of the teachers' contribution to understanding how a particular curriculum Unit might be introduced (the 'starting point') and the work progressed.

> ... the way in which those who were developing the Units would work ... would be to have some fairly sketchy ideas and take them to teachers in a few schools and then go and talk to them and collect the work and bring it back and really write the Unit from that. So there was a big input ... because you couldn't get those examples of children's work that you write into the Units without doing that ...[102]

The involvement of teachers in these ways, however, fell far short of meeting the criticisms of the approach to curriculum reform levelled by, for example, Stenhouse, and, as Parker-Jelly was later to acknowledge, this had implications for the impact which the Science 5–13 Project had on the work of primary schools in general beyond the end of its funded life.

The Science 5–13 Project produced 25 books intended to provide teachers with various kinds of help in teaching science to children aged five to thirteen. One of these books provided an introduction to the Project, 17 were Units offering teachers ideas about how to achieve the Project's objectives, six were background or resource books and one was intended to help teachers understand the Project's ideas and materials. The focus of the Project output was teachers rather than pupils, since 'one of the Project's tenets was that teachers could best help children to learn science by selecting experiences and activities appropriate to the abilities, and engaging the attention, of individual children'.[103]

The Schools Council Science 5–13 Project and its precursor, the Nuffield Junior Science Project, differed significantly in the ways in which they sought to assist primary teachers develop the science component of the primary curriculum. Whereas the latter might be seen as identifying what could be achieved and, in so doing, offering teachers examples of 'good practice', the former adopted a greater degree of structure based upon the use of curriculum objectives clustered within a framework derived from Piagetian stage theory. The Project's use of

Piagetian ideas is discussed in Chapter 6. For the present, it may be noted that the three stages used by the Project differed slightly from those conventionally associated with the Piagetian approach to cognitive development and that, like the Nuffield Junior Science Project, Science 5–13 recognised the importance of experience in facilitating progression from one stage to another.

> Our Stages are chosen so as to divide ... development into three more convenient parts than would have been the case had we kept to Piaget's stages. Since we follow quite closely Piaget's ideas about development, our Stages 1, 2 and 3 have similar properties to Piaget's stages.[104]
>
> With appropriate experiences, the change from one form of thinking to another will take place more readily than without them.[105]

Since it was the task of the teacher to provide these experiences for their pupils, it was important that primary school teachers were aware of at least the rudiments of the Piagetian stage theory of cognitive development and be able to match the experiences they were to provide with the relevant stage of a pupil's intellectual maturity. Wastnedge claimed in 1965 that it had been made very clear to him in the preceding three or four years that 'the majority of teachers attending courses and certainly all lecturers with whom I have spoken, are very much *au fait* with the various Piagetian operational stages'.[106] Maggie Ing in 1978 asserted that 'Every teacher knows of Piaget ...' and added that 'Piaget's stages of conceptual development have been very influential (since) ... some summarized version of his work had been taught to student teachers for many years.'[107] Roy Richards, interviewed in 1995, agreed, stating of Piagetian theory:

> I think ... certainly in the sixties, by then it had quite an influence and all the training colleges would do it with their students and I think if you talk to many teachers they will know of all people something of his stage development theory.[108]

Somewhat curiously, Richards further recalled that it wasn't necessary to 'know much about Piaget if you don't want to when you're involved as a teacher in the Project'.

> You can just get into doing 'Ourselves' or whatever else you like ... and yet at the same time if someone was keen on that sort of

> theoretical thing ... they could go into that and you'd get a variation among teachers.[109]

From the broad aim of 'Developing an enquiring mind and a scientific approach to problems', the Project team developed eight, more specific aims. Of these, six related to purely behavioural aspects of learning, one was purely knowledge-related, and the remainder something of an amalgam of the two. From these eight aims were derived no less than about 150 objectives.[110] Many of these objectives were content-specific, for example, those referring to an 'Awareness of the meaning of words which describe various types of quantity' and to a 'Knowledge of sources and simple properties of common forms of energy'.[111] Other objectives, the Project material asserted, were 'clearly content-free'.[112] Examples include the 'Ability to find answers to simple problems by investigation' and a 'Willingness to observe objectively'.[113] Harlen, who played a central role in the development of these objectives, noted in her evaluation of the project that 'Only a minor fraction of the total number of the project's objectives relate to "knowledge": by far the majority deal with the many other different kinds of behaviour involved in learning science.'[114]

All of the 150 or so objectives were assigned to one of the three, Piaget-derived Stages referred to above, and identified accordingly. For example, under the broad objective of 'Attitudes, interest and aesthetic awareness', a 'Willingness to ask questions' was labelled objective 1.01 to indicate that it was appropriate for a child at the first Stage of intellectual development. Likewise, a 'Willingness to co-operate with others in science activities' (2.01) was an objective for a child at Stage 2, and 'Acceptance of responsibility for their own and others' safety in experiments' (3.01) for a child judged to be at Stage 3.

All except one of the curriculum Units produced by the Project covered Stages 1 and 2 together, or Stage 3 separately. The Units for Stages 1 and 2 encompassed a wide range of non-scientific topics drawn not only from science but also from mathematics, geography, history, English, dance, drama and music. A Unit such as *Minibeasts* could be linked to art and craft via the making of models and the aesthetic appeal of spiders' webs; to mathematics via measurement, calculation, weighing and timing involving the movement of small creatures; to dance/drama and music, for example, by children imitating the movement of insects; with history, especially the history of science and scientific biography; with technology, for example, by constructing a simple microscope; with English, via poetry and other forms of written work.[115] Some Units showed an awareness of wider primary school concerns, such as the development of a child's vocabulary,[116] and the Stage 3 Units, intended for older pupils, including those in the early years of secondary education, reflected the increased emphasis upon a subject-based curriculum. Thus, in the Stage 3 Unit, *Changes*, science teachers were advised, perhaps somewhat unrealistically, to 'Ask the teacher taking geography if he would mind referring children to you when dealing with maps, "finding your way", or a compass.'[117]

The specification of numerous objectives derived from a much smaller number of aims is of considerable interest and it was to be the source of some difficulty in the Project's communication with teachers. It is clear that the list of objectives was not to be regarded as some kind of syllabus and that teachers were not expected to attempt to achieve them all with their classes.

> We do not intend ...
> That this book should in any way represent a course ...
> That *all* children should carry out *all* the suggestions in the book.[118]

The same message was repeated in various ways in other curriculum Units produced by the Project. Thus, in *Structures and Forces, Stages 1 and 2*, teachers were advised that

> Almost always further investigation will arise from the starting experiment ... and it will certainly be worth following these rather than trying to stick to this chapter as a text, which it is not intended to be.[119]

Likewise, in the same Unit at Stage 3, teachers were reminded that

> It should be understood that this Unit does not represent a 'course' or a text to work steadily through from beginning to end, even though it has an ordered arrangement of material.[120]

Equally, the objectives could not be described as behavioural objectives, although the behavioural ancestry of specifying curriculum outcomes in these terms cannot be denied. Harlen was familiar with Bloom's influential *Taxonomy of Educational Objectives* from her Master's degree studies, but she is clear that the Science 5–13 objectives were not 'classified anywhere like ... that *Taxonomy*' and that they were 'nothing like the behavioural objectives that were being promoted in the United States at that time'.[121] They were, however, about expressing the Project's objectives in terms of changes in children's behaviour'.[122]

> Having an aim cannot lead to satisfaction unless it is possible to recognize its achievement. So aims are most effective when they are expressed in terms of expected changes in children, and changes which can be observed. This means that where possible they must indicate changes in what children can do, in what opinions they express, in their preferences, in their skills – in other words, in their 'behaviour', where this word is used in its technical sense, meaning all the various kinds of response a person can make.[123]

This technical use of objectives was a source of some difficulty for many teachers. According to Parker-Jelly, those few teachers who enjoyed frequent and sustained contact with the Project team in the task of producing the first draft of project materials, 'became great in their enthusiasm for the idea of working with objectives in mind, even though the concept was new to them and in many cases initially quite difficult to grasp'. Indeed, the firm commitment of these teachers to working in this way was instrumental in the Project team's decision to publish a full set of objectives for primary science, derived from an internal working document, and it found expression in the use made of objectives as an organising focus for the early trial Units. However, the response of the 500 or so trial teachers to this approach to representing and organising curriculum ideas was much more mixed.

> Many teachers found the treatment of objectives somewhat confusing and in some cases it was clear that its organisation formed an unintended barrier to guidance offered on the pragmatic front.[124]

The outcome, again according to Parker-Jelly, was a substantial revision of subsequent trial Units 'in order to communicate to teachers a more obvious concern for the pragmatic while adopting what might be described as an objectives-by-stealth approach to the reflective'. Her conclusion is of some importance, although unsurprising.

> Favourable response to the objectives content (*sic*) was ... largely dependent on the extent to which teachers employed, or were willing to develop, child-centred methods and the extent to which they had sustained contact with people able to communicate the practical advantages of working with objectives in mind.[125]

As far as the Project team was concerned, the use of objectives in conjunction with the various 'starting points' identified in the curriculum Units was a means of providing the extra guidance that many teachers had found lacking in the Nuffield Junior Science Project. The role of the teacher remained central to the successful teaching of primary science.

> The teacher takes a crucial part. Hovering around, sympathetic to the working atmosphere, he (*sic*) can be ready with the right question at the right time, he can come forward to teach a skill, he can enter into a lively discussion (but more as an equal than to pontificate), and he can draw together the threads of an argument.[126]

That 'crucial part' was elaborated in a number of the Units, for example, in *Structures and Forces, Stages 1 and 2*.

> An experiment should not be set up to demonstrate a preconceived answer but in order to find out. Of course, the teacher has an objective and knows what is *likely* to happen, but in most cases (by asking the right questions usually) that activity can be one of satisfactory discovery by the children.[127]

Despite the presentation of objectives as a means of providing a focus for teachers' work in primary science, the potential tension between this approach and some of the assumptions underlying progressive pedagogy cannot be ignored, not least because the Project team was itself aware of it. The Nuffield Junior Science Project had actively discouraged the use of 'end-points', claiming that 'starting points' rather than 'end points' would allow the science curriculum to better serve the needs of children of primary school age.[128] In the Science 5–13 Project, the use of objectives necessarily drew attention to 'end points' or outcomes, an emphasis that many teachers might have found difficult to reconcile with at least the more radical ideas about child-centred education and spontaneity of learning.[129] Writing in 1981, Blenkin and Kelly claimed that child-centredness implies turning attention 'away from the end-product of the educative process and concentrate it on the individuals who are the objects of that process', adding that

> ... what we are claiming is wrong with the objectives model of curriculum planning *per se*, whatever form of objectives it favours, is that ... it is essentially an instrumental approach to education and thus regards the activities of education as means to certain ends, however those ends are defined, and therefore as extrinsic to the processes of education itself.[130]

However, Blenkin and Kelly, acknowledging that the 'pre-specification of objectives played a major part in the evolution of the Science 5–13 project', were willing to concede that 'those objectives on examination prove to be rather more loosely framed than at first sight they appear to be and in practice they have been used to support an approach to the teaching of science in the Primary school that is enquiry-based'.[131] As far as the Project team was concerned, it is clear that

> Being firmly of the opinion that it is for teachers to decide what is best suited to their children, we stopped well before the statements became so detailed as to prescribe exactly what a child should know and do, before the statements began not only to refer to *why*, but also to *what*, *when* and *how*.[132]

Indeed, the purpose of objectives for the team was stated, succinctly and in bold type, in the publication, *With Objectives in Mind.*

> **Working with objectives takes some of the insecurity out of discovery situations,**[133]

and there was no unresolvable conflict between the use of objectives and a child-centred approach to teaching and learning.

> The objectives are intended to be in the teacher's mind so that she can take any opportunities which arise to work towards them, and thus their statement does not conflict with the project's child-centred philosophy.[134]

Given the difficulties which the use of learning objectives presented for the Project, it is pertinent to ask why such an approach to curriculum reform was adopted. Part of the answer has already been given, that is, the specification of objectives provided a structure which was otherwise lacking. However, according to Blenkin and Kelly, broader factors were also in play.

> The statement of clear course objectives ... was a major feature of most of the curriculum projects that emerged during that period of widespread innovation that followed the establishment of the Schools Council ... The allocation of public money to curriculum development on this scale brought with it the requirement that a proper account be given of how that money was being spent. For this reason, as well as because of considerations of a purely educational kind, evaluation was a central concern of most new

> projects from the outset and a proper evaluation was interpreted as requiring a clear statement of goals, aims, purposes, objectives.[135]

While this kind of accountability was unquestionably important, curriculum objectives and formative evaluation (see below) had been part of the project from the outset. According to Wynne Harlen, the evaluator, the Project director and his team were 'entirely free' to find the means of implementing their terms of reference[136] and the working atmosphere was one in which 'we weren't conscious of control or anything other than encouragement'.[137] In addition, the granting of funds to extend the work of the Project on a number of occasions are indicative of at least some measure of ongoing appraisal of its work.

The decision to specify objectives conferred at least two other advantages upon the Science 5–13 Project. By the end of the 1960s, criticism of progressive, informal methods in education was gaining ground. A contributor to the first of the so-called Black papers warned that where children were encouraged to work independently at their own pace, there would always be those who did 'little more than copy passages from the encyclopaedia and stick cut out pictures in their books'.[138] By specifying objectives, the Project was able to defend itself against the caricature that pupils were allowed to wander around the classroom doing as they pleased, flitting from one activity to another while not learning anything of substance. Again, Harlen's retrospective view is that criticism of the kind presented in the Black papers had little or no impact upon the work of the Science 5–13 Project, although it did exert some influence upon a subsequent project, *Progress in Learning Science*.[139] It is perhaps important, however, to acknowledge that in making use of curriculum objectives, Science 5–13 was at odds with the stance reflected in the seminal Plowden report published in 1967. Blenkin and Kelly criticised this report for its lack of aims[140] and Robert Dearden, two years after its publication, pointed out that 'Out of its five hundred and fifty-five pages, the Plowden Report devotes just three and a half to a discussion of aims'. He argued in return that

> A good statement of aims ... is badly needed ... it seems to me that statements of aims must be general. This is not a fault about them but surely precisely their function. They have to provide overall orientation and direction for a highly complex activity, which is what I take education to be.[141]

With some justification, members of the Project team might have claimed that 'providing overall orientation and direction for a highly complex activity' was exactly what they had set out to do.

The second advantage stemmed from the value of objectives in the process of formative evaluation to which the Project was committed. Harlen, as the person principally responsible for this innovative feature of the Project's work, was charged with 'clarifying the objectives of the Project and providing information as to how the materials were achieving their intended purposes'.[142] After much discussion, it was decided that the evaluation would address four issues, namely changes in pupils' 'behaviour', the opinions and reports of teachers, the interactions between teachers, pupils and the Project materials, and the learning environment.[143] For the trials of the first set of Units, the Project used 12 English areas which had been involved in the piloting of the Nuffield Junior Science materials, together with four other areas in Scotland,[144] although later trials involved a much larger number of areas and many more schools. In testing pupils, control and trial groups were used to measure the achievement of the objectives associated with particular Units. Harlen's conclusion was that 'The overall test results were satisfying for the project, since they indicated that the materials were helping children to achieve the objectives.'[145] However, further analysis showed that some objectives were being achieved more readily than others, suggesting that some Units offered more effective learning experiences than others. Why this was so was explored via a factor analysis of the qualitative information contained in the reports from teachers who used the Project materials and from observers who had observed them teach. The analysis again revealed a positive correlation between factors associated with a child-centred and informal approach (for example, 'The class timetable was fully integrated' and 'The desks or tables in the classroom were arranged in irregular groups') and the effective use of the Project materials. Such use (for example, 'The children's attitude to science activities test score increased during the trial') was also positively related to the teacher's liking for, and understanding of what the project was about (for example, 'The teacher appreciated very well the meaning of objectives'). In contrast, factors indicative of a more formal approach to teaching correlated with a negative attitude towards the material and a poor understanding of the objectives.

Information of this kind was made available to the authors of the various Units as they embarked upon revision. A cluster analysis of data from the successive trials of the second set of Units generated similar findings, as did the third and fourth sets of Units, although somewhat different techniques of analysis were used. For example, when preference forms were used to trial the material designed for use with infants (*Early Experiences*) and the third set of Units, the evaluator concluded that 'Teachers with a high score on attitude towards giving children freedom to learn through active exploration tended to be those who used the activities as intended, while the reverse was true for those with a low score'.[146] The link which the formative evaluation established between progressive pedagogy and the effectiveness of the project materials enabled those staffing in-service courses to offer teachers advice about the 'favourable conditions' which correlated with the realisation of the various curriculum units produced by the Project.

The formative evaluation undertaken by Harlen was an important and, as noted above, innovative feature of the Science 5–13 Project. However, its methodology was not without criticism. For example, Richards and Abell, writing in 1973, were concerned at the use of trial schools which had formerly been involved with the Nuffield Junior Science Project.

> (Some) trial schools were chosen because in the past they had been involved in the Nuffield Junior Science Project, though no real attempt was made to assess the extent to which systematic science teaching was still taking place in these schools. The control schools were those known to be interested in science and actively teaching it. In this case there was more likelihood of the children in control schools being better prepared for science and therefore the odds were laid against the trial schools in this situation.[147]

Harlen, however, had seen this issue as conferring advantages upon the evaluation rather than as a methodological weakness.

> One advantage of conducting trials in the same areas as the previous project was that, in those areas, it would be easy to find classes which had already had some experience of active discovery methods and in which, it was hoped, some kind of learning through discovery was already going on. These were the kind of classes wanted for the trial so that the value and effect of the materials would be evaluated without the influence of introducing a new way of working.[148]

It was for this same reason that, when using trial schools which had not at an earlier stage used the Nuffield Junior Science materials, Science 5–13 sought to identify teachers who were familiar and comfortable with progressive, informal approaches to primary teaching.

Given the association between Science 5–13 and progressive

pedagogy, what can be said about the response of the wider community of primary teachers to the published materials? The Science 5–13 Project required primary school teachers to come to terms with the use of a large number of objectives as a strategy for science curriculum reform and demanded some familiarity on their part with at least the outlines of the Piagetian stage theory of cognitive development. In addition, it required them to teach aspects of a subject, science, of which few could command any significant academic expertise or draw upon substantial pedagogical experience. To adopt and use successfully the Science 5–13 curriculum materials, therefore, required a high level of teacher commitment. To put the issue rather differently, the Project's 'target teacher model was a highly sophisticated one' and, in Parker-Jelly's judgement, one in which 'experience has shown ... the expectations were too high for teachers in general'.[149] Harlen, interviewed in 1995, concurs with this judgement, commenting that 'Science 5–13 was the ideal ... It would have been wonderful if every teacher was like the top 5 per cent who could use it.'[150] Gibby has claimed that 'there were many teachers who felt that the large number of specific objectives listed bewildered them', adding that the attempts to measure whether such objectives had been achieved were time-consuming, costly and of doubtful validity.[151] Roy Richards has acknowledged that if teachers saw objectives as the principal focus of their work, they were likely to have been discouraged: 'if you've got that great mass of objectives and you look at it like that, (it would) frighten you to death'.[152] However, Harlen, also commenting with the benefit of hindsight, has queried whether 'teachers ever referred to objectives like that ... they would just go for the activities ... they're not the first thing teachers think about'.[153]

To be able to make appropriate use of the Science 5–13 materials with a pupil, a teacher first needed to assign that pupil to one of the levels of cognitive development identified and characterised by the Project team. He or she then needed to use the Units to guide the pupil towards an activity (with an objective in mind from that activity) appropriate to the identified level which, it should be noted, bore no simple relation to chronological age. The members of the Project team were, of course, well aware that these were not straightforward tasks:

> It is all very well to urge that children's science experience should match their stages of development in scientific ideas, but this is no easy task for a teacher. There are two sides to the problem: one is to be able to recognise the stage a particular child has reached with respect to a certain area of experience, and the other is to know

> what kind of activity is suited to this stage of development. Only when these two things are known can 'matching' take place.[154]

and they offered help by providing a list of diagnostic statements which were intended to 'help to direct teachers' observation to things that children may or may not do which would be indicative of Stages reached by children'. However, the research base required to support the matching strategy upon which the success of Science 5–13 depended was poorly-developed and much more fundamental work needed to be done. In part, this was the remit of another Project, *Match or Mismatch*, set up by the Schools Council in 1973, directed by Harlen and charged with 'the production of materials aimed at helping teachers to observe and record the development of children's ideas and concepts in relation to science'.[155]

Although one visitor to the United Kingdom in 1976 concluded that the 'Science 5–13 Project was the most important development in primary school teaching in Britain',[156] Paul Black concluded only seven years later that the materials produced by the Project, along with those of other initiatives including the Nuffield Junior Science Project, had 'fallen at the first hurdle – that of convincing teachers to take them seriously'.[157] Upon what was Black's judgement based? A survey of the science taught in primary schools in the south-west of England in 1976 revealed that 60 per cent of male and 90 per cent of female primary teachers were unaware of the existence of the Science 5–13 Project, a result which the investigator described as 'very significant since the 5–13 Project is based at Bristol and one would have hoped that local teachers were reasonably aware of it'.[158] Furthermore, Bristol schools were used for the trials of the first, second and third sets of Units, and in the trials of *Children and Plastics, Stages 1 and 2* and *Ourselves, Stages 1 and 2*.[159] A Schools Council survey in 1978 found that of 740 randomly-selected schools, nearly 70 per cent of teachers to whom Science 5–13 would be relevant had never used any of the Project materials, and postal returns from a larger sample of 1,146 schools generated a corresponding figure of 65 per cent. When Howard Bradley surveyed 215 schools (136 replies) in Derbyshire, Lincolnshire and Nottinghamshire in 1976, he was able to identify some positive features of Science 5–13 but came to the conclusion that 'only one third of the teachers in schools having a policy of using Science 5–13 do actually (make) use of it'. He also found that over half of the teachers in the survey had either never heard of the Project or had heard of it but knew no details about it, and that while 15 per cent were familiar with the details and made occasional use of the Project materials, only two per cent were familiar with Science 5–13 and used it often.[160] Black, in 1983, reported a survey which had shown that 'Science 5–13 has been studied seriously in 30 per cent of schools and is being used by 22 per cent while the corresponding figures for Nuffield Junior Science are 20 per cent and 7 per cent respectively'.[161]

These various figures for the uptake of the Project materials by primary schools need to be set alongside not only the claim that it was the 'most important development in primary school teaching in Britain', but also the enthusiasm shown towards the Project by many of the institutions and organisations providing initial and in-service training for primary teachers. Parker-Jelly, for example, claimed that by 1983 'It was rare ... to find an initial course for primary teachers that does not make use of Science 5–13 materials', with 'method' courses including the publications in their bibliographies and practical use being made of the Units in student workshop activity. In judging this claim and its extension to in-service activities,[162] it is important to recall that Parker-Jelly was a member of the Science 5–13 team.

Since curriculum materials can only be used when teachers are aware of their existence, the lack of awareness of the work of the Science 5–13 Project is significant. It suggests a failure by the Project and/or its sponsor, essentially the Schools Council, to promote and disseminate the innovation for which they were responsible. For Parker-Jelly, the 'slow and patchy' spread of the Project reflected 'insufficient attention to the large-scale planned spread and up-take of its work', a shortcoming which she attributed to the failure to allocate substantial resources to dissemination, and to the fact that a Unit, *Understanding Science 5–13*, intended to help those new to the Project, was never published.[163] Within the Schools Council, it was not until the early 1970s that the full importance to be attached to disseminating the materials produced by its various curriculum projects, and allocating resources accordingly, came to be appreciated. In 1974, the *Times Educational Supplement* reported the Schools Council's publication of a report outlining plans to spend between £100,000 and £200,000 on the dissemination of their curriculum projects in 'an attempt to meet what Sir Lincoln Ralphs, the Council's chairman, has described as a "pressing concern" with teachers' ignorance of the Council's work'. Tony Light, the Secretary to the Schools Council noted in particular the failure of the Science 5–13 Project to reach more than 300 out of a possible 24,000 schools that could have been involved.[164]

Ennever replied to this criticism by asserting that the figures were inaccurate and claiming that of the 738 classes involved in the Science

5–13 Project, very few were in the same school. About 63,000 copies of the trial material had been produced and 141 of the 147 Local Education Authorities in England and Wales, together with some Scottish Authorities, had purchased copies. Nearly a quarter of a million copies of the final editions of the project materials had been sold, of which about one third had been overseas sales. Ennever's conclusion was that 'we must have reached more than 300 schools'.[165]

Given Black's comment above, it is appropriate to ask whether the large but unquantifiable sums of money that had been spent on a Project of eight years' duration can be justified. Parker-Jelly, a by no means impartial judge, claimed in 1983 that 'the extent of the project's success (had) more than justified the large sum of money involved'.[166] Both Harlen and Roy Richards are equally convinced that the Project was of seminal importance. In 1995, Richards cited in evidence the continuing sales of the Project's publications.

> I think that one of the great things that helped Science 5–13 was that most of the 25 books are books of things to do, so those kept on selling and the publishers still publish (them) which is a remarkable thing … after all this time … You can scarcely go into a school in the land, a primary school, that hasn't got them.

He also drew attention to the influence of the Project's ideas and materials upon subsequent developments in primary science education.

> I don't think I can emphasize too much … the fact that if you're going to teach science, you need to know what to teach, what activities (to use), and here is a whole repertoire of activities which has profoundly influenced all the succeeding projects and all the … publishers' projects that have come since. If you look, you can trace them all back to these books.[167]

Harlen's opinion is similar.

> … the sales were good … I think one tends to recognize that … it did have … an enormous impact … Whether … you take it as measured by … the number of schools taking it up is a different matter, but it influenced thinking … about primary science enormously … In colleges of education, in the Inspectorate … it was very influential, there's no doubt, and it's still influential in other countries … I've been to the centre of Australia and found it on the bookshelves … I think it had a very considerable impact

> ... on thinking and without that ... a very important step in the various things that have happened since ... would have been missing.

She also adds the challenging point that the success or otherwise of a curriculum project cannot be measured in some simple way by counting the number of teachers or schools who were using the project materials.

> If ... you got a large number of teachers to use it ... you would have had to come down to a common denominator ... of usability with teachers. That would have meant that it wasn't innovative ... By definition, something that's innovative is not for everyone ... There was a secondary project called 'Combined Science' ... (This) had a high take-up but in fact it was nothing more than asking teachers to do what they were already doing.[168]

What cannot be doubted is that the Nuffield and Schools Council primary science projects identified a number of pioneering and influential figures within the emerging field of primary science education. One of these, Wynne Harlen, was to be a member of the Working Party appointed by the Secretaries of State for Education and for Wales to construct the science component of the national curriculum introduced under the Education Reform Act 1988. The projects also made important contributions to the development of a professional and research understanding of many of the issues involved in teaching science to young children, some of which were explored further in two subsequent projects, the Progress in Learning Science Project (to which reference has already been made) and the Learning Through Science Project (directed by Roy Richards). The aim of this latter Schools Council Project was 'to help teachers consider the importance of science as part of the planned curriculum of a school, and to assist school staffs in the task of planning and implementing a policy for science'[169] and it sought, in part, to address some of the problems that had arisen during the work of the Science 5–13 Project.

> 'Learning Through Science' is concerned with giving a continuous stimulus to work in the primary and middle school field, and takes up the need that was felt for a national focus to develop the work begun by the Science 5/13 team. A further need which became increasingly apparent was for pupil material to accompany the Science 5/13 Units. During original trials of these, teachers made it clear that they would have liked the trials to be backed by materials designed for use by children. The project will, therefore,

> extend the work of the Science 5/13 Project by producing material for direct use by children.[170]

The Learning Through Science project also encouraged individual primary schools to develop a policy for school science. Such a policy was intended to do more than 'prevent unnecessary repetition of activities'[171] from year to year. It would formalise a school's commitment to science as a component of the education of its pupils and perhaps make the curriculum less vulnerable to changes in staffing, a point given added significance by Richards' claim, in 1995, that 'The greatest difficulty I've always had … was … persuading schools to do science.'[172]

The Nuffield Junior Science Project and the Science 5–13 projects provided resources for primary teachers at a time when these were much needed and they catalysed the writing of a range of primary science schemes made available commercially in the usual way via established educational publishers likely to be familiar to most primary teachers. There is some evidence to suggest that the materials produced by Science 5–13 were valued by those teachers who already had something of an interest in teaching primary science. For example, Bradley's survey, referred to above, showed that half of the schools which adopted a Science 5–13 policy had science 'specialists' (that is, science curriculum leaders) on the staff, whereas such specialists were found only in a quarter of the primary schools as a whole in his sample. In addition, 38 per cent of the schools that adopted a Science 5–13 policy taught science as a recognisably separate part of the curriculum, and another 32 per cent presented science as a planned component of broader topics.[173] The quality of this science education, however might perhaps be questioned, since Bradley's survey also showed that no less than 70 per cent of the schools that had adopted Science 5–13 taught science in ways that were inimical to the Project's philosophy of activity-based, discovery learning.

The 'patchy and slow' response to Science 5–13 suggests strongly that primary teachers and their schools were less than enthusiastic about including science as a component of a curriculum which, from the perspective of the 1990s, was astonishingly free from external constraints. It would, however, be a mistake to infer from this that most primary teachers were necessarily hostile to primary science education. Science 5–13 was a complex and, in many ways, daunting Project. The constraints of time to familiarise oneself with the Project and its philosophy, together with the confidence and experience needed to choose activities wisely in the interests of pupils were almost certainly at work. As Ingle and Jennings expressed it in 1981, 'many teachers understandably feel the need for some form of positive encouragement ... that, at the end of the day, they have selected wisely and well'.[174] The importance of the interrelated dimensions of professional confidence and experience has been well-captured by Brown in an observation which touches equally upon the limitations of a centre–periphery strategy for curriculum reform and the difficulty of constructing a statutory national curriculum which adequately meets the needs and circumstances of all pupils and schools.

> The problems seem to arise when teachers who are without experience or confidence in science work are expected to take these materials and make selections from them. They may be expected to organize science experiences for pupils over a wide age and ability range and the circumstances in which they work may vary from the all age, one class village school to the large urban primary. These variations permit of no one right answer – a science curriculum needs to be devised to fit each. It should take into account the strengths and interests of the staff in the schools as well as the physical constraints of accommodation and resources.[175]

In addition, science was seen as competing for time with the traditional subjects of reading, writing and number work, to which most primary teachers, their recent critics notwithstanding, have always attached importance. As Shirley Toulson, a supporter of the Science 5–13 Project, acknowledged in 1974,

> Among primary teachers the most serious criticisms are likely to be that the days aren't long enough to fit in any new work, and that reading and writing must come first.[176]

There is likely to be a variety of reasons for the generally disappointing level of response of primary schools to a curriculum initiative such as the Science 5–13 Project but Toulson's comment perhaps hints at the heart of the matter, namely the conservatism of most primary teachers. This conservatism relates not only to the content of the primary curriculum but also to primary pedagogy. The evidence suggests that, despite all the rhetorical impact of progressivism, most teachers use a variety of traditional teaching methods and that while they may place the child at the centre of the education process, they do not espouse classroom 'activity' and 'informality' in an uncritical way. Bennett's study of teaching styles in primary schools in Lancashire and Cumbria in 1976 led him to conclude that

> From the responses of 88 per cent of the 871 schools sampled, a fairly generous estimate is that some 17 per cent of teachers teach in the manner prescribed by Plowden, while at the other end of the teaching continuum approximately one in four teachers teach formally. The majority of teachers use what have been termed mixed styles, incorporating elements of both formal and informal practice.[177]

Bennett was able to report that group work was considerably less popular than individual work by pupils and that, in general, pupils' work was teacher-directed for 77 per cent of the time and 'child-directed' for the remainder. Freedom for pupils to move around, talk and leave the classroom was uncommon, with two-thirds of the primary teachers restricting these activities. Moreover, a subject-centred timetable predominated.[178]

Bennett's findings are placed in a wider context by Brian Simon's response to Black paper claims that student involvement in the unrest of the later 1960s, and much else, was attributable to their experience of informal (and, therefore, by implication, undisciplined) methods of education. He describes such claims as historically inaccurate, commenting that

> Of course it is the case that the Hadow reports of 1931 and 1933 ... had both stressed a 'child-centred' approach with the famous phrase on 'activity and experience' central to each of them. Indeed, Professor R.J.W. Selleck has argued that a kind of watered down progressivism had become the 'intellectual orthodoxy' among training college lecturers, HMIs etc. by 1939, but the reality, as opposed to the rhetoric, appears to have been rather different ... The students of 1968 were, in fact, the products of the streamed, divided, hierarchical system from which we only began to emerge in a significant way in the mid-1960s.[179]

By 1987, 20 years after the publication of the Plowden report, a review of the relevant research findings by Sylva led her to conclude that 'we are left with two widely agreed observations; that the Plowden ideal has never been fully implemented in Britain ... and that the few studies which have directly addressed its effectiveness in terms of pupil progress have found it wanting'.[180]

If, therefore, the professional practice of most primary teachers has been far from 'progressive' it is perhaps hardly surprising that a science teaching project reflective of a progressive ideology while simultaneously seeking to establish a new curriculum component, should meet with something less than enthusiasm from the profession as a whole. Experience has confirmed that access to good quality science curriculum materials and resources will not, of itself, effect change. As Skilbeck has observed, schools also need 'curriculum development *capability* and ... working *conditions* where what was in principle possible and desirable could occur in practical ... ways'.[181] Black's question[182] of whether the 'feeble plant' of primary science 'just needed light, air and water' or should be pulled up again so that 'another look could be taken at the roots' was to be answered, at least in the short term, by the element of compulsion introduced by the national curriculum.

NOTES

1 D.H. Morrell and A. Potts, *Britain's New Schools* (London, 1960), 5–6.
2 Department of Education and Science, *Children and their Primary Schools, A Report of the Central Advisory Council for Education (England)* (London, HMSO, 1967), 394.
3 D. Layton, *Interpreters of Science: A History of the Association for Science Education, ASE/Murray* (London, 1984).
4 M. Waring, *Social Pressures and Curriculum Innovation: A Study of the Nuffield Foundation Science Teaching Project* (London, 1979).
5 The Association of Women Science Teachers (AWST) and the Science Masters' Association. The two organisations merged in 1963 to form the Association for Science Education. For details of the merger, see D. Layton (1984) op. cit.
6 Nuffield Junior Science Project 1, *BAAS Conference Programme* (1961), back page.
7 Ministry of Education, *Science in Primary Schools*, Pamphlet No. 42 (London, HMSO, 1961).
8 Association for Science Education, *Bulletin*, 7 (Nov. 1963), 18–21. The statement was also published by the School Nature Study Union in *Natural Science in Schools*.
9 For details, see D. Layton, op. cit., 116–17. The ASE now publishes a *Primary Science Review*.
10 N. Isaacs, 'The Case for Bringing Science into the Primary Schools', in W.H. Perkins (ed.), *The Place of Science in Primary Education, Proceedings of the BAAS Conference, September 1961* (London, 1961), 5.
11 'Science for the Young', *The Guardian*, 5 July 1961.
12 P. Gordon, 'Tradition and Change in the Curriculum', in D. Lawton *et al.*, *Theory and Practice of Curriculum Studies* (London, 1978), 126.
13 Association for Science Education, Primary Schools Science Committee: Policy Statement, *Bulletin*, No. 7, Nov. 1963, 19.
14 R. Lowe, *Education in the Post-War Years, A Social History* (London, 1988), 95.
15 *Junior Science Project 1* (hereafter *JSP 1*), draft of speech by J.F. Kerr, to BAAS Conference, dated 2 August 1961, 2.
16 *JSP 1*, E.J. Wenham, Questionnaire, June 1962.
17 J.F. Kerr, 'Training for Learning through Scientific Investigations', in W.H. Perkins (ed.), op. cit., 1961, 33.
18 Ministry of Education, op. cit. (1961), 31.
19 E.R. Wastnedge, *Nuffield Junior Science: Teacher's Guide 1* (London, 1967), 9 and 22.

20 M. Waring, Background to Nuffield Science, *History of Education*, 8, 3 (1979), 223.
21 *JSP 7*, Ron Wastnedge, Reply to Irene Finch, 29 Oct. 1965, 1.
22 The Nuffield Foundation, 'The Teaching of Science and Mathematics', 1961, reprinted in Association for Science Education, *Bulletin*, No. 1, April 1962 (unnumbered pages).
23 *JSP 1*, letter from J.F. Kerr to Nathan Isaacs 31 Oct. 1962; letter to J.F. Kerr from Dennis Chisman, Education Officer, Royal Institute of Chemistry, 19 Nov. 1962.
24 *JSP 10*, The Nuffield Foundation, 'The Teaching of Science in Primary Schools', Item No. 127.
25 *JSP 4*, Letter from R.A. Becher to J.F. Kerr, 9 Oct. 1963. Becher was Assistant Director of the Nuffield Foundation. See also, Nuffield Foundation, *Report for the Year Ended 31 March 1964* (Oxford, 1964), 71.
26 Interview of E.R. Wastnedge by BS, 11 May 1995, Carlisle.
27 *JSP 10*, Meeting of Team Leaders, 5 Dec. 1963, 2.
28 *JSP 2*, appendices to Nuffield Foundation 'Statement for the Consultative Committee to be held 29 April 1964', written by Eric Rogers, Frank Halliwell and W.F. Dowdeswell, the Organisers of the O-level physics, chemistry and biology Projects respectively.
29 *JSP 2*, Draft Press Announcement, made jointly by the D.E.S. and the Nuffield Foundation, 1964, 2.
30 *JSP 9*, E.R. Wastnedge, 'Statement for the Consultative Committee to be held 19 April 1964', 1.
31 Ibid., 2.
32 Association for Science Education, *Bulletin*, No. 7, Nov. 1963, 19.
33 Malcolm Hardstaff was initially responsible for the work involving secondary schools. He was joined by J.W. Bainbridge in Sept. 1965. See *JSP 4*, 'Consultative Committee Meeting', 23 Sept. 1964, 5 and ibid., 'Items to be discussed at Consultative Committee', 27 Oct. 1965, 3.
34 *JSP 7*, Letter from Wastnedge to J.A.G. Banks (HMI), 3 Feb. 1966, 1; Notes with draft of letter to publishers from Brian Young (Director of the Nuffield Foundation), 1.
35 Ron Wastnedge, 'Nuffield Junior Science: The End of a Beginning?', in C. Richards and D. Holford (eds), *The Teaching of Primary Science: Policy and Practice* (London, 1983), 141.
36 N. Isaacs, *Nature*, 23 July 1927, quoted in E.R. Wastnedge, op. cit., 1967, 295.
37 E.R. Wastnedge, op. cit., 1967, 16.
38 E.R. Wastnedge, op, cit., 1983, 141–2.
39 E.R. Wastnedge, *Teacher's Guide 2* (London, 1967), 62–4 and 135–43.
40 *JSP 6*, F.F. Blackwell, 'Basic Planning Outline' – Teacher's Sourcebook of Apparatus and Ideas', Jan. 1964, 2.
41 *JSP 9*, 'Committee Meeting, 28 January 1964', Paper discussed 'Junior Science Section, 5–13 age range', by E.R. Wastnedge, 4, and *JSP 8*, letter from E.R. Wastnedge to John Maddox (Nuffield Foundation), 8 Oct. 1964, 1–2.
42 *JSP 8*, 'Draft letter to Chief Education Officers of Consultative Areas'.
43 Ibid., 2.
44 *JSP 14*, Cutting from *The Science Teacher*, May 1965, 111.
45 *JSP 9*, Consultative Committee Meeting, 11 Nov. 1965, 2.
46 *JSP 8*, Draft letter to the Chief Education Officers of the Science Pilot Areas, n.d., 1–3 and *JSP 14*, M. Collisand and A.C. Seward, Report on Work in the Pilot Area of Folkestone, February–October 1965, 5 Oct. 1965, 1.
47 *JSP 9*, Item to be discussed at Consultative Committee Meeting, 27 Oct. 1965, 2.
48 E.R. Wastnedge, op. cit., 1983, 145.
49 *JSP 9*, Leader Course held at the College of Domestic Arts, Llandaff, Cardiff, 21–27 April 1965, report by E.R. Wastnedge, 15 May, 1965, 3.

50 E.R. Wastnedge (ed.), *Nuffield Junior Science: Teacher's Guide 1* (London, 1967), 11.
51 *JSP 4*, Consultative Committee Meeting, 23 Sept. 1964, 1.
52 *JSP 3*, letter from E.R. Wastnedge to R.A. Becher, 24 Nov. 1953, 2.
53 *JSP 6*, F.F. Blackwell, Basic Planning Outline 4 – Prepared Apparatus and Equipment, Jan. 1964, 1.
54 *JSP 9*, Committee Meeting, 28 Jan. 1964, 7.
55 *JSP 6*, F.F. Blackwell, Basic Planning Outline 1 – Teachers' Source Book of Apparatus and Ideas, January 1964, 3, and *JSP 2*, The Teaching of Science in Primary Schools. Discussion document produced by the Nuffield Foundation after discussion which took place on 26 April 1963 (no author specified), 2–3.
56 *JSP 7*, Pilot Stage 1965–66, Area Leader's Report from London Pilot Area, no date, 1–2, 6; ibid., Pilot Stage 1965–1966, Area Leader's Report, Cardiff Area, no date, 1–2; *JSP 9*, Pilot Stage 1965–1966 Area Leader's Report, Liverpool, no date, 1–2; ibid., Pilot Stage 1965–1966, Area Leader's Report, Bristol, no date, 1–2; *JSP 16*, Pilot Stage 1965–1966, Area Leader's Report, Folkestone, no date, 1–2 (hereafter, Area Reports and Area).
57 *JSP 9*, Area Report, Liverpool, 3.
58 *JSP 7*, Area Report, London 3; *JSP 9*, Area Report, Bristol, 2; *JSP 16*, Area Report, Folkestone, 2.
59 *JSP 9*, Report on Work in Chelmsford Schools, no author, 1.
60 *JSP 7*, E.R. Wastnedge, Proposed Areas of Direct Help and Advice to Teachers, 2 June 1965, 1.
61 *JSP 7*, Letter from A.G. Banks to John Maddox, 2 Nov. 1965; R.W. Crossland, An Individual Study of the Nuffield Foundation Primary Science Project, *School Science Review*, 53 (March 1972), 628.
62 R.W. Crossland, Ibid., 628–9.
63 Ibid., 631.
64 See Vol. 2 of the Project's *Teacher's Guide* and *JSP 2*, Nuffield Foundation, Summary of the discussion on the teaching of science in the primary school, held at Nuffield Lodge, 26 April 1963, 3. The idea of starting points was not confined to the Project. See, for example, ATCDE, AWST, London Association of Science Teachers, SMA, *Science in the Primary Schools* (London, 1959), 14, 25; Ministry of Education, *Science in Primary Schools*, 9; *JSP 6*, F.F. Blackwell, Basic Planning Outline 3;Teaching Aids, Jan. 1964, 1.
65 Ibid., 629.
66 Ibid., 629–30.
67 Ibid., 630.
68 E.R. Wastnedge, (ed.), op. cit., 1967, Vol. 1, 184–5.
69 E.R. Wastnedge, op. cit., 1983, 145–6.
70 J. Conran, 'Primary Science 1950–82: A Personal View', in C. Richards and D. Holford (eds), op. cit., 1983, 22–3.
71 P. Black, 'Why Hasn't It Worked?', *Times Educational Supplement*, 3 Oct. 1980, reprinted in C. Richards and D. Holford (eds), op. cit., 1983, 30.
72 S. Parker-Jelly, 'Science 5–13: Reflections on Its Significance', in C. Richards and D. Holford (eds), op. cit., (1983), 147.
73 In addition, the Plastics Institute contributed £2,000 towards the cost of work on the unit, 'Plastics'. W. Harlen, *Formative Evaluation* (London, 1975), 2, 6–7.
74 L.F. Ennever and W. Harlen, *With Objectives in Mind* (London, 1972), 4.
75 W. Harlen, op. cit. (1975), 2.
76 L. Ennever, 'Science 5/13', *Education in Science*, 33 (June 1969), 27.
77 E.R. Wastnedge, 'Nuffield Junior Science: The End of a Beginning?', in C. Richards and D. Holford (eds), op. cit. (1983), 144.
78 E.R. Wastnedge. Interview with B.S., Carlisle, 11 May 1995.

79 Roy Richards, Interview with B.S., London, 2 May 1995.
80 E.R. Wastnedge, Interview with B.S., Carlisle, 11 May 1995.
81 Sheila Parker-Jelly, 'Science 5–13: Reflections on Its Significance', in C. Richards and D. Holford (eds), op. cit., 152.
82 W. Harlen, op. cit. (1975), 7–8.
83 Roy Richards, 'The Swinging of a Pendulum: discovery science with young children', *Education 3–13*, 1, 1 (April 1973), 28.
84 Schools Council Science 5/13, *Changes, Stage 3*, A Unit for Teachers (1973), 11.
85 L. Ennever and W. Harlen, op. cit. (1972), 17.
86 Schools Council Science 5–13, *Metals*, Stages 1 and 2 (1973), 1.
87 Schools Council Science 5–13, *Working with Wood*, A Unit for Teachers, Stages 1 and 2 (1972), 1. Italics in original.
88 Roy Richards, interview with B.S., London, 2 May 1995.
89 Schools Council Science 5–13, *Science, Models and Toys*, Stage 3, A Unit for Teachers (1974), 1.
90 W. Harlen, 'Science and Scientific Thinking across the Curriculum', *Cambridge Journal of Education*, 7, 3 (1977), 131.
91 L. Ennever and W. Harlen, op. cit., 39.
92 E.R. Wastnedge, interview with B.S., Carlisle, 11 May 1995.
93 W. Harlen, interview with B.S., Edinburgh, 9 May 1995.
94 J. Gammage, *Science 5/13 Project*, Monograph No. 1, Wollongong Institute of Education, 5.
95 B. MacDonald and R. Walker, *Changing the Curriculum* (London, 1976), 14.
96 Schools Council, *The First Ten Years, 1964–1974* (Bath, n.d.), 24.
97 Quoted in R. Ingle and A. Jennings, *Science in Schools* (London, 1981), 54.
98 B. Gibby, 'Curriculum Evaluation with Reference to Some Projects', in D. Lawton *et al.*, *Theory and Practice of Curriculum Studies* (London, 1978), 173.
99 M. Skilbeck, *School-Based Curriculum Development* (London, 1974), 85.
100 L. Ennever, 'A Case Study of a Project', *Secondary Education*, 4, 2 (March, 1974), 87.
101 S. Parker-Jelly, op. cit., 148.
102 W. Harlen, interview with B.S., Edinburgh, 9 May, 1995.
103 W. Harlen, *Formative Evaluation* (London, 1975), 1.
104 L. Ennever and W. Harlen, op. cit., 13.
105 L. Ennever and W. Harlen, op. cit., 17.
106 *JSP 7*, E.R. Wastnedge, Reply to Irene Finch, 29 Oct. 1965, 5.
107 M. Ing, 'Theories of Cognitive and Moral Development', in D. Lawton *et al.*, *Theory and Practice of Curriculum Studies* (London, 1978), 80 and 81.
108 R. Richards, interview with B.S., London, 2 May 1995.
109 Idem.
110 L. Ennever and W. Harlen, op. cit., 59–65.
111 Ibid., 62–3.
112 W. Harlen, *Formative Evaluation*, 8.
113 L. Ennever and W. Harlen, op. cit., 60, 62.
114 W. Harlen, *Formative Evaluation*, 28.
115 Schools Council Science 5/13, *Minibeasts, Stages 1 and 2*, A Unit for Teachers (1973).
116 Schools Council Science 5/13, *Science from Toys, Stages 1 and 2 and Background*, A Unit for Teachers (1972), 6.
117 Schools Council Science 5/13, *Changes, Stage 3* (1973), 25.
118 Schools Council Science 5/13, *Metals, Stages 1 and 2* (1973), 1.
119 Schools Council Science 5/13, *Structures and Forces, Stages 1 and 2* (1973), 53.
120 Ibid., *Unit 3*, 1.
121 W. Harlen, interview with B.S., Edinburgh, 9 May 1995.
122 W. Harlen, *Formative Evaluation*, 17.

123 L. Ennever and W. Harlen, op. cit., 22.
124 S. Parker-Jelly, op. cit., 149–50.
125 Ibid., 150.
126 R. Richards, 'The Swinging of a Pendulum', op. cit., 23.
127 Schools Council Science 5/13, *Structures and Forces, Stages 1 and 2*, 56.
128 *JSP 2*, Nuffield Foundation, Summary of the discussion on the teaching of science in the primary school, held at Nuffield Lodge, 26 April, 1963.
129 G.M. Blenkin and A.V. Kelly, *The Primary Curriculum* (London, 1981), 20.
130 Ibid., 72.
131 Ibid., 81–2.
132 L. Ennever and W. Harlen, op. cit., 22. For the same reason, the Project also decided against producing primary science kits, ibid., 6–7.
133 Ibid., 26.
134 W. Harlen, 'Does Content Matter in Primary Science?', in C. Richards and D. Holford, op. cit., 61.
135 G.M. Blenkin and A.V. Kelly, op. cit., 68.
136 W. Harlen, *Formative Evaluation*, 3.
137 W. Harlen, interview with B.S., Edinburgh, 9 May 1995.
138 C.M. Johnson, 'Freedom in Junior Schools', in C.B. Cox and A.E. Dyson, *Fight for Education* (London, 1969), Black Paper, 49.
139 W. Harlen, interview with B.S., Edinburgh, 9 May 1995.
140 G.M. Blenkin and A.V. Kelly, op. cit., 69.
141 R. Dearden, 'The Aims of Primary Education', in R.S. Peters, *Perspectives on Plowden* (London, 1969), 21 and 23–4.
142 W. Harlen, *Formative Evaluation*, 14.
143 Ibid., 25.
144 Ibid., 30.
145 Ibid., 36.
146 Ibid., 43–4, 46, 56, 72–3, 87.
147 C. Richards and B. Abell, 'Science 5/13: an evaluation of an evaluation?', *School Science Review*, 54, 188 (March 1973).
148 W. Harlen, *Formative Evaluation*, 30.
149 S. Parker-Jelly, op. cit., 153.
150 W. Harlen, interview with B.S., Edinburgh, 9 May 1995.
151 B. Gibby, 'Curriculum Objectives', in D. Lawton *et al.*, op. cit., 154.
152 R. Richards, interview with B.S., London, 2 May 1995.
153 W. Harlen, interview with B.S., Edinburgh, 9 May 1995.
154 L. Ennever and W. Harlen, op. cit., 16.
155 Idem.
156 J. Gammage, op. cit., 1.
157 P. Black, 'Why Hasn't It Worked?', in C. Richards and D. Holford, op. cit., 30.
158 T.J. Harvey, 'Science in the primary school – an estimate of the amount taught and the teacher's attitude towards it', *School Science Review*, 57, 201 (1976), 772.
159 W. Harlen, *Formative Evaluation*, Appendix D, Information about participants in the unit trial, 100–25.
160 H. Bradley, *A Survey of Science Teaching in Primary Schools – Pointers for I.N.S.E.T.*, University of Nottingham Institute of Education, 1976, 5–6, 8.
161 P. Black, op. cit., 30.
162 S. Parker-Jelly, op. cit., 151.
163 Ibid., 154.
164 *TES*, 17 March 1974, copy stored in the *JSP 22* Archive.
165 L. Ennever, reply to *TES* article of 17 March 1974, Letter to the Editor, 12 June 1974. Copy in the *JSP 22* Archive.
166 S. Parker-Jelly, op. cit., 156.

167 R. Richards, interview with B.S., London, 2 May 1995.
168 W. Harlen, interview with B.S., Edinburgh, 9 May 1995.
169 Schools Council, *Learning Through Science. Formulating a Schools Policy* (1980), 5.
170 Ibid., 3.
171 Ibid., 8.
172 R. Richards, interview with B.S., London, 2 May 1995.
173 H. Bradley, op. cit., 2, 3.
174 R. Ingle and A. Jennings, op. cit., 53–4.
175 C.A. Brown, 'A sandwich course for primary science', *School Science Review*, 63, 223 (1981), 342.
176 S. Toulson, 'The Influence of Science 5–13', *Dialogue*, 18 (Autumn, 1974), 5.
177 N. Bennett, *Teaching Styles and Pupil Progress* (London, 1976), 149.
178 Ibid., 43.
179 B. Simon, 'The Primary School Revolution: Myth or Reality?', in E. Fearn and B. Simon (eds), *Education in the Sixties*, Proceedings of the 1979 Annual Conference of the History of Education Society of Great Britain (Leicester, 1980), 16–17.
180 A.H. Halsey and K. Sylva, 'Plowden: History and Prospect', *Oxford Review of Education*, 13, 1 (1987), 10.
181 M. Skilbeck, *School-Based Curriculum Development* (London, 1984), 83.
182 P. Black, op. cit., 32.

5

Elementary science and the training of teachers

Teacher education has received attention from a number of historians of education, notably Asher Tropp,[1] P.H.J.H. Gosden[2] and H.C. Dent.[3] Given these and other scholarly historical studies of the education and training of teachers, attention in this chapter is focused upon the relationships between these wider developments and the teaching of science to young children in elementary and primary schools. However, it is convenient, by way of introduction, to note the major shifts that have taken place in the training of teachers for work in public elementary and primary schools during the period with which this book is concerned.

Alexander sees the initial training of teachers of young children as having passed through three stages. The earliest, nineteenth-century, approach to such training was essentially an 'apprenticeship' system, whereby intending teachers gained most of their training by observing and imitating experienced teachers at work in the classroom. The second stage, which has prevailed for most of the twentieth century, may be called the 'teaching practice' model. Here, students were presumed to acquire academic and professional competence in a specialised training institution, such competence then being demonstrated and practised for extended periods in schools. The current approach to primary teacher education is described by Alexander as a 'school-based study' or 'school experience' model, based upon partnerships between schools and institutions of higher education, but with the former playing a more substantial and seminal role in the training process than was the case under the 'teaching practice' model.[4] Jeffreys, writing in 1961, offered a somewhat different and international perspective upon these changes.[5] He identified four broad features which have marked the history of teacher training, namely a separation of the professional training of teachers from secondary education, the delaying of such training until the age 17 or 18, a lengthening of the period of training and, finally, a narrowing of the differences between the training required of those intending to teach in primary and secondary schools. All of these features can be discerned in the developments which have taken place in England and Wales.

PUPIL TEACHERS

The pupil-teacher system, introduced in 1846,[6] enabled elementary school pupils of at least 13 years of age to become apprenticed for a period of five years to a practising teacher, who would receive payment for instructing them. The more able of the pupil teachers could proceed, after success in an examination, to a training college with the financial aid of a 'Queen's Scholarship'.[7]

The regulations governing admission as a pupil teacher required candidates to prepare themselves for examination in reading, recitation, English grammar, history, geography, arithmetic, algebra (boys only), geometry (boys only) and needlework (girls only). Music and elementary science were optional subjects, the syllabus for the latter being presented under two headings, physics and chemistry. There is no evidence of how many, or what proportion, of pupil teachers elected to study elementary science but the numbers are likely to have been small. In the Queen's Scholarship examination, elementary science was one of no less than 17 'subjects' for which the candidate was required to present himself or herself for assessment. In 1905, the relevant syllabus was divided into two sections. The first section specified topics such as matter, force, motion and inertia, the mechanical powers (i.e. levers, pulleys, inclined plane and screw), energy, heat and temperature, radiation, elementary chemistry and terrestrial magnetism. The second section was presented in three parts (elementary chemistry, elementary astronomy and elementary biology) of which the scholarship candidate was required to study one. It was expected that all candidates would have obtained 'an experimental knowledge of the Chemistry and Physics set forth' in the syllabus which had been so arranged that 'the necessary experiments can be conducted without any expensive apparatus or materials'. The 'list of illustrative experiments' associated with the syllabuses for physiography and elementary biology issued by the former Department of Science and Art was commended to those preparing for the scholarship examination in elementary science, together with the advice that they 'should have performed some of these or similar experiments for themselves.'[8]

In his evidence before the Newcastle Commission (1858–61), Matthew Arnold referred to pupil teachers as 'the sinews of English primary education',[9] and the greatly increased demand for public elementary school teachers resulting from the 1870 Education Act led the Committee of Council to penalise schools which did not employ a sufficient number of them.[10] As a result, in the period 1870–95, the number of pupil teachers rose from just over 14,000 to 34,000. From 1884 onwards, a growing number of pupil teachers received a part of their training away from the school in specialised pupil-teacher centres, with only half of each day spent in a school.[11] A day pupil-teacher centre was opened by the London School Board in 1885, and this set an example which was followed over the next 15 years by several of the larger School Boards. By 1902, just over half the pupil teachers in training were being partly taught in centres, working, it is claimed, at higher standards than those who were not.[12]

However, even as the number of pupil-teacher centres increased, the pupil-teacher system itself came in for mounting criticism. According to the minority report of the Cross Commission, the teachers trained by the pupil teacher route 'were badly taught and taught badly'.[13] By the end of the nineteenth century, this minority view had come to prevail and support for the pupil-teacher system was in decline.[14] The requirements for acceptance as a pupil teacher were modest. The candidate had to be approved by an HMI, be medically fit, and pass a Board of Education examination in the subjects indicated above.[15] Science, in any form, is notable by its absence as a compulsory component of this examination, even though, by the last decade of the nineteenth century, elementary science was an approved 'class subject' under the Code governing the work of public elementary schools and several alternative schemes of work were available (See Chapter 1). As late as 1905, Morant, the Permanent Secretary to the Board of Education, announced that the Board would pay more attention to pupil-teacher centres, and he specified the subjects to be studied therein. These now included elementary science and incorporated a reference to the importance of practical work, although the emphasis was to be on English, history, geography and, if possible, a foreign language.[16] The reality, however, was that, between 1904 and 1907, pupil-teacher centres were being closed and the training of elementary school teachers increasingly undertaken in the training colleges, many of them newly established by some of the larger local education authorities.[17] The outcome was that the number of pupil teachers being trained declined rapidly in the years before 1914, by which time the system was obsolete, although it lingered in some areas until the Second World War. In 1906–7, the pupil-teacher system still produced 11,018 pupil teachers, a figure that can be set alongside the 164,271 teachers working in public elementary schools only four years later.[18] By

1912–13, the number of pupil teachers in training had fallen to below 1,500, a rate of decline that was exacerbated by the raising of the minimum age of acceptance of pupil teachers, to 15 in 1900 and to 16 in 1904 (except in a few rural areas)[19] and which was so rapid that it contributed to a shortage of teachers in elementary schools.[20] In 1913, the Board of Education warned that 'Exceptional difficulty in staffing many schools during the next few years is now inevitable.'[21]

According to Aldrich, an important factor contributing to the lack of confidence in the pupil-teacher system was that, in addition to their youth and inexperience, the students were confined to elementary schools throughout their own schooling, apprenticeship and future teaching, and were thus 'denied any real access to the type of education available to their social superiors'. In 1898, a Departmental Committee had acknowledged the narrowness of the education of pupil teachers and had recommended that, in future, their training should provide them with some experience of secondary education because

> The traditions of primary teaching are still, through no fault of the teachers, narrower than is consistent with sound education; and we believe that better methods, greater spontaneity, a wider outlook ... would result from the more frequent employment in primary schools of persons whose experience has not been exclusively or chiefly primary ...[22]

However, for those students taking the normal two-year course in a college, the syllabus of which was prescribed by the Board of Education, the training remained narrowly conceived. Apart from foreign languages,

> the curriculum otherwise was based, subject by subject, on the curriculum of the elementary school in order that the teacher could teach every subject. He could not expect to have any great mastery of any one part of the curriculum, and he had to learn what he did learn in stereotyped ways. The teaching in the schools was in fact based upon the 'lesson', and the college student had to learn from the Master of Method how to give a lesson, how, that is, to break up information into the right fragments for digestion by the pupil.[23]

The Master of Method was also responsible for visiting the student teachers in their practice schools 'to ensure uniformity of standard in assessing the teaching value of the students'.[24] An important part of the school practice was the so-called criticism lesson, the instructions for which were often laid down in great detail. Such lessons were given at the training college or in a school, usually in the afternoon, and students took it in turn to teach a class in front of some of their fellow students, a member of the education staff and a tutor associated with the topic of the lesson.

TOWARDS A COLLEGE-TRAINED PROFESSION

In 1903, the Board of Education required that all future elementary school teachers receive a 'sound, general education in a Secondary School for three or four years'. Local education authorities were urged to provide secondary school scholarships for intending teachers and, by 1906, these accounted for almost half (48.5 per cent) of the total of 23,500 scholarships available to secondary schools in England and Wales.[25] In addition, the free place regulations, introduced in 1907, required that 25 per cent of the places in grant-maintained secondary schools be given, free of tuition and entrance fees, to pupils who had spent the previous two years at a public elementary school. By 1916–17, almost a third of the 200,000 pupils attending grant-aided secondary schools paid no fees, although many of these were technically scholarship holders.[26] By 1911, nearly 40 per cent of students entering training colleges had been educated in a secondary school until the age of 17.[27] This meant that the training colleges could gradually assume a higher level of general education among their incoming students and give more emphasis to their professional training. The change was noted by the chairman of the governors of Crewe College of Education when it was opened in 1908.

> There used to be the old apprenticeship system of pupil teachers; now, however, they have the bursar system. A very striking difference between the two systems was that under the apprentice system pupils taught and studied at the same time; the training College was required to broaden and guide the teaching of young pupils who had already been taught; for the most part it occupied itself with the teaching of academic subjects. But the leading feature of the bursar system was that the bursars had a more adequate education in the secondary schools and while they required of course that their studies should go on, they required above all things to be taught the art of teaching ...[28]

The subjects to be taught in the training colleges were specified by Regulations issued annually by the Board of Education, and those of 1904 mark an important development in teacher education. The Board assumed a greater degree of control over the appointment of staff to the colleges and remodelled the curriculum to provide a much more liberal course of study than had been permitted previously. Elementary science was made compulsory, along with English language and literature, history, geography, the principles and practice of teaching, reading and recitation, physical training, manual instruction (for men), needlework (for girls), arithmetic and elementary mathematics, and each college had to have at least one well-equipped laboratory.[29] There was, however, considerable freedom to construct alternative schemes of study within the prescribed framework and, in the case of elementary science, 'even more latitude' was given than to other subjects, leaving each college free to devise its own course after careful consideration of the needs of its students and the facilities available for science teaching.[30] This extra latitude included the mode of assessment of students' work, elementary science being a subject in which attainment was inspected rather than judged by means of a written examination.

> No scheme is laid down by the Board of Education ... Students will be expected to be able to carry out experiments selected from that portion of the approved syllabus which has been worked through up to the date of the Inspector's visit or to perform such experiments of similar character as the Inspector may consider suitable. The Science note-books of every student must be available for the Inspector's investigation. These experiments should show clearly the experiments performed by each student and the order in which the experiments were performed. The Inspector is instructed to base the report which he may make not only on the experiments which he sees performed on the occasion of his visit and on the oral answers to any questions he may put to students during his inspection, but also on the evidence afforded by those note-books that the practical work of the students has been systematic and properly supervised.[31]

The inevitable result of this curriculum flexibility offered to the colleges was diversity in the science courses provided for intending teachers, although, in some respects, this was less than might have been anticipated. In 1913, the Board of Education commented that while 'some students took a course in physics and chemistry', the kind of work which had found 'most favour ... and made most advance in recent years' was best described by the 'necessarily vague title of Nature Study', although much of the work was of a low standard.[32]

In 1907, as part of its policy to raise the standard of the work in the training colleges, the Board of Education required that the staff 'be such as to provide adequately for each of the following branches of study: (1) education; (2) English language and literature; (3) history and geography; (4) mathematics; (5) science'.[33] The two-year training college course was divided into Ordinary and Optional subjects of study. Elementary Science, 'including hygiene', was one of the Ordinary subjects to be studied by all students in accordance with a scheme of work approved by the Board of Education. Providing that the training college could satisfy the Board that its staff and facilities were adequate, two-year students could also prepare for examination in not more than two Optional subjects. These Optional subjects included physics, chemistry, botany, hygiene and rural science, in a list of 21 options. In these subjects, the instruction 'must be of a practical and experimental character' and the proficiency of the students 'will as a rule be tested partly by inspection of their practical work during the course of training, and partly by means of written examination ... No credit will be given for this examination in any case where the practical work appears to be insufficient or unsatisfactory.'[34]

The commitment to at least some form of science education as part of the initial training of elementary school teachers seemed secure, and it was strengthened by a requirement that Certificate students could be excused the study of elementary science only if they could produce evidence that they had received instruction in practical science to a standard which was acceptable to the Board of Education.[35] The course of elementary science indicated by the Board in 1907 relied heavily on nature study but it also included simple experiments in physics and chemistry that elementary school teachers were expected to perform with their pupils in the classroom.

However, in 1913, in response to pressure from the colleges, the teacher-training Regulations were amended to allow students to take fewer subjects and to study those selected to a more advanced level. The two-year course was reorganised into General subjects (Group A), Professional Subjects (Group B) and Additional Subjects (Group C). Elementary science appeared in Group A, along with English, history, geography, mathematics and (in the Welsh colleges) Welsh. Students were required to study three subjects from this group, one of which had to be English. In addition, elementary science was excluded from the Board's Final examination for the two-year Certificate course, those students taking a course of study in this subject being 'arranged in groups by the Training College Authorities according to their proficiency'. Science thus ceased to be a compulsory component of the two-year course leading to Certification as a teacher, although some attention to nature study was required as part of the 'Principles of Teaching Course', as indicated by the following extract from the Regulations.

> A. Methods and principles of teaching the following ...
> Observation lessons and Nature Study; place of investigation and of information; indoor and outdoor work; selection of material appropriate for schools differently situated; connection with gardening.
> *or*
> B. Methods of instruction and training suitable to Infants and Junior Classes
> Nature Study; choice of material for town and country children; the observation lesson; connection of nature study with expression lesson; lessons on natural phenomena leading up to geography.[36]

The consequences of this compulsory attention to nature study in the Principles of Teaching course are indicated by the questions set in the corresponding part of the examination for the Teacher's Certificate. The following examples are taken from the middle section of a paper divided into three parts. Candidates were required to answer six questions, including at least one from each section.

> For what uses in connection with nature study could you employ a small patch of ground attached to a school, in cases where a full course of gardening is impossible?
>
> Describe a 'school visit', real or imaginary, to some place of historical or geographical interest or for nature study. State what previous preparation is necessary, and what subsequent exercises in school are founded on the visit.[37]

Although the list of Group C (Additional) subjects included physics, chemistry, botany and rural science, and colleges were required to provide at least one room equipped for general science teaching,[38] the Regulations of 1913 represent a lost opportunity to remedy what was to prove almost a century-long neglect of physical science in the training of elementary school teachers.

The impact of the 1913 Regulations soon became clear. Of the 3,392 student teachers who sat the Board's final examinations in 1915, only 1,731 (51 per cent) were examined in Elementary Science and most of these (1,549) were women. The numbers of students examined in more advanced courses in physics or chemistry were very small, amounting to no more than 53 (chemistry) and 56 (physics) of the total of 3,392 students.

The retention of instruction in the methods of teaching elementary science within the 'Principles of Teaching' course is of some interest. It reflects an enduring belief that the advantages of studying science go beyond the learning of scientific facts to the development of a scientific habit of mind, and that such a habit of mind, sometimes equated with 'scientific method', was much needed in approaching the more general issues involved in teacher training. In 1907, the Board of Education could do no better than invoke and interpret Matthew Arnold in support of its wider case for a more scientific approach to teacher training.

> When Matthew Arnold declared in 1868 that the want of the idea of science, of systematic knowledge, was the capital want of English education and of English life, he was thinking of science as a method and not as a prescribed portion or subject of a curriculum. It cannot be doubted that this want has been seriously prevalent in a large portion of the education and training hitherto provided for Elementary School Teachers.[39]

In 1913, as in 1907, the Board's view was that what mattered in the scientific education of would-be elementary school teachers was an 'enquiring outlook',[40] rather than a sound, if necessarily modest, understanding of important scientific ideas. However, as the Board was only too well aware, what could be done in practice depended upon the resources available within the training colleges, and these were acknowledged to be often very inadequate.[41]

CLOSER ASSOCIATION WITH THE UNIVERSITIES[42]

The inadequacy of resources to teach science was particularly severe in some of the older training colleges, notably the denominational colleges, established in the nineteenth century. By 1860 there were 34 training colleges, a number which increased to 43 in the next 30 years.[43] By 1900, when there were 61 colleges, training 5,608 students, these institutions had endured 20 years or more of criticism of a different and rather broader kind.[44] Gosden has described some of the problems as follows:

> The fact that they were residential led them too often into being little worlds of their own – at no time did their average size reach 100 students – (they were) almost completely cut off from outside educational thought and activity.[45]

In addition, they often recruited their staff from their former pupils, with the result that while, 'Such teachers were no doubt well able to ensure continuity in the ideals and traditions of their college, their lack of acquaintance with any form of education other than that given in elementary schools produced a narrow, mechanical and illiberal approach.'[46] Jones has referred to similar problems, drawing attention to 'the lack of adequate skills ... insufficient facilities for practice in teaching, and especially the segregation which living in a separate institution necessarily involved'.[47] From 1890, following a recommendation by the Cross Commission and subsequent approval by the Education Department, day training colleges (later to evolve into University Departments of Education) of a non-denominational character were established in connection with universities. The principal educational advantage of these day training colleges was seen to be the integration of student teachers with students following other courses, although as a form of non-residential provision, they also addressed some of the other concerns referred to above. By 1903, 2,000 intending teachers were training in these day training colleges.[48]

By the early twentieth century, there were thus two routes leading to professional qualification as an elementary school teacher, based upon a teacher-training college and a university, both of which were expanding their teacher-training provision. The grant-aided elementary school teachers in training were a particularly important source of funds for the newer 'civic' universities who perceived elementary teacher training as 'a vast field waiting to be cultivated'.[49] As a result of the 1902 Education Act, and the Board of Education Regulations of 1903 and 1904, the newly-established Local Education Authorities (LEAs) were given powers to establish colleges or to aid existing institutions,[50] a move later described in a Ministry of Education publication as a 'turning point in the history of training colleges'.[51] Between 1904 and 1914, Local Education Authorities opened 22 colleges,[52] and by 1938 this number had increased to 28. In 1913–14, a total of 87 training colleges trained 11,728 students,[53] almost all of whom followed a two-year course.[54]

> The most common route for elementary teachers by the 1920s was from elementary school to secondary school (on a scholarship) and then either straight to college for a two-year course, or to an elementary school as a 'student teacher' and then to college.[55]

The various routes to qualification as an elementary teacher and the Board's ongoing policy of raising the standards required for certification meant that, in the inter-war period, elementary schools contained a mixture of untrained certificated teachers, uncertificated supplementary teachers, and university or college-trained certificated teachers.[56] The numbers of all except trained certificated teachers were in decline, and this decline was actively encouraged by the Board of Education. As early as 1909, steps were taken to abolish supplementary teachers, a category of teaching staff which Sandiford described in 1910 as 'the great blot on the English Elementary School system',[57] whose only qualifications for the job were reaching the age of 18 and being vaccinated. Their demise was hastened by restricting their activities to the infant department, or to the youngest class in a rural all-age school. At the same time, men ceased to be recognised as supplementary teachers whilst women were given until 1914 to gain further qualifications, be restricted to teaching the infant classes or to leave teaching.[58] Uncertificated teachers with five years' experience, who had previously been allowed to sit for the Board's Acting-Teaching certificate, now had to take a one-year academic, professional qualification, although, when teachers were in short supply, these regulations were often relaxed. For example, an uncertificated teacher in a London school in 1913 was permitted to remain because of 'the length of service and practical skill shown' on condition that he attended a course of lectures organised by the London County Council on two evenings a week.[59] The effect of the Board's attempts to raise the standards of the elementary school teaching profession is illustrated by an incident in a London school in 1922, when a recommendation that a retiring headteacher be replaced by a well-respected and successful member of staff at the same school was vetoed by the London County Council because of the candidate's lack of formal qualifications.[60] By 1938, more than 80 per cent of the 167,000 teachers employed in public elementary schools were certificated.[61] The growth in the numbers of qualified teachers in elementary education between 1900 and 1950 is shown in Table 5.1.

The training of public elementary school teachers in a university was initially provided in conjunction with a three-year degree course but, in 1921, this was extended to four years with the bulk of the professional training taking place in the final year.[62] This university-based, four-year course gradually displaced the two-year, day training college course, although the latter did not finally end[63] until 1951.

In a number of respects, the interwar years were a difficult time for the teacher-training colleges. Their work was not widely known, and where it was known, it was frequently heavily criticised. A particularly savage attack came from L.C. Knights,[64] co-editor of the influential *Scrutiny*. All too often the colleges were regarded as 'backwaters, rather than as an essential part of the educational system', offering 'a link between the elementary and secondary schools' and serving 'as an

TABLE 5.1
QUALIFICATIONS OF TEACHERS IN GRANT-AIDED ELEMENTARY SCHOOLS (000s), 1900–1950

Year	Certificated		Uncertificated		Supplementary		Total	
	men	women	men	women	men	women	men	women
1900–01	25.2	41.3	5.4	29.5	–	18.0	30.7	88.7
1910–11	34.4	67.9	6.3	39.9	–	14.4	40.7	122.2
1920–21	34.4	83.1	2.5	34.3	–	13.5	36.9	131.0
1930–31	40.5	87.7	3.9	32.4	–	7.3	44.4	127.4
1937–38	45.4	88.9	4.0	26.6	–	4.9	49.4	120.4
1950	60.6	110.6	0.9	5.4	–	1.8	61.5	117.8

Source: Ministry of Education, *Education 1900–1950. The Report of the Ministry of Education and the Statistics of Public Education for England and Wales for the Year 1950* (London, HMSO, 1951), Cmd. 8244, 248.

interpreter of the theoreticians to the practitioners'.[65] They were also at the centre of an ongoing debate about the best way to train teachers for a publicly-funded education service which, in response to the Education Act of 1918 and the various Hadow reports, was undergoing important changes in both its philosophy and organisation. A pamphlet, produced by a group under the chairmanship of R.H. Tawney on behalf of the Labour Party and the Trades Union Congress, argued for a separation of the academic and the professional in the training of teachers,[66] prompting the colleges, via their association, to defend their commitment to concurrent training. Tawney's view that the segregation of teachers in training was undesirable and that a university degree followed by professional training constituted a better route to qualification was countered by the claim that the 'concurrent carrying' of the academic and the professional and 'turning them into one course' constituted the distinctive strength of the colleges' work.[67]

These issues were explored by a Departmental Committee on the training of teachers which reported in 1925. Most of the Committee favoured the retention of the two-year course but the minority view, recommending a one-year professional course following either a degree or a Higher School Certificate (HSC), initially found favour with the Board of Education, and the HSC route was permitted by the Regulations issued in the summer of 1925. Eventually, after some pressure from the Training College Association and the Council of Principals, the matter was left to the discretion of the Joint Examining Boards, set up as a result of the Departmental inquiry and intended to bring the colleges into closer association with the universities.[68] In practice, the Boards achieved little in the way of ending the isolation of the colleges, partly because the Board of Education retained control of the approval of syllabuses and examinations.[69] The McNair report of 1944 described the lack of co-operation as follows.

> The fact that the several colleges of a group are all represented on the same Joint Board has not, in general, resulted in their having any closer relations with one another, save in the matter of examinations, than they had when they were more directly under the Board of Education. There is no co-operation between them about staffing, nor do they share amenities.[70]

Set up by the Board of Education to inquire into the supply, methods of recruitment and training of teachers and youth leaders, the McNair Committee[71] came up with two alternative schemes for the governance and administration of teacher training. The proposal that the existing Joint Boards should be reorganised under a Central Training Council was rejected in favour of a number of Area Training Organisations (ATO) responsible, through university-based Schools (later Institutes) of Education, for all the teacher training in the area in which they were located.[72] The scheme involving the universities prevailed because 'their standards commanded universal respect and their established independence enabled them to resist the encroachments of centralization',[73] a political stance towards teacher training that stands in stark contrast to that which has framed policy in this field in the 1990s. The Area Training Organisations were responsible for supervising courses, planning and co-ordinating facilities in the areas for which they were responsible, and promoting the continuing education of qualified teachers.[74] There is little doubt that the McNair recommendations brought the universities and colleges of education into closer co-operation and raised the standards of the academic work in many of the colleges.[75] Furthermore, the Primary and Secondary Schools Regulations of 1945 required that all except temporary teachers be qualified[76] and the Burnham salary settlements of 1947 and subsequently, led to improved salaries for teachers, although the wider issue of the status of teachers continued to receive little attention.

The McNair Committee also focused attention on an issue which had exercised the 1925 Departmental Committee, namely the balance to be struck between the academic and professional components of the college curriculum. Committed to raising the status of the teaching profession, the McNair Committee recommended both the lengthening of the college training course from two to three years and a strengthening of the academic work. The latter recommendation led in 1949 to the revision of the course leading to the Teacher's Certificate.[77] The new Regulations required students to study one subject (and in exceptional cases two) 'to as high a pitch as can be attained' and an examination in this 'main course' was to be the only test of academic knowledge during the course. There was also to be a test 'devised to examine the proficiency of students with regard to the teaching of all the ordinary subjects ...', but these tests would explicitly *not* be the subject of 'academic study', because, it was said, the colleges 'could not do everything'.[78] In part, of course, the change in the Regulations reflected the fact that many of the students in the colleges were now being prepared to teach in secondary modern, rather than elementary schools. As the Board of Education later noted:

> The teacher can no longer hope or expect to prepare himself by learning specifically at college all he will need to know for the education of the children he will teach. The emphasis is therefore on the teacher as an educated person with interests, ideals, and ideas, who has had the chance of reaching at least in one field of study the highest standard of which he is capable, and of acquiring in others some experience of the ways in which children learn and grow.[79]

As for the lengthening of the college course from two to three years, the problems and priorities facing the education service in the twenty or so years after the end of the Second World War were so severe that this was not a realistic policy option. Teachers were in desperately short supply and a massive school-building programme was underway as schools struggled to cope both with the bulge in the post-war birth rate and the trend for pupils to remain longer at school. As the National Advisory Council on the Training and Supply of Teachers, set up as a result of the McNair report, recognised, the 'possibility of any such reform would ... depend on the size of the teacher force required at the time'.[80] That time came for students entering the colleges in September 1960, following an announcement by the Minister of Education, Lord Hailsham, in June 1957. The firm commitment to extending the college course was, as Manzer has observed, an example of policy that was achieved because of the convergence of opinion on all sides in the 'educational sub-government'.[81]

The links between the training colleges and the universities received renewed attention in the report of the inquiry under Lord Robbins into Higher Education. Acknowledging that the colleges were 'only doubtfully recognised as part of a system of higher education' while 'having attained standards of work and a characteristic ethos that justify their claim to an appropriate place in it',[82] the Robbins Committee recommended that those college students whose three-year course was close in standard to that of a pass degree should be given the opportunity to graduate after following a four-year concurrent course. Such a degree, however, was to have its own distinctive characteristics.

> Though the academic standard of the degree must be broadly related to what is customary in universities, the nature of the course and the approach to the various subjects should be such as to suit the needs of future teachers.[83]

Thus, in Browne's phrase, was 'the B.Ed. launched'.

The launch, however, was not entirely smooth, partly because of controversy about the control and government of the training colleges, now to be retitled colleges of education, the emergence of the polytechnic sector of higher education and the establishment of the Council for National Academic Awards (CNAA). In addition, Alexander has observed how the new courses concentrated on a main subject and education theory at the expense of professional studies and teaching practice.[84]

> ... the academicisation of education studies, apparently a prerequisite for upgrading the three-year certificate to a degree, gave it a momentum away from those needs of the intending teacher which had provided its earlier rationale. By the 1960s the content of education courses increasingly reflected the intellectual preoccupations of education theorists and researchers rather than the needs of intending teachers – what was available by way of theory rather than what was required.[85]

The 1970s were to bring further and more turbulent changes for the colleges of education, many of which were the 'third institution' in a city or region, alongside a university and polytechnic. Following the publication of the James report[86] in 1972 on teacher education and training, the government issued its response in a White Paper entitled *Education: A Framework for Expansion*. No document can perhaps have been so ironically titled. For the colleges, the 1970s brought reorganisation, closure and amalgamation as central government sought to reduce the numbers of teachers being trained in response to demographic changes affecting the school population. In a period of 'constant inconstancy', the future of an individual college depended less upon some set of principles than upon the kind of accommodation it was able to reach with a supportive university or polytechnic, as well as the degree of wider political support it was able to command. Newly-founded and venerable institutions alike were affected and, with some justification, the Association of Teachers in Colleges and Departments of Education complained that

> There have been no policies for teacher training, only policies for teacher supply ... as a result the system and the institutions of which it is composed have never enjoyed an atmosphere of stability, certainty or confidence. When institutions can only rapidly expand or rapidly contract, they can neither develop as institutions nor concentrate on the work they are supposed to do.[87]

By the 1990s, many colleges changed yet again, ceasing to become 'mono-technic' institutions and metamorphosing into colleges within a higher education system that nominally no longer made a distinction between universities and the former polytechnics. In the 1990s, central government took firm and direct control of teacher education, funding its work through a Teacher Training Agency, encouraging a variety of routes to qualification, defining the work of a teacher in terms of statutory competences to be acquired, and allowing teacher supply to be determined by the operation of market forces, rather than in response to any central planning. Not surprisingly, many of those closely involved in teacher education saw parallels with the nineteenth century and presaged the weaknesses and limitations of which Edmond Holmes had written so eloquently in 1911 (see p. 31).

POLICY AND SCIENCE EDUCATION IN THE TRAINING OF TEACHERS

The impact of central policy initiatives in the field of teacher training upon the science education offered in the training colleges is best illustrated by examples drawn from a number of individual institutions. Avery Hill College was opened in 1906 by the London County Council which had purchased the mansion and the Avery Hill estate in 1902 for the sum of £25,000. When the County Council became an education authority following the passage of the Education Act of 1902, responsibility for the house and estate was transferred by the Council from its Parks and Open Spaces Committee to the Education Committee for the purposes of establishing the Council's first residential training college. Avery Hill set out to train women teachers via a two-year course for either infant school teaching or the girls' departments of elementary schools.[88] The first year of training concentrated on academic development with the compulsory study of English language and literature, history and geography, algebra, geometry, chemistry, physics, nature study, hygiene, drawing, music, drill, needlework and the theory of education, although the time devoted to some subjects was minimal. A high priority seems to have been accorded to science since the college opened with three laboratories,[89] the stables of the former mansion being converted into a laboratory dedicated to nature study work. However, the lack of serious attention given to science subjects in the Board of Education's Examination for the Teacher's Certificate and the poor science background of the incoming college students inevitably had a restricting influence on any attempts by the College to encourage science education. Of the 80 students who passed the Avery Hill training course in 1915, only 42 had taken and passed elementary science, only one in chemistry, and six in botany.[90] By 1921, an LCC inspector was commenting upon the high number of students being trained at Avery Hill without receiving any instruction in science. For a handful of students in the 1920s and 1930s, training in physics and chemistry was available, but they often had to be sent to Woolwich Polytechnic for this.[91] The situation did not substantially improve up to the Second World War. For example, all of the 59 students training for infant schools in 1929 took nature study, and, of the 102 who were training to teach girls over the age of seven in public elementary schools, only 27 took biology and as few as three took physics. Five years later, of the 134 training to teach girls in elementary schools, only 58 took biology.[92] The timetable followed by the girls preparing in 1932–33 to teach elementary school pupils over the age of seven is illustrated[93] in Table 5.2.

During the Second World War, the college widened the scope of its science education by introducing a course on Science in the Home and in Industry which included visits to mines, factories, dyeworks and chemical plants.[94] In the 1950s, the science work at the college, particularly that in biology, attracted praise from the London County Council which tried, although unsuccessfully, to get the Ministry of Education to grant special recognition to science at Avery Hill.[95] In 1960, the college followed other comparable institutions in introducing a three-year course and, in 1962, opened its doors to graduate students who wished to train as teachers by taking the postgraduate certificate in education awarded by the University of London. The B.Ed. degree, validated by the Council for National Academic Awards, followed in 1975, but, despite this and many other initiatives, the college was merged in 1985 with Thames Polytechnic, then also under the control of the Inner London Education Authority.

TABLE 5.2
AVERY HILL TRAINING COLLEGE: WEEKLY TIMETABLE 1932–33 AND SPECIAL SUBJECT CHOICES FOR THOSE TRAINING TO TEACH GIRLS IN ELEMENTARY SCHOOLS

Year 1	Periods per week
Educational Psychology	1
Child Welfare	1
Hygiene	1
Special Subject	3
Language	1
Speech Training	1
Story Telling	1
Physical Training	2
Arithmetic	1
Handiwork or Music	2
School Practice discussion	1
School Practice	1 morning and 1 afternoon
Year 2	
Educational Psychology	1
Hygiene or Child Welfare	1
Special Subject	3
English	1
Geography	1
History	1
Tutorial Groups in one of the above three subjects	1
Discussion on Method	1
Physical Training	2
Arithmetic	1
Music or Handiwork	2
School visits	1 day per week

Unlike Avery Hill, which may be taken as representative of the training colleges opened by some of the larger Local Education Authorities in the early years of the twentieth century, the church colleges at Cheltenham were founded by The Church of England Training School Association in 1847 to 'prepare a class of instructors who, while enlightened and spiritually minded men, shall be furnished with a sound and not superficial knowledge of the subjects which they will be called to handle'.[96] Despite this reference to men, the College of St. Mary and St. Paul had a women's department (St. Mary's Hall) until the departments separated in 1921 as St. Paul's and St. Mary's Colleges for men and women respectively. A chemical laboratory was opened at the College in 1893, and four more laboratories were added by 1914, St.

Mary's acquiring its own elementary laboratory in 1905. An inspection in 1901 had placed the College 'among the first rank', and the science teaching was especially praised, although the scale of the laboratory provision cannot be regarded as typical: in 1902, the college was described as the 'best equipped of any Training College for Science'.[97] Prior to the First World War, it was possible for female students at Cheltenham to study physics and chemistry to an advanced level, although very few chose to do so. By 1925, only biology was available at this level to the female students. It seems likely that this 'restriction of women's subjects owed itself ... to the belief of Anna Monk, Principal of St. Mary's College from 1921 to 1938, that the place of college-trained women teachers was in the primary school', and to the gradual evolution of St. Paul's College into an institution training teachers for work with older pupils in elementary and, later, modern schools. Nonetheless, an inspection in 1938 described the science teaching at St. Mary's as of exceptional quality. An interesting, but not unrepresentative, development in the College syllabus in 1920 was the addition of gardening, which reflected enduring national concerns with rural life and the drift of the rural population into towns.[98] The numbers of students at St. Mary's College studying various subjects in 1938 is shown in Table 5.3. In general, the data lend some support to Sandiford's comment, made nearly twenty years earlier, that

> The curricula of English training colleges in comparison with those of American normal schools indicate a greater emphasis on literature and perhaps mathematics, while there is considerably less attention paid to science, history of education, and psychology,[99]

although the weakness of mathematics is striking.

Crewe College of Education, which opened in 1908, gave special emphasis from the outset to 'outdoor pursuits', and this was reflected in its syllabus, which, in addition to English, History and Mathematics, included Physical Exercises and Hygiene, Rural Science, Biology, Nature Study, Gardening, Drawing and Handiwork. An Annual Field Study Week at Llanberis began in the first year, and old photographs show students at Llanberis occupied in botanical, geographical and geological work.[100] When the College was first opened, £150 was spent on scientific apparatus and kindergarten material.[101] An HMI Report of 1923 was especially impressed by 'a general course of Open Air Science embracing some Meteorology, Botany, Zoology, Geology, Surveying, Archaeology, Anthropology and Scout Craft.'[102] A new science room was opened[103] in 1928 when the college employed a specialist science teacher.[104] During

TABLE 5.3
NUMBER OF STUDENTS STUDYING VARIOUS SUBJECTS, ST. MARY'S COLLEGE, CHELTENHAM, 1938

Subject	Ordinary 1st year	2nd year	Advanced 1st year	2nd year
English	72	63	20	10
History	46	37	14	7
Geography	31	14	14	6
Mathematics	10	12	–	–
Elementary Science	32	23	–	–
Biology	–	–	9	5
French	–	–	4	4
Music	41	36	18	7
Art	50	28	8	6
Needlework & Handiwork	78	53	–	–
PT*	75	73	17	–

* Compulsory Professional Course.

the 1930s, the College syllabus reflected the national trend of combining academic with professional studies. Two-year students were offered *English Language and Literature*, History, Geography, Mathematics, Biology, *Principles and Practice of Teaching*, *Hygiene*, Art, Handiwork and Needlework, Gardening, Music and *Physical Training*, those subjects identified in italics being compulsory. Although, in session 1941–42, the College switched to recruiting females only, and from 1946 until the late 1950s confined itself to training teachers for primary schools, science remained a part of the syllabus,[105] with a Science Society thriving throughout the 1940s and 1950s.[106]

The work of the diocesan training college at Chester is of some interest, since, during the mid-nineteenth century, Chester College included a remarkably forward-looking and successful science school which came to be something of a showpiece for the institution. The work of the science school, however, depended critically upon Arthur Rigg, the College Principal, and, when he retired in 1869, the school declined, although it lingered for financial reasons until December 1883. By the 1930s, there was little to distinguish the work at Chester College from that at other comparable institutions, and a specimen timetable from this period in no way privileges science in the curriculum. (See Figure 5.1.)[107]

The City of Leeds Training College was established in temporary premises in Leeds in 1907, before being accommodated in its own,

FIGU
A SPECIMEN TIME
(CHESTER

			9–9.45	9.45–10.30	10.30–11.15		11.30–12.15
MONDAY	2	ROLL CALL 7.40AM CHAPEL 7.45AM BREAKFAST 8AM	Education	Science Geography (adv.)	Science French	INTERVAL 11.15 – 11.30am	Adv. PT (Theory)
	1		Handiwork (adv.) French	Handiwork (adv.) History (adv.)	Handiwork (adv.) Geography (adv.)		History (ord.) Mathematics (adv.)
TUESDAY	2		English (ord.)	Art (ord. & adv.) Reading (α)	Art (ord. & adv.) Mathematics (adv.)		Geography (ord.)
	1		Education	Rel. Knowledge	English (ord.)		Art (α) PT (β)
WEDNESDAY	2		Education	Rel. Knowledge	Mathematics (ord.) English (adv.)		Hygiene
	1		Handiwork (adv.) Geography (adv.) English (adv.)	Handiwork (adv.) Handiwork (sub.)	Handiwork (adv.) Handiwork (sub.)		Art (β) Reading (α)
THURSDAY	2		English (ord.)	PT (Theory)	Art (ord. & adv.) Mathematics (adv.)		Art (ord. & adv.)
	1		PT (Theory)	Science French Music (adv.)	Science History (adv.)		Mathematics (adv.) History (ord.)
FRIDAY	2		Music (ord.)	Science History (ord.)	Science History (adv.)		Mathematics (ord.) English (adv.)
	1		English (ord.)	Adv. PT (Pract.)	English (adv.) Mathematics (adv.)		Geography (α) Music (β)
SATURDAY	2		Handiwork (ord.) French	Handiwork (ord.)	Handiwork (ord.)		Rural Science Mathematics (adv.) Art (adv.)
	1		Education	Handiwork (ord.)	Handiwork (ord.)		Rural Science

Criticism Lessons and Demonstration Lessons on one afternoon

RE 5.1
TABLE OF THE 1930s
COLLEGE)

12.15–1.00	DINNER 1.05pm		4.45–5.30	5.30–6.15	TEA 6.15pm CHAPEL 7pm	7.15–8.00	PRIVATE STUDY 8–9PM SOCIETIES 9–10PM DORMITORIES 10PM
Mathematics (ord.) History (ord.)		2.30–3.15 PT	Handiwork (adv.) History (adv.)	Handiwork (adv.) Reading (β)		Handiwork (adv.)	
Adv. PT (Pract.) Music (adv.)			Geography(α) Music (β)	Music (α) Geography (β)		Nature Study Rural Science (8–9)	
PT (Pract.)			Rel. Knowledge	Rural Science			
Art (α) Reading (β)		Science 2.45–4.15	Rural Science	Hygiene		Adv. PT (Theory)	
Music (ord.) Geography (adv.)			Adv. PT (Pract.)	Rural Science		Handiwork (adv.)	
Art (β) PT (α)			Mathematics (ord.)	Adv. PT (Pract.)			
Adv. PT (Pract.) French			Handiwork (adv.) Science	Handiwork (adv.)			
History (sub.)		2.30–3.15 PT (α) 3.15–4.00 PT (β)	Rel. Knowledge	Science			
Adv. PT (Pract.)			Science Geography (adv.)	Geography (ord.)			
Music (α) Geography (β)			Mathematics (sub.)	Mathematics (ord.) French			
Rural Science Art (adv.							
Rural Science							

of each week 2 – Second Year. 1 – First Year.

somewhat grand, buildings in 1912. The college survived a number of crises in its early years and, until the new teacher training Regulations were introduced in 1913, all its students studied elementary science in the form of nature study. The advanced courses, offered by the college as a means of extending students' general education, included history, English and mathematics, but not science. In 1928, the work of the college became subject to the approval of the Board for the Final Examination of Students in Yorkshire Training Colleges, set up following the recommendation of the Departmental Committee in 1925 and one of the largest regional Boards of its kind in the country. In 1930, the subjects of study for the Teacher's Certificate in the Yorkshire Colleges were divided into two groups, professional and general, the latter being subdivided into A and B lists. Elementary science appeared in the A list, along with English, history, geography, mathematics, French, physics, chemistry and biology. Every student was examined in all three professional subjects (principles and practice of teaching, hygiene and the theory and practice of physical education), in four of the general subjects and in two short professional courses in two of the general subjects.[108]

Scrutiny of the Regulations, Syllabuses and examination papers for the interwar years provides a glimpse of the kind of work undertaken by students following the two-year Certificate course and offers some insight into the standards expected. It is clear that the flexibility allowed by the Board of Education to training colleges to devise their own schemes of work in elementary science led to some discernible differences in emphasis, even when, as in Yorkshire, the work of a number of colleges was subject to the approval of a single regional authority. At Bingley Training College in 1936, for example, two alternative courses were offered, one entitled 'Biology' and the other, 'Nature Study and Gardening'. The first section of the biology syllabus, intended only for those students without any previous knowledge of physics and chemistry, prescribed the study of the 'physical and chemical properties of air and water with reference to the part they play in plant and animal life'. The remaining three sections were concerned with (i) the processes of living things (respiration, movement, reproduction, and so on) studied for a range of plant and animal groups, (ii) an elementary account of evolution and genetics and (iii) 'short independent work showing personal observation or reading'. The course in Nature Study and Gardening was much as its title implies, with considerable emphasis upon plant propagation, flower and vegetable cultivation and a requirement that students cooperate in the 'cultivation and development of a model school garden for children up to eleven, the garden to include grass, paths, flowers, vegetables, fruits, etc.'. At Ripon Training College, in the same year, the syllabus for elementary science required all students to learn some basic physics and chemistry, to undertake some work on soils, plants and animals, and to engage in field work 'on a small area to illustrate interdependence and the struggle for existence'. At the City of Leeds Training College, students following the ordinary course of elementary science in 1936 would have studied relatively little biology in a syllabus which is noteworthy for its brevity. The limited knowledge of physical science required of the Certificate students at the College is illustrated by the following extract from that syllabus which is complete in its reference to the topics drawn from physics and chemistry.

> The atmosphere and its constituents. Their relation to combustion and to the life of animals and plants. The properties of water and its constituents. Chalk, quicklime, slaked lime, limewater. Chemical theory only taken in sufficient detail to explain simple chemical changes.
> Pressure. The barometer. Vapour pressure and its relation to boiling. Expansion. Simple experiments on specific heat and latent heat. Conduction, convection and radiation. Idea of wave motion. Wave length. Frequency.
> Colour.
> Simple experiments in magnetism and electricity.

At York Training College, the course of Elementary Science assumed 'an adequate previous training in Physics and Chemistry', and the syllabus was structured around botanical biology, zoological biology, biological principles, variation, evolution and heredity, and the 'Application of Biological Principles to School Hygiene'. Where, as at the City of Sheffield Training College, the Elementary Science syllabus was subtitled 'Physics and Chemistry', it is clear that the course was designed to provide an adequate, if modest, basis for the teaching of science in senior, rather than primary, schools.[109]

Because students' work in elementary science was not assessed by means of a written examination, it is not possible, as with a number of other components of the Teacher's Certificate, to use examination papers to gain an insight into the standards demanded of students. However, when students left college having failed, or not completed, their work in elementary science and wished to be re-examined in this subject, it was necessary for the college to set an examination paper. Several of these examination papers have survived. At Bingley Training College, for example, a theory and a practical paper were set in 1934 for the re-examination of one student. The hour-long theory paper required the student to answer one question from each of two sections, of which the following are representative.

> SECTION A
> Give a short outline of the cultivation of the carrot, and of the potato. How would you prepare the soil and generally treat these crops?
>
> SECTION B
> Describe the changes which take place in the germination of the bean seed. What are the essential conditions for the germination of seeds?

The practical examination, lasting for two and half hours, was divided into 'Laboratory Work' and 'Garden Work', although the distinction was not always evident from the questions set. The former presented six questions, each requiring the candidate to respond to such instructions as 'Weigh accurately the given sample of seeds', 'Test the leaf sample for the presence of Starch' and 'Identify the vegetable seeds provided'. The 'Garden Work' was similarly succinct in its demands, the candidate being asked to respond to a further set of six instructions such as 'Name 6 weeds on any one vegetable plot', 'Name 6 weeds in the lawn' and 'Make sowings of the bean carrot and cabbage seeds provided'.[110]

Examination questions of this kind, and those set annually in other subjects for the Teacher's Certificate, are not suggestive of high standards. While comparison is necessarily difficult, the work in elementary science is certainly significantly below that of the contemporary School Certificate examination in General Science and, in the final examination of other subjects such as mathematics, the standard seems to have been somewhat below that demanded in the corresponding subjects at the Principal level of the Higher School Certificate examination. Connell, writing about the City of Leeds Training College, has noted that when the College introduced an advanced course in general science in 1938, it was acknowledged that those students who 'had taken the Higher School Certificate Examination needed no further study in their specialist science subjects'.[111]

For most of the twentieth century, the shortcomings in the scientific education offered by the training colleges to those intending to teach young children have embraced issues of both quality and quantity, and have proved remarkably difficult to overcome. As long as science, especially physical science, was not regarded as an important element in the curriculum of elementary or primary schools, there was no pressure upon the colleges to provide the necessary training. Likewise, when more advanced science courses were available on an optional basis to students training in the colleges, students were unlikely to choose them since they would not be seen as central to their eventual work with young children in the schools. There is, of course, the broader question of why the scientific education of such children was held in such low esteem that even in some of the new training colleges established in the 1960s, the serious study of science was regarded as appropriate only for those intending to teach in secondary schools.

Part of the answer seems likely to lie in the failure of those concerned with science education to make and advance the case within a society which, in Snow's analysis, has difficulties in accommodating science as an integral part of culture.[112] From this perspective, issues such as the inadequate scientific background of primary school teachers and the limitations of the teacher training provided in the colleges are not so much causes of the lack of progress in advancing science within the primary curriculum as symptoms of a much deeper cultural ambivalence towards science and the contribution that it might make to the education of young children. Organisations such as the Royal Society and the professional institutes concerned with physics, chemistry and biology were, until the latter half of the twentieth century, interested only in the scientific education provided in universities and selective secondary schools. In much the same way, membership of the professional science teaching organisations, The Science Masters' Association, The Association of Women Science Teachers and, later, the Association for Science Education were, until relatively recently, drawn almost entirely from grammar and independent schools. The attention of these organisations, associations and institutes broadened to include primary science only when their principal interests seemed threatened, for example by an anticipated or immediate shortage of qualified scientific personnel (including graduate science teachers), by fundamental changes in schooling (notably the rapid development of comprehensive secondary education), or by concerns about the public understanding and image of science in the aftermath of a series of environmental and other science-related disasters. Perhaps fittingly, since it had played such an influential role in promoting science in elementary schools in the later nineteenth century, it was the British Association for the Advancement of Science which, in 1961, provided a forum for an initial exploration of the contribution that science might make to the education of children in primary schools (see Chapter 4).

What cannot be doubted is that the scientific education of those teaching in primary schools was seen as a significant obstacle to the widespread adoption of the primary science initiatives of the so-called curriculum development era of the 1960s and 1970s. Kerr, for whom the duty of the training colleges was to produce teachers able

> to play a major role in raising the level of the scientific literacy of the people; that is to say, the level at which people can recognise and handle the facts and the concepts of science,[113]

claimed that primary teachers' lack of scientific knowledge was 'one of the major obstacles to any extension of science teaching at the Primary stage', adding that any remedying of this deficiency would be an important part of the work of the Nuffield Junior Science Project.[114] Wastnedge, the Organiser of the Project (see Chapter 4), recalled in 1995 that '... in those days there were students, particularly women, who came to college never having done more than say two years of general science in schools and most of the women came with no physics or chemistry ... You got garbled versions of science.'[115] Richards, also from the perspective of 1995, identified the same difficulty '... there's always this problem of teacher's lack of science background and that's still there to the present day. It is a big problem', adding that,

> The greatest difficulty I've always had in this game was persuading schools to do science. I'd go and give talks round the country. Very often I'd have quite a lot of head teachers and they would nod and they would say all this was excellent ... and then they'd go away and they wouldn't do it ... very often because of the lack of background knowledge of the teachers getting it started ...[116]

The data in Table 5.4 offer some context for these recollections. In 1952, the overwhelming majority of candidates at Ordinary and Advanced levels of the GCE in physics and chemistry were boys. The relative position changed little by 1975, despite large increases in the numbers of boys and girls entered for examination.

Surveys of the work done in the training colleges in 1962 to prepare primary teachers to teach science showed that almost half of the colleges sampled provided less than thirty hours of primary science teaching during an entire three-year course. In addition, only 40 per cent of the colleges required all their students to have at least some training in science. Another survey of eight training colleges found that while almost all colleges included nature study in their programmes, only five per cent required any significant study of the physical sciences.[117]

TABLE 5.4
NUMBER OF PASSES IN GCE O- AND A-LEVEL SCIENCE EXAMINATIONS IN 1952 AND 1975

Subject		O level				A level			
		1952	%	1975	%	1952	%	1975	%
Physics	(Boys)	12,720	88.2	61,406	78.2	8,925	87.6	23,954	81.8
	(Girls)	1,715		17,121		1,258		5,342	
	(Total)	14,435		68,527		10,183		29,296	
Chemistry	(B)	11,838	79.7	45,087	68.1	7,743	84.9	16,891	70.7
	(G)	3,006		21,133		1,372		6,937	
	(T)	14,844		66,220		9,115		23,828	
Biology	(B)	5,283	26.0	45,972	40.1	4,390*	61.8	11,616	50.5
	(G)	15,002		68, 471		2,714		11,407	
	(T)	20,285		114,443		7,104		23,023	

* Includes Botany and Zoology.

Commenting upon this problem, Wastnedge has recalled that '... there was a crying need for teachers to know more science and there still is ... very rarely did you meet one who had much science background and then they tended to be relying on the notes they had from their grammar school days ... you tended to get watered-down secondary school physics taught.'[118] Writing in 1983, Redman and his colleagues involved earlier with the Oxford Primary Science Project went somewhat further, attributing primary teachers' reluctance to accommodate science within the primary curriculum to their own experience as pupils at school.

> There are still doubts in the minds of many teachers as to the proper place of science in the primary school. Part of the trouble stems from the memory they have of the science in their own school careers. This was a subject with a special mystique of its own and one they found difficult. It required special rooms and facilities and used a jargon which they never felt they fully understood.[119]

The importance of this school experience of science to the future primary teacher is emphasised by Ingle and Jennings, who suggest that among the 'many reasons' for the limited impact of the primary science curriculum initiatives of the 1960s and 1970s

> can be included the poor 'image' that most primary school teachers have of any science that they did at secondary school, and the fact

> that science is frequently not regarded by head teachers as an important part of the primary school curriculum.[120]

Redman adds that while, in the 1960s, the project members *expected* primary school teachers to have had little or no scientific background, they had not anticipated just how poor that background would be. For the project team, there was, therefore, a major problem of communication and mutual understanding.

> ... individuals who have been trained in science and pursued scientific activities have (difficulty) in appreciating the standpoint of people whose training and careers have been orientated towards the humanities and away from the sciences.[121]

A further difficulty, however, and one not identified by Redman and his colleagues, was the ambiguity about the importance to be attached to the acquisition of scientific knowledge, both in the training of primary teachers and in the science taught in primary schools. Wastnedge, although agreeing that a good background knowledge in science made for richer teaching, did not believe that a teacher needed to have such a background to help children to engage in the 'inquiry' to which the Nuffield Junior Science Project attached such importance.[122] Crossland, in his evaluation of the impact of this Project, found that some of those involved did not think that the lack of scientific knowledge was necessarily a hindrance. For a few, such ignorance even had its advantages, while, for others, having a specialist scientific background could amount to a liability.[123]

> I do not feel that academic knowledge has been a major factor in determining an individual teacher's success with the Project. Most teachers have appreciated that one of the main aims of the Project is to inculcate in the children a scientific attitude and method. Actual scientific content of the material is a means to this end. While, therefore, many teachers have shown a readiness to improve their own scientific knowledge, this lack of knowledge has not hindered the development of the Project to any great degree. (Chief Education Officer)

> The teacher should find the work more interesting as he is able to learn and discover with the children. (Junior Head)[124]

Comments such as these can be understood only in the context of a progressive primary pedagogy, and its attendant commitment to pupil activity and experience, rather than to the acquisition of scientific knowledge. In this context, Crossland's broad conclusion is hardly surprising. He found that those teachers who were familiar and comfortable with progressive methods of teaching were not handicapped by their lack of scientific knowledge, whereas those who were both inexperienced in science *and* unfamiliar with progressive methods tended to impose what little they knew upon the work.[125]

The data in Table 5.4 assume an added significance in the light of the dominance of the primary school teaching profession by women (see Table 5.5) and the consequent relatively rapid turnover of staff. In the 1950s, about half of all female teachers left the profession within five years of qualification, upon marriage or on the birth of their first child. In the following decade, statistics of this kind were used to underpin a government campaign[126] to attract married women 'returners' to work in a school system facing an acute shortage of teachers.

TABLE 5.5
PRIMARY SCHOOL TEACHERS IN THE MAINTAINED SECTOR (ENGLAND)

	Female (%)
1955	75.7
1960	76.0
1964	75.0
1975	76.8
1979	77.9
1990	81.7

Source: R. Lowe, *Education in the Post-War Years: A Social History* (1988), 95; *Statistics of Education.*

Some data are available about the academic background and subjects of study of those students who entered the training colleges in the early 1960s. Table 5.6 shows the percentages of students in teacher training in 1961 who followed courses in a number of academic subjects.

The familiar gender divide between physical and biological science is much in evidence as is the relative upopularity of mathematics among women students. The data need to be set alongside the fact that students intending to teach in primary schools spent much less time than their secondary counterparts on their main courses and rather more on the so-called curriculum courses 'studied mainly with a view to learning how to teach them'.[127] Given the breadth of the primary teacher training course, the qualifications of the students upon entry acquire a further

TABLE 5.6
PERCENTAGES OF STUDENTS IN TEACHER TRAINING (1961) BY ACADEMIC SUBJECT STUDIED

Academic subject studied	Men	Women
English	13	24
French	3	3
History	18	17
Geography	20	16
Religious knowledge	6	10
Social studies	2	2
Technical subjects	50	48
Mathematics	19	9
General Science	7	2
Physics	10	2
Chemistry	6	2
Biology	8	12

(Total percentages exceed 100 because many students followed more than one course)
Source: Committee on Higher Education, Appendix Two (B) (1963), 228.

significance. In 1961/2, 27 per cent of the students (41 per cent men, 20 per cent women) following a three-year teacher training course had one or more Advanced level passes in science as their only qualification at this level. This figure of 27 per cent includes mathematics and compares with 62 per cent for arts subjects. When the science data are further analysed by gender, only seven per cent of the students following the three-year course had one or more Advanced level passes in physical science, compared with 23 per cent of the men.[128]

It is evident that raising the overall level of competence of primary teachers to teach science, especially physical science, requires both a long-term and a short-term strategy. The former, which must have as its focus the course of initial training required of all future teachers, was not to be put in place until the 1990s, when a statutory commitment to a broad and balanced science education at school was followed by a requirement that all primary teachers study science as part of their programmes of initial training. The latter is necessarily dependent upon what can be achieved with teachers already in post, that is, by means of in-service training.

PRIMARY SCIENCE AND IN-SERVICE EDUCATION

It is not difficult to identify a range of activities which, during the second half of the nineteenth century, offered opportunities to teachers and others to improve the standard of their education and training, although the nature and scale of the provision inevitably showed some geographical variation. From the 1880s onwards, some of the larger School Boards employed peripatetic science demonstrators who visited elementary schools to assist teachers with the practical aspects of science teaching (see Chapter 1). However, such assistance was confined to cities such as Birmingham, London and Liverpool and was thus 'the exception rather than the rule'.[129] In the North of England, institutions such as Owens College, Manchester and the Yorkshire College of Science in Leeds were able to build upon the earlier success of other organisations, such as the Mechanics' Institutes, in providing classes in elementary science.[130] The Yorkshire College of Science established Saturday 'teachers' classes' in mathematics and science in Leeds in 1875–76. In 1882, the College instituted first a 'chiefly elementary' course and then a complete curriculum of London Matriculation classes, also for teachers, held on Saturdays and in the evenings, in mathematics, English, physics, chemistry, French, German, Latin and Greek. In the 1880s, the government paid part of the fees of some science teachers to allow them to attend classes in physics, chemistry, mathematics, geology and biology for two days each week, and from 1884–85 the College offered a three-year training course for assistant teachers in elementary schools (mainly ex-pupil teachers) with the support of the Leeds School Board (which compelled students' attendance).

It was not, however, until the early twentieth century that the 'necessity for the progressive education of the teacher in service' came to be widely realised.[131] By this time, two somewhat different types of in-service course had evolved. The first was intended to improve a teacher's effectiveness in a particular subject area such as drawing, science and infant work. The second, often run by, or in association with, a local university, was intended to raise teachers' understanding of individual disciplines by bringing them into contact with scholars in the relevant fields. In London in the year 1906–7, 5,099 teachers enrolled for courses of the first type and 2,615 for the second.[132] In the capital, as elsewhere and notably in Leeds and the West Riding of Yorkshire, courses were also organised by the local education authorities to improve the qualifications of uncertificated and supplementary teachers in their employ. Although these initiatives were important, not all of the newly-established local education authorities were so forward-looking and it is not possible to dispute Sandiford's conclusion in 1910 that 'much remained to be done'.[133]

In the years leading up to the Second World War, there was a steady, although uncoordinated, growth in the number of courses of different types offered by a range of providers, prominent among which were the Board of Education, the universities and the larger local education authorities.[134] However, it is highly likely that few, if any, of these courses would have been concerned with promoting the teaching of science, other than nature study, to young children.

After the Second World War, many of the training colleges, working in conjunction with the Institutes of Education set up following the McNair report, introduced 'supplementary courses' for qualified teachers.[135] Successful completion of these courses often led to the award of a Certificate by the Institute in the subject of the course. As examples, the City of Leeds Training College introduced a supplementary course in religious studies in 1953 and another in science in 1956. Not all supplementary courses were subject-orientated. Some were cross-curricular and led to a qualification in such fields as the education of 'backward children', educational administration and primary education. However, early support for these courses declined once the initial teacher training course was extended to three years and they were ended by the Department of Education and Science in 1966. It is difficult to be sure of the extent to which these supplementary courses addressed the teaching of science in primary schools but scrutiny of some of the surviving historical records does not identify this as a significant commitment.

Although HM Inspectorate held national science courses for primary school teachers from 1951 onwards, the initial response from the profession was disappointing[136] and it was not until the 1960s that the importance of in-service education to curriculum reform came to be more widely appreciated, and appropriate institutional arrangements, notably teachers' centres and local authority support services, put in place. Even so, Cane described the provision in the early 1970s as 'frequently piecemeal and uncoordinated', and claimed that 'one can point to just a few geographical locations or subject areas for which the provision is promising'.[137] In Cane's judgement, one of the problems was that 'most LEAs do not appoint staff full-time to tackle in-service education on the scale required. Many authorities do not have advisors for important parts of the school curriculum.'[138] The 'scale required' is indicated by the results of a survey conducted by the National Foundation for Educational Research in 1967 which revealed that 80 per cent of the teachers sampled acknowledged their need for some form of in-service training. The same survey also revealed the inadequacy of the provision, with between one-sixth and one-quarter of the experienced teachers reporting that they had not undertaken any form of in-service training, and most of the remainder referring to participation in only one or two courses or working parties, often of very brief duration. The same report found that teachers believed that enthusiasm in the profession was underestimated and that many more teachers would willingly attend in-service courses if only suitable courses were provided on an adequate scale.[139]

Given the very limited scientific background of most primary teachers, in-service training was of particular significance for the Nuffield Junior Science Project and the subsequent Schools Council Science 5–13 Project, although it is important to recognise that the initiatives associated with these Projects were part of a much wider, if uneven, commitment to improving the quality of work in the schools through programmes of in-service education. The Nuffield Junior Science Project initially provided introductory courses for three or four people drawn from each of its pilot areas. So-called second phase areas were the focus of further courses, organised by the Schools Council between December 1965 and the summer of 1966.[140] To meet the in-service needs of teachers in the longer term, however, the Project looked to teachers' centres, established by, or in association with, a local education authority and/or Institutes of Education.[141] A Schools Council Working Paper, published in 1967, identified three functions for such centres. The 'most important' was to 'focus local interest and to give teachers a setting within which new objectives can be discussed and defined, and new ideas, on content and methods ... can be aired'. The second function was to contribute to the evaluation and development of national curriculum projects, thereby giving 'nationally initiated work a solid foundation in widespread teacher experience and judgement'. Finally, teachers' centres were to play an important role in the dissemination 'of research and development in progress elsewhere'.[142] In framing the work of the teachers' centres, the same Working Paper suggested that the Nuffield Primary Science Project was one of the 'areas of interest 1967–70' in which the 'Council would see an urgent need for local activity'.[143]

The work of teachers' centres was endorsed by both the Plowden Committee (1967) and the James Committee (1972).[144] The number of such centres grew rapidly, from 45 in 1966 to more than 280 by the end of the decade and to over 600 by the early 1970s.[145] By 1980, most local education authorities had established teachers' centres, although these differed greatly in their resources, accommodation and programmes, and a few of the larger authorities had established specialist science centres.[146] For Wastnedge, the Organiser of the Nuffield Junior Science Teaching Project, the establishment of teachers' centres and the in-service training associated with them was one of the most successful aspects of the Project's work.

> It was teachers who had problems, and yet we established that, with support, all teachers, from the newest probationer to those approaching retirement (for example, a 64-year-old lady in Kent), could undertake the work successfully.[147]

In the mid-1970s, the role and effectiveness of in-service training in helping teachers to use Science 5–13 more effectively was the subject of a study by Griffiths. Not surprisingly, he found that '... nearly half of the teachers in the study sample had no training in the teaching of science during their initial training period' and that only a small proportion (13 per cent) of the sample had some expertise in science teaching, namely, a science degree or a college main course in science.[148] Griffiths' survey involved five groups of teachers, comprising a control group, a group which received the Science 5–13 Project materials only, and three other groups whose Project materials were supplemented by various forms of in-service training. The control and materials-only group performed similarly, whereas the three groups supported by in-service training achieved a change in their attitude towards ways of teaching, and towards organising activities and materials for science in their classrooms. Griffiths' conclusion was that in-service education is effective in changing teachers' attitudes, and, perhaps more significantly in the context of his work, that 'giving ... new curriculum materials to teachers without any in-service support is ineffective'.[149] An interesting aspect of Griffiths' study was the finding that primary teachers' scientific background seemed not to be related in any direct way to changes in teachers' attitudes towards primary science.[150] It is a finding that resonates with the view of Wynne Harlen, evaluator on the Science 5–13 Project and director of one of Science 5–13's follow-up projects, Match and Mismatch. When asked if primary teachers' lack of science background had been a restriction on the adoption of primary science programmes, she replied that 'the best teachers, best in terms of our evaluation of them ... were non-scientists ... a good confident teacher can handle science.'[151]

Despite Griffiths' findings and the rapid growth in the number of teachers' centres, there was considerable evidence, throughout the 1970s, that only modest progress was being made in establishing science within the primary curriculum. The Schools Council drew attention to the observation that

> Where the Nuffield Junior Mathematics and Junior Science Projects are being followed in the same area, mathematics is often progressing better. In many cases the reason for this bias can be traced to the thin scientific knowledge of many primary teachers. Without adequate background knowledge, teachers have difficulty preparing for pupil-centred lessons and some compromise from earlier ideas, perhaps by providing a skeleton on which average teachers can build a course or advise on pupil-centred activities, might be desirable.[152]

A survey carried out by Bradley in the early 1970s showed 'that there were very few "science" specialists in Primary schools', and that 'science' played only a small role in their work. Bradley also identified a large group of women to whom science was unattractive, even distasteful, and another group who regarded their lack of scientific training as a sufficiently grave handicap to prevent them from attending in-service courses concerned with primary science. Little time was given to science in the primary classroom and the suggestion that science might be taught in a way which integrated it with the rest of the primary curriculum was judged to be unworkable.[153]

The DES Primary Education Survey of 1978 found that less than a fifth of primary schools had teachers in posts with special responsibility for the science component of the primary curriculum, although 43 per cent of schools reported having written guidelines for a scheme of work in science.[154] The conclusion was that few of the primary schools visited in the course of the survey

> had effective programmes for the teaching of science. There was a lack of appropriate equipment; insufficient attention was given to ensuring proper coverage of key scientific notions; the teaching of processes and skills such as observing, the formulating of hypotheses, experimenting and recording was often superficial. The work in observational and experimental science was less well matched to children's capabilities than work in any other area of the curriculum.[155]

In 1981, Ingle and Jennings reported that

> although some science is attempted in a majority of classes, such work is seriously developed in but one class in ten. In a minority of classes some imaginative and excellent work is being carried out, but in many schools, science is limited to 'nature study'. This should, perhaps, not surprise us when we remember that women

> greatly outnumber men as primary school teachers, and that if they studied a science course beyond the age of thirteen it was probably biology ... Consequently, much work, especially that of a physical science nature proposed in curriculum projects, is unfamiliar and even frightening to many primary teachers, whose expertise centres around the three Rs.[156]

They attributed their findings to teachers having 'too little confidence in their ability to teach science effectively, probably because their own scientific knowledge and experience is often very limited'.[157] The Department of Education and Science came to essentially the same conclusion.

> The most severe obstacle to the improvement of science in the primary school is that many existing teachers lack a working knowledge of elementary science appropriate to children of this age. This results in some teachers being so short of confidence in their own abilities that they make no attempt to include science in the curriculum. In other cases, teachers make this attempt but the work which results is superficial since the teachers themselves may be unsure about where a particular investigation or topic in science could lead.[158]

Acknowledging that 'despite efforts by the Nuffield Foundation and the Schools Council, work in science is weak', the Department of Education and Science took the view that a slow but steady build-up from the points of strength of individual teachers was 'probably the only sure way forward'.[159] The 1978 HMI report accordingly recommended that in-service training should be a continuous part of a teacher's career, both formally through courses and informally by learning from colleagues and visitors. While this recommendation is neither surprising nor innovative, it seems clear that it was unlikely to offer an effective solution to long-standing and deep-seated difficulties.

Throughout the 1980s, the accommodation of science within primary schools remained uneven and very variable in quality.

> At present the content of primary science is left almost entirely to chance, a state of affairs which puts a considerable strain on conscientious teachers who lack sufficient background and experience of science.[160]

A series of reports confirmed that science continued to make disappointingly slow progress towards securing a satisfactory place within the primary curriculum. When the Assessment of Performance Unit revealed that 'although few schools admitted to no science, few gave more than five per cent of the time to it',[161] the HMI Science Committee quoted this finding and sought to explain it by asking

> whether it is reasonable to expect all or even most teachers to teach science without support of a kind and quantity that is wholly lacking at the present time. Many of the teachers who, to their credit, are willing to attempt the teaching of the subject nevertheless fail to understand its nature and requirements. It may be that this lack of background explains why two fully fledged curriculum development projects (Nuffield Junior Science and Schools Council Science 5–13) with their attendant in-service training programmes have failed to engender a large scale development of science in primary schools, despite much dedicated effort on the part of LEAs, advisers and teachers.[162]

The reference to a lack of support is of some significance. It reflects a degree of frustration with attempts to put in place systematic and well-funded programmes of in-service education, despite a number of central government initiatives towards this end.

Despite some improvements, the scientific education provided in initial training courses also continued to fall short of what was required,

> the expertise of the primary school teachers in service (being) heavily weighted towards the humanities and aesthetic subjects. Science is less well served.[163]

In addition to this curriculum bias in initial teacher education, there was concern that where science courses were provided for student-teachers, the work was 'too content orientated, with a secondary bias and lacking relevance to the primary schools'.[164] In 1983, it was suggested officially 'that all primary teachers should be equipped to take a particular responsibility for one aspect of the curriculum (such as science, mathematics or music), to act as consultants to their colleagues on that aspect and, where appropriate, to teach it to classes other than their own'.[165] In reality, this was another solution which was incommensurate with the problem to be solved and one which, in any event, presented a number of staffing and other difficulties for primary schools, especially small primary schools in rural areas.[166]

The adequacy of the scientific background of new entrants to the primary teaching profession was closely related to the relatively small number of men, especially male graduates, who chose to work in this sector. Of 189,000 nursery and primary school teachers in service in 1981, only about 9,000 were male graduates. Moreover, as Table 5.7 shows, primary schools, unlike their secondary counterparts, were overwhelmingly staffed by non-graduates (158,000 or 84 per cent).

TABLE 5.7
FULL-TIME TEACHERS ANALYSED BY SCHOOL TYPE, SEX AND GRADUATE STATUS

England and Wales, thousands, March 1981

	Nursery & Primary			Secondary		
	Men	Women	All teachers	Men	Women	All teachers
Graduate	9	21	31	75	53	128
Non-graduate	34	124	158	59	58	117
Total[a]	43	145	189	134	110	244

a: Because of rounding, some totals are not the exact sum of their constituents.
Source: DES, *Teaching Quality* (HMSO, London, 1983), 3.

By the later 1980s, a 'slow but steady build up from the points of strength of individual teachers' had become politically unacceptable as 'the only sure way forward'. The earlier large-scale investment in primary science curriculum development and in in-service education were judged to have been much less successful than might reasonably have been expected. Allied with enduring inadequacies in the scientific education of most intending primary teachers, a more radical solution to problems of primary science for all was almost inevitable. It was to come initially through the national curriculum introduced following the passage of the Education Reform Act 1988 and subsequently through direct government intervention in the courses of initial[167] and in-service[168] training of teachers for primary schools. Whether these central systemic initiatives amount to a sufficient, as well as a necessary, condition for raising the quality of primary science education remains to be seen.

NOTES

1 A. Tropp, *The School Teachers. The Growth of the Teaching Profession in England and Wales from 1800 to the present day* (London, 1957).
2 P.H.J.H. Gosden, *The Evolution of a Profession. A Study of the Contribution of Teacher's Associations to the Development of School Teaching as a Professional Occupation* (Oxford, 1972).
3 H.C. Dent, *The Training of Teachers in England and Wales 1800–1975*, (Sevenoaks, 1977).

4 R. Alexander, *Primary Teaching* (London, 1984), 96–7.
5 M.V.C. Jeffreys, *Revolution in Teacher-Training* (London, 1961), 3–4.
6 L.G.E. Jones, *The Training of Teachers in England and Wales. A Critical Survey* (London, 1924), 17.
7 P.H.J.H. Gosden, op. cit., 195.
8 Board of Education, *Regulations and Syllabus for the King's Scholarship Examination 1905*, PP LXXV (1905), 672–3.
9 Quoted in L.G.E. Jones, op. cit., 12.
10 R. Aldrich, 'The Evolution of Teacher Education', in N.J. Graves, I*nitial Teacher Education. Policies and Progress* (London, 1990), 14–15.
11 S.J. Curtis and M.E.A. Boultwood, op. cit., 374.
12 A. Tropp, op. cit., 164–5.
13 S.J. Curtis and M.E.A. Boultwood, op. cit., 374.
14 R. Aldrich, op. cit., 15.
15 H.C. Dent, op. cit., 50.
16 Ibid., 53.
17 A. Tropp, op. cit., 185.
18 E.W. Jenkins, *From Armstrong to Nuffield. Studies in Twentieth-Century Science Education in England and Wales* (London, 1979), 216.
19 J. Lawson and H. Silver, *A Social History of Education in England* (London, 1973), 381; H.C. Dent, op. cit., 48, 50.
20 E.W. Jenkins, op. cit., 216.
21 Board of Education, *Regulations for the Preliminary Education of Elementary School Teachers* (London, HMSO, 1913), vi.
22 Quoted in P.H.J.H. Gosden, op. cit., 197.
23 Ministry of Education, *Education 1900–1950. The Report of the Ministry of Education and the Statistics of Public Education for England and Wales for the Year 1950* (London, HMSO, 1951), 82.
24 City of Leeds Training College, *Report of the Master of Method, 1910–11*, Leeds LEA papers, Brotherton Library, University of Leeds.
25 In 1900, about 5,500 children received 'assistance from public funds', principally in the form of scholarships available under the Technical Instruction Acts, to finance their secondary education. While this figure cannot be compared directly with that for 1906 quoted in the text, the figures undoubtedly indicate a substantial increase in the numbers of scholarships available. For a review of the passage from the elementary schools to the secondary school, see Board of Education, *Report for the Year 1911–12* (London, HMSO, 1912), 24–8.
26 Not all free (i.e. non fee-paying) places were 'free places' in the special sense of the 1907 Regulations, which provided that, where private or LEA scholarships and awards for intending teachers did not make up the required 25 per cent of places, the gap was to be bridged by an appropriate number of 'free places'.
27 Board of Education, *Regulations for the Training of Teachers for Elementary Schools* (London, HMSO, 1913), vi.
28 *A College in Green Fields. The Story of Crewe College of Education, 1908–1974* (1974), 2.
29 E.W. Jenkins, op. cit., 217.
30 Board of Education, *Report for the Year 1912–13* (1913), 35–6.
31 Board of Education, *Regulations for the Training of Teachers and for the Examination of Students in Training Colleges*, PP LXXV (1904), 611–12.
32 Ibid., 38.
33 Quoted in P. Sandiford, *The Training of Teachers in England and Wales* (Teachers College, Columbia University, Contributions to Education, No.32., New York City, 1910), 74.
34 Board of Education, *Regulations for the Training of Teachers and for the Examination*

of Students (London, HMSO, 1907), 64.
35 Ibid., 15.
36 Board of Education, *Regulations for the Training of Teachers for Elementary Schools* (London, HMSO, 1913), 72–3.
37 City of Leeds Training College, Examination for Board of Education Teacher's Certificate 1909, Principles of Teaching, Syllabus No. 1. Question Paper. Leeds LEA, paper, Brotherton Library, University of Leeds.
38 Ibid., xiv.
39 Board of Education, *Regulations for the Training of Teachers and for the Examination of Students in Training Colleges* (London, HMSO, 1907), xiii.
40 Board of Education, *Regulations for the Training of Teachers and for the Examination of Students in Training Colleges* (London, HMSO, 1907), xiv.
41 Board of Education, *Regulations for the Training of Teachers and for the Examination of Students in Training Colleges* (London, HMSO, 1907), xv–xvi.
42 For a detailed account of some of the events referred to in this section of the chapter, see W.R. Niblett, D.W. Humphreys and J.R. Fairhurst, *The University Connection* (London, 1975), *passim.*
43 R. Aldrich, op. cit., 17
44 M. Craft, 'A Broader Role for Colleges of Education', in J.W. Tibble (ed.), *The Future of Teacher Education* (London, 1971), 8.
45 P.H.J.H. Gosden, op. cit., 198.
46 Ibid., 198.
47 L.G.E. Jones, op. cit., 25.
48 Ibid., 25.
49 D.S.L. Cardwell, *The Organisation of Science in England* (London, 1957), 162.
50 R. Aldrich, op. cit., 17.
51 Ministry of Education, *Education 1900–1950. The Report of the Ministry of Education and the Statistics of Public Education for England and Wales for the Year 1950* (London, HMSO, 1951), 83.
52 M. Craft, op. cit., 8.
53 E.W. Jenkins, op. cit., 215.
54. Ibid., 216.
55 J. Lawson and H. Silver, op. cit., 388.
56 For details, see A. Tropp, op. cit., 154–5.
57 P. Sandiford, op. cit., 107.
58 Ibid., 107.
59 P. and H. Silver, *The Education of the Poor, The History of a National School 1824–1974* (London, 1974), 145. A further example involves the training college at Leeds where the LEA wished to appoint a highly successful teacher and the former head of the Pupil Teacher Centre as Principal. However, the Board resisted the appointment because the candidate was a non-graduate. The matter dragged on, with both the LEA and the Board holding to their respective positions, until the candidate reached retirement age, his appointment as 'Acting Principal' being renewed annually until the end of the 1914–18 War. See E.W. Jenkins, *A Magnificent Pile; A Centenary History of the Leeds Central High School* (Leeds, 1985).
60 P. and H. Silver, op. cit., 158.
61 Board of Education, *Teachers and Youth Leaders. Report of the Committee appointed by the President of the Board of Education to consider the Supply, Recruitment and Training of Teachers and Youth Leaders* (London, HMSO, 1944), (known as the McNair report), 10.
62 S.J. Curtis and M.E.A. Boultwood, op. cit., 376.
63 Ministry of Education, *Education 1900–1950. The Report of the Ministry of Education and the Statistics of Public Education for England and Wales for the Year 1950* (London, HMSO, 1951), 83.

64 L.C. Knights, 'Will Training Colleges Bear Scrutiny?', *Scrutiny*, Vol. 1, No. 3, Dec. 1932, 247–63.
65 J.D. Browne, *Teachers of Teachers. A History of the Association of Teachers in Colleges and Departments of Education* (London, 1979), 14. Browne forms her opinion principally on the basis of comments published in the Association's journal.
66 TUC and Labour Party, *The Training of Teachers* (London, 1922).
67 For details, see J.D. Browne, op. cit., chapter 2.
68 S.J. Curtis and M.E.A. Boultwood, op. cit., 377–8.
69 M. Craft, op. cit., 8.
70 Board of Education, *Teachers and Youth Leaders*, 16. (See n. 61).
71 S.J. Curtis and M.E.A. Boultwood, op. cit., 378.
72 Ibid., 379.
73 L. Connell, *Carnegie, A History of Carnegie College and School of Education, 1933–1976* (Leeds, 1983), 26.
74 Ministry of Education, *Education 1900–1950. The Report of the Ministry of Education and the Statistics of Public Education for England and Wales for the Year 1950* (London, HMSO, 1951), 88.
75 W.A.C. Berry, *The Development of Teacher Training in England and Wales since 1944, with particular reference to the establishment of B.Ed. degree courses for students in Colleges of Education* (Lecture given by Berry, Secretary, University of Birmingham, Institute of Education, 26 July 1966, Bristol), 1.
76 Ministry of Education, *Education 1900–1950. The Report of the Ministry of Education and the Statistics of Public Education for England and Wales for the Year 1950* (London, HMSO, 1951), 79.
77 P. Renshaw, 'The Objective and Structure of the College Curriculum', in J.W. Tibble, op. cit., 54.
78 T.W. Eason, in J.W. Tibble, op. cit., 85–6.
79 Ministry of Education, *Education 1900–1950. The Report of the Ministry of Education and the Statistics of Public Education for England and Wales for the Year 1950* (London, HMSO, 1951), 84.
80 National Advisory Council on the Training and Supply of Teachers, Paper 69, Oct. 1952.
81 R.A. Manzer, *Teachers and Politics*, Manchester University Press, 1970, quoted in Browne, op. cit., 103.
82 *Higher Education*, Report of the Committee appointed by the Prime Minister under the Chairmanship of Lord Robbins, 1961–3 (London, HMSO, 1963), para. 308.
83 Ibid., para. 327.
84 R.J. Alexander, op. cit., 85.
85 Ibid., 115.
86 *Teacher Education and Training*, a Report of a Committee of Inquiry under the chairmanship of Lord James of Rusholme (London, HMSO, 1972).
87 J.D. Browne, op. cit., 229.
88 D. Shorney, *Teachers in Training 1906–1985. A History of Avery Hill College* (London, 1989), 62, 91.
89 Ibid., 65.
90 Ibid., 339–40.
91 Ibid., 87.
92 Ibid., 122–3.
93 Ibid., 341.
94 Ibid., 147.
95 Ibid., 213. Because of the shortage of science teachers in secondary schools, the Ministry of Education encouraged a number of training colleges to institute a three-year, integrated course in order to give more able students a more extensive preparation for science teaching than was possible in the normal two-year course.

Institutions offering these courses came to be known as 'wing' colleges. The students who completed their training in these colleges found employment in secondary modern or, where graduates could not be secured, in grammar schools.

96 C. More, *The Training of Teachers, 1847–1947. A History of the Church Colleges at Cheltenham* (London, 1992), 15.

97 Ibid., 93.

98 Ibid., 84.

99 P. Sandiford, op. cit., 83.

100 Crewe College of Education, *A College in Green Fields. The Story of Crewe College of Education, 1908–1974* (Crewe, 1974), 7.

101 Ibid., 1.

102 Ibid., 11.

103 Ibid., 3.

104 Ibid., 4.

105 Ibid., 17, 19.

106 Ibid., 24.

107 J.L. Bradbury, *Chester College and the Training of Teachers 1839–1975*, Chester College (Chester, 1975), 133–8 and Appendix VI. One noteworthy development of the interwar period was the link established with the University of Liverpool. However, only one student graduated by means of this link and that was in science. (Ibid., 186). A number of comparable links, some more successful than others, were established in various parts of the country.

108 L. Connell, *A Century of Teacher Training in Leeds 1875–1975* (Leeds, 1996), 144.

109 Board for the Final Examination of Students in Yorkshire Training Colleges, *Regulations and Syllabuses 1936* (1936), 34–47. Some 'trade-off' between Ordinary and Advanced subjects was possible.

110 Board for the Final Examination of Students in Yorkshire Training Colleges, Final Examination 1934, Bingley Training College, *Elementary Science* (for an ex-student). University of Leeds Archives.

111 L. Connell, op. cit., 170.

112 C.P. Snow, *The Two Cultures and the Scientific Revolution* (Cambridge, 1959).

113 J.F. Kerr, 'Training for Learning Through Scientific Investigations', in W.H. Perkins (ed.), *The Place of Science in Primary Education*, Proceedings of the BAAS Conference, Sept. 1961 (London, 1962), 33.

114 *JSP 9*, Meeting of Consultative Committee, 28 Jan. 1964, 1.

115 E.R. Wastnedge, Interview with B.S., Carlisle, 11 May 1995.

116 Interview with Roy Richards, 2 May 1995, London.

117 *JSP 1*, E.J. Wenham, Questionnaire, June 1962.

118 B.S. interview with E.R. Wastnedge, Carlisle, 11 May 1995.

119 Stewart Redman *et al.*, 'Young Children and Science: The Oxford Primary Science Project', in C. Richards and D. Holford, op. cit., 131.

120 R. Ingle and A. Jennings, op. cit., 36.

121 S. Redman, op. cit., 136.

122 E.R. Wastnedge, 'The Nuffield Foundation Science Teaching Project IX: Science in primary schools', *School Science Review*, 168 (1968), 347.

123 R.W. Crossland, 'An Individual Study of the Nuffield Foundation Primary Science Project', *School Science Review*, 53 (1972), 635.

124 Ibid., 635

125 Ibid., 636.

126 R. Lowe, op. cit., 104. The Crowther report (Ministry of Education, *15 to 18*) provides interesting data about a variety of social trends, including patterns of marriage.

127 Committee on Higher Education, *Appendix Two (B)*, Cmnd. 2154 (1963), 224 and 228.

128 Ibid., 82.
129 R. Ingle and A. Jennings, op. cit., 16.
130 Many of the classes were held under the auspices of the Yorkshire Union of Mechanics' Institutes and the Yorkshire Board of Education and took place in the larger West Riding towns and cities such as Leeds, Bradford, Halifax, Wakefield and Huddersfield. P.H.J.H. Gosden and A. Taylor, *Studies in the History of a University 1874–1974* (Leeds, 1975), 251.
131 P. Sandiford, op. cit., 116.
132 Ibid., 118–19.
133 Ibid., 119.
134 Ministry of Education, *Education 1900–1950. The Report of the Ministry of Education and the Statistics of Public Education for England and Wales for the Year 1950* (London, HMSO, 1951), 90.
135 M.V.C. Jeffreys, op. cit., 16–17.
136 R. Wastnedge, 'The Nuffield Foundation Science Teaching Project', 342.
137 B. Cane, 'In-Service Education for Teachers', in Tibble, op. cit., 134.
138 Ibid., 151–2.
139 Ibid., 135, 141.
140 *JSP 9*, Items to be discussed at Consultative Committee, 27 Oct. 1965, 2.
141 *JSP 3*, Memorandum to R.A. Becher from E.R. Wastnedge, April 1964.
142 Schools Council, *Curriculum Development*, Working Paper No. 10 (London, 1967), 6.
143 Ibid., 14. The other Nuffield Science, Mathematics and Language Projects were similarly suggested.
144 DES, *Teacher Education and Training*, 108.
145 L. Weber, *The English Infant School and Informal Education* (NJ, 1971), 153; E.R. Wastnedge, 'Nuffield Junior Science: The End of a Beginning?', in C. Richards and D. Holford, op. cit., 145.
146 Biological and environmental field centres were also in existence at this time. R. Ingle and A. Jennings, op. cit., 146.
147 E.R. Wastnedge, 'Nuffield Junior Science: The End of a Beginning?', 145. See n. 145.
148 B.M. Griffiths, *A Study of the Effectiveness of Different Methods of Inservice Education and Training Designed to Introduce the Schools Council Science 5/13 Project Into Primary Schools*, Unpublished M. Phil. thesis, University of Nottingham (1978), 57.
149 B.M. Griffiths, op. cit., 103.
150 Ibid., 101.
151 Wynne Harlen, interview with BS, May 1995, Edinburgh.
152 Institute of Education, SC 328/352/08, *Annex to Junior Science Field Report*, n.d., 1.
153 B.M. Griffiths, op. cit., 16.
154 DES, *Primary Education in England: a survey by HM Inspectors of Schools*, (London, HMSO, 1978), 37, 40.
155 DES, *Primary Education in England* (London, HMSO, 1978), 58.
156 R. Ingle and A. Jennings, op. cit., 88.
157 Ibid., 132.
158 DES, *Primary Education in England* (London, HMSO), 62.
159 Ibid., 125.
160 J. Kerr and E. Engels, op. cit., 48.
161 DES, *Science in Primary Schools. A discussion paper produced by the HMI Science Committee* (London, HMSO, 1984), 4.
162 Ibid., 18.
163 DES, *Teaching Quality* (London, HMSO, 1983), 9.
164 M. Whittaker, op. cit., 252.
165 DES, *Teaching Quality* (London, HMSO, 1983), 10.

166 Ibid., 11–12.

167 Since 1996, all initial primary teacher-training courses must include a minimum of 150 hours in primary science. From 1998, all new entrants born after 1979 should have a Grade C pass in GCSE Science or its equivalent.

168 In 1990–91, for example, the Department of Education and Science earmarked funds under the Local Education Authorities' Training Grant Scheme (LEATGS) to support a new kind of in-service programme of teachers of science (and mathematics) in primary schools in order to strengthen the work required by the National Curriculum. In 1990–91, the 'designated courses' funded by the LEATGS were attended by 2,635 science and 2,461 primary teachers of science and mathematics respectively. See Department of Education and Science, *Designated Courses in Mathematics and Science for Primary Teachers, April 1990–April 1991, A Report by HMI* (London, DES) 1992.

6

Learning theories and the scientific education of young children

In the Foreword to this book, attention was drawn to the fact that the terms 'elementary' and 'primary' are not interchangeable and that primary education is a comparatively recent development within the education system of England and Wales. There are, of course, many factors which underpin this development which, despite important earlier initiatives, has been such a marked feature of the second half of the twentieth century. Among these factors have been ideas about childhood and, in particular, about how children learn and should be taught.

Theories of learning have contributed in a number of different ways to the rationale and practice of primary education. They have provided a new 'child-centred' language with which primary teachers and others can conceptualise and describe the everyday work of the primary classroom. They have also provided a new educational philosophy to justify that work and the curriculum and pedagogy which characterise it. As Alexander has noted, 'Working with primary teachers and children one gains a powerful sense of professional consensus over the kinds of educational practices connoted by the word "primary".'[1]

This is not, of course, to claim that most, or even many, elementary or primary school teachers have readily espoused extant or emergent theories about how children learn and been eager to apply them in their classrooms. As the Plowden report noted of the early twentieth century:

> A considerable body of liberal thinking on the education of children was available to teachers. Rousseau, Pestalozzi, Froebel, Whitehead, Dewey, Montessori and Rachel Macmillan, to mention only a few, had all written on lines that encouraged change and innovation. Yet it may be doubted whether the direct influence of these or of any other writers was great. It was rare to find teachers who had given much time to the study of educational theory, even in their training college days. Perhaps the strongest influence was that of Froebel, mediated through the Froebel training colleges which bore his name.[2]

What is, however, clear, is that during the twentieth century, and particularly after 1944, teachers of young children increasingly came to think about, and to conduct at least some of their work in ways that have come to be called 'progressive'. Such progressivism was not confined to primary teachers or to those responsible for their education and training. Progressive ideas, although not unchallenged, were to become part of the language of politicians and Her Majesty's Inspectorate of Schools, and they were to find architectural expression in the school building programme undertaken as part of post-war reconstruction after 1945. They also represented a loose coalition of claims, assumptions and practices which went far beyond the somewhat narrower and earlier notion of 'child-centred' education. The essential features of that coalition have been described by Cunningham in the following terms.

> ... a reduction in the traditional authoritarianism of the teacher, alternatives to the dominant pedagogical form of the class lesson, removal of punishment and unnecessary drill and discipline, dissolution of the formal timetable and a shift in curriculum emphasis from the routine of the three Rs to more creative expressive activity.[3]

This chapter reviews some of the changes that have taken place during the twentieth century in ideas about how children learn and examines the implications of these changes for how, and, in some instances, what, science they should be taught.

THE DECLINE OF FACULTY PSYCHOLOGY

At the beginning of the twentieth century, science education in public elementary schools was dominated by object teaching and nature study, the former in decline and the latter gaining rapidly in importance in response to official encouragement by the Board of Education and the energetic support of the School Nature Study Union. Faculty psychology, which dominated educational thought in the nineteenth century, structured the mind around a number of faculties such as observation, reasoning and accuracy, each of which could be trained by appropriate exercises, much as an athlete could develop muscles by following a suitable training programme. The object lesson was derived from the ideas of Pestalozzi and introduced to England at a school in Cheam by Rev Charles and Elizabeth Mayo in the 1830s.[4] It was regarded as particularly well-suited to developing the faculty of observation, and 'object teaching', often of the most sterile and unimaginative kind, dominated elementary school science education for the greater part of the second half of the nineteenth century. Competing with object teaching, but equally dependent upon a faculty psychology, was the heuristic approach of H.E. Armstrong. Armstrong sought to place pupils as far as possible in the position of the scientific discoverer and placed his emphasis upon the development of a widely-applicable scientific method.

However, as noted in Chapter 1, by the early years of the twentieth century, both faculty psychology and heurism were in decline. The former suffered at the hands of the Herbartians and was also undermined by the findings of some experimental psychologists, notably Thorndike and Woodward, which cast doubt upon the claims made about the transfer of training. As for the latter, the Board of Education warned[5] in 1900 of a 'slavish adherence' to heurism, and the British Association scheme of work in elementary science was judged in 1909 to have led to 'considerable repetition' and, occasionally, to teaching which was 'grotesquely unsuited to the ages and abilities' of some pupils attending public elementary schools in London.[6] There were also unmistakable signs that in the hands of inexperienced or inadequate teachers, the heuristic method was being misapplied, and teachers, unquestionably the weakest point of heurism,[7] were themselves divided about the effectiveness of Armstrong's approach, some judging it to fail completely, others, after some years of teaching, seeming to be more convinced than ever of its value.[8] Writing in 1958, Thompson claimed that 'Either from lassitude or a desire to do things by established methods, many teachers never made a genuine attempt' [at heurism].[9]

THE GROWTH OF PROGRESSIVE IDEAS

By 1900, the ideas of Froebel, Pestalozzi and Herbart, all of whom had been dead for many years, were beginning to have a significant influence upon elementary education in England. Although the late nineteenth-century 'naturalist' disciples of J.H. Pestalozzi (1746–1827) and F. Froebel (1782–1852) were far from unanimous in their views, they[10] all shared the belief that the prime aim of education was to develop the latent powers of each pupil 'in accord with the laws of nature'.[11] The 'naturalists', therefore, placed their emphasis on freedom, rather than method, and on self-development rather than faculty training, thereby helping to generate 'a new spirit', the essentials of which were a 'reverence for the pupil's individuality and a belief that individuality grows in an atmosphere of freedom'.[12] Such ideas, while not themselves destructive of faculty psychology, clearly threatened to infuse it with such a generous spirit as to alter its significance for the curriculum.

Pestalozzi, through experience with his son, and a number of years working in schools, had advocated an approach to teaching young children which emphasised co-operation between teacher and pupil, activity by the child, and the observation of nature to facilitate learning. He stressed that children should be educated to develop their individual talents, rather than to serve some economic or other end. He modified Rousseau's ideas, arguing that children should be encouraged to have self-control from an early age,[13] and prioritised moral and religious education over the intellectual.[14] As for the scientific education of children, Pestalozzi advocated the observation of natural phenomena and, at home with his son, he brought snow into the house so that it could be observed melting.[15] Pestalozzi's emphasis upon 'natural phenomena' was misunderstood by many of his later followers who frequently confronted children with artefacts and natural objects, far removed from, and often quite alien to, their everyday experience. Pestalozzi tested his views by implementing them in a number of schools. Through his reputation and with the support of like-minded others, he opened a school at Burgdorf in 1799, which was moved to Yverdun in 1805, closing 20 years later when Pestalozzi was eighty years old. Both Froebel and Herbart visited the school at Yverdun.[16] Pestalozzian views were popularised in England by the Rev Charles Mayo (1792–1846), who had worked at the school at Yverdun. When he came back to England he set up a school at Epsom, later moving to Cheam, where he practised Pestalozzian ideas and also publicised them.[17]

Like Pestalozzi, Froebel developed his educational ideas whilst teaching[18] and emphasised the importance of 'the natural' in education.[19] Both Pestalozzi and Froebel used the metaphor of the child as a plant to be nurtured, with the teacher as the gardener, providing all the necessary requirements for growth in the child's environment, and having faith that the child itself had the capacity to grow from within.[20] The infant schools which Froebel established from the mid-nineteenth century onwards, the 'kindergarten',[21] emphasised the importance and value of play and activity in learning. They made use of group and individual methods of teaching and emphasised the development of the child rather than the acquisition of a body of factual knowledge. Froebel's enduring contribution to the education of young children was his view that they could and would learn through the activity of play. There had been some popularisation of Froebelian theory in England from the mid-nineteenth century, with Sir William Mather opening the first free kindergarten in Manchester in 1873,[22] but it was the work of Madame Michaelis which was particularly influential. She came to England in 1874 after teaching in kindergarten in Switzerland and Italy, and founded the Froebel Society.[23] She also established a kindergarten and Preparatory School in Croydon, followed by a training college for kindergarten teachers in Notting Hill.[24]

The learning theory espoused by J.F. Herbart (1776–1841) did not become known in England until the end of the nineteenth century, although it was formulated almost a century earlier.[25] J.J. Findlay specifies the timing:

> In 1890 scarcely any English teacher knew of Herbart's existence [but by 1896] almost everyone in the Training Colleges was talking and teaching the new pedagogics.[26]

Herbart began from the premise that children were born without predetermined tendencies or innate abilities. For him, the mind of the newborn child has 'originally neither concepts, nor feelings, nor desires. It knows nothing of itself, and nothing of other things; also in it lie no forms of perception and thought, no laws of willing and action, and not even a remote predisposition to any of these.'[27] Children acquired knowledge and skills through a process of assimilation, the four steps of which were developed by Herbart's later followers into five: *preparation*, *presentation*, *association*, *generalisation/systematisation* and *application*.[28] The 'Herbartian steps' were widely used to structure individual lessons. 'Preparation' required the teacher to refer to the existing knowledge to which the subject matter of the lesson, the 'new' knowledge, was to be related. During the next step, pupils were presented with the 'new' knowledge to be learnt. This was followed by 'Association' when the 'new' knowledge was analysed and related to the pupils' existing knowledge. During the fourth step of 'Generalisation/Systematisation' the 'new' knowledge was reviewed and related to a wider context. The final step involved the application of the newly-acquired knowledge to a variety of contexts, and the rehearsal of the various skills that had been learned.[29]

One of the principal difficulties for the naturalist view of education was the imprecise role it prescribed for the teacher and it was here that the differences between the various 'English' naturalists showed most clearly. Although Herbart himself had been influenced by Pestalozzi and Froebel, and had even visited Pestalozzi's school at Yverdun, his view that the child was born without predisposition or innate qualities and that the role of the teacher was an active, crucial one, was at odds with the naturalist view that the role of the teacher was that of a guide, charged with bringing out what was present but latent within the child.[30] For the 'naturalist', the teacher's task was 'simply to interfere as little as possible' with the 'natural development' of the pupil. In this respect, the teacher was at a significant disadvantage when compared with colleagues who subscribed to the ideas of the Herbartian school. The Herbartian teacher was given not only a positive, directing role in pupil development, but also a well-defined plan for organising instruction, based upon the five steps.[31] As Herbart himself stressed unequivocally: 'I have no conception of education without instruction ...'[32]

At some risk of over-simplification, for the naturalist, the child developed. For the Herbartian, he or she was to be made by the teacher. The different approaches resulted in different curriculum preferences and teaching strategies. Herbart favoured literature and the arts since they promoted his desired moral emphasis, whilst the naturalists attached importance to the study of natural phenomena. Such importance pointed towards object lessons, and later, towards nature study with its added advantage of direct contact with the natural world and the opportunity for what a later generation would call 'active learning'. The practical advantage of Herbartianism to the teacher is obvious and many elementary school teachers were quick to recognise it. HMI Potter, writing[33] much later of this period, records that the five steps were the 'fashionable' lesson pattern and Selleck has commented[34] that, in the ten years after 1897, Herbartianism supported a minor publishing industry. The *Journal of Education* observed in 1911 that 'all students of education were stepping to the tune of the five steps' not long after they had been introduced.

The success of Herbartian ideas cannot be understood simply in terms of the enthusiasm of its advocates or their appeal to the practical and professional instincts of teachers. For the Herbartians, education was essentially moral education, with the good to be cultivated by the teacher. This was a message readily welcomed by many who, at the turn of the century, saw society as 'undermined and enfeebled' and 'no longer assured of certain certainties'.[35] Herbartianism, in effect, offered to counteract the consequences of apparently crumbling moral and religious beliefs. The late nineteenth century witnessed a decrease in the birth-rate, a decline in the average family size from 6.1 children in the 1860s to 4.1 in the 1890s,[36] and a temporary increase, followed by a stagnation, in the infant mortality rate. These statistics, allied with a number of other factors, such as the continuing drift from the land to the towns, the findings of an interdepartmental committee[37] set up to investigate physical deterioration, and the claims of the Eugenics Society, helped sustain fears about a decline in the 'genetic quality' of the Imperial race. Furthermore, social surveys, notably those of Charles Booth and B.S. Rowntree, were showing that at least one-third of the population was living in poverty, at a time when state aid was limited to the Poor Law. Inculcating, at an early age, ideas about thrift, self-help and temperance and limiting the size of 'genetically inferior' working-class families, were seen as ways of alleviating social problems, and elementary schooling was assigned an important role in the process. The Herbartian emphasis on history and literature in elementary education derived from the claim that it was these subjects that held the greatest potential for moral education. Armstrong's heurism and his emphasis upon the teaching of scientific method was the focus of a direct attack from a leading Herbartian, F.H. Hayward. For Hayward and his fellow Herbartians, Armstrong's heurism simply missed the point. Exercising a child's mind in the analytical way demanded by the teaching of scientific method was not the principal purpose of elementary education. Rather the mind was to be fed 'with a rich repast of historical and biographical ideas'.[38] This was too much for Armstrong who had initially ignored the Herbartian onslaught on façulty psychology. He saw the Herbartians as responsible for a 'new crusade', favouring literary studies at the expense of workshop or laboratory instruction and he was to spend much of the remainder of his long life thundering against what he described as the 'revival of the literary cult'.[39]

While the views of the so-called practical educationists, the naturalists, and a group named the pragmatists who derived their ideas from the writings of John Dewey (1859–1952) had much in common, they also often contradicted and undermined one another. Nonetheless, as Selleck states, '... out of the confusing mixture of theories, beliefs and practices which was the "New Education", there evolved a view of education which can be labelled "progressive".'[40] There were as many different ideas about teaching methods as there were advocates of 'progressive' teaching. However, the term has come to mean a method or approach to education which emphasises freedom (for both the teacher and the pupil), the importance of the individual, flexibility (of the timetable and curriculum), informality in all respects, including approach, timetable, curriculum and relationship between pupil and teacher, and active learning by the child. Advocates of 'progressive' or informal education were opposed to the authoritarian role of the teacher found in traditional schools, and many criticised the formal timetable with class lessons and an emphasis on the 3Rs. These broad principles were the extent of any agreement on how teaching methods should change, and much of it was hostile to the practice of many schools, although there was often little agreement about a replacement.

From the First World War until the mid-1920s, pioneers advocated new methods of teaching such as Caldwell Cook's 'Play Way' and Helen Parkhurst's 'Dalton Plan', as a means of teaching younger children.[41] Maria Montessori's ideas, developed with slum children in Italy from 1906, were popularised in England by Bertram Hawker, who after visiting Montessori's children's house in Italy, returned to England and set up a class based on her principles in his own home. He was also largely responsible for the establishment of the Montessori Society in England.[42] Montessori, like John Dewey, believed that a child's development depended on adjustment to his or her environment and that the role of the teacher was to act as a guide in this process, with the child playing an active role.[43] New schools were set up, such as A.S. Neill's 'Summerhill' (founded in 1921), J.H. Simpson's 'Rendcomb', and Dora and Bertrand Russell's 'Beacon Hill' (founded in 1927).[44] Homer Lane established 'The Little Commonwealth' in Dorset in 1912, a school which emphasised self-government by the pupils, with staff having a minimum amount of authority.[45] Lane's view of the child as being innately good led him to believe that 'The freer a child is the more it will be considerate and social, the more its chief interests will be progressive, and the more its fundamental instincts ... will have social outlets.'[46] The school remained open only until 1918 but was an important and influential educational experiment. A.S. Neill (1883–1973) in Summerhill also emphasised the child's freedom:

> ... we set out to make a school in which we should allow children freedom to be themselves. In order to do this, we had to renounce all discipline, all direction, all suggestion, all moral training, all religious instruction. ... All it required was ... a complete belief in the child as a good, not an evil, being.[47]

Influenced by the ideas of the nineteenth-century naturalists, teachers in a number of schools experimented with new methods of teaching and organisation. For example, in 1914, N. MacMunn published *A Path to Freedom in the School*, in which he described how after being influenced by the writings of Rousseau and Montessori, he relaxed the formal class lesson, and had children working individually and with a partner.[48] New societies were formed, such as the New Education Fellowship (NEF) in 1921,[49] and a wealth of literature was produced, including the NEF's official publication *New Era* and T.P. Nunn's *Education: Its Data and First Principles*, which provided a 'textbook for the progressives'.[50]

Nunn was a supporter of nature study, involved actively with the School Nature Study Union, and influential on nature study advocates such as Clothilde von Wyss, a colleague of Nunn's at the London Day Training College (later the London Institute of Education).[51] Nunn detected in the history of science, as in the minds of children, three 'motives', of 'wonder, utility and systematisation',[52] and elaborated the view that the interest of children in science exhibited a rhythm corresponding to the rhythm of its history. The notion that children learn in stages was not new, and can be traced back to Rousseau, through Pestalozzi and Froebel. Homer Lane also developed the idea of stages, claiming that early childhood was the 'Age of Imagination' (very similar to A.N. Whitehead's Romance Stage) followed by the Age of Self-Assertion, through transition and adolescence to the Age of Loyalty, then on to puberty.[53] In addition, according to Whitehead, 'different subjects and modes of study should be undertaken by pupils at fitting times when they have reached the proper stage of mental development'.[54] For von Wyss, nature study provided an appropriate setting for children's natural tendencies and for her modified three stages of children's development. Wonder and curiosity, up to the age of seven, were followed by a stage marked by intense physical energy, up to about the age of ten, and the third stage, up to about twelve years old, was characterised by the desire to investigate, understand and impose some order upon the natural world.[55] The idea that a certain kind of approach was appropriate for younger children derived from this view that children learn in stages, that is, that they learn in different ways at different ages (or intellectual stages). This idea was developed much more fully, and in a rather different way, by Jean Piaget, whose work *Language and Thought of the Child*, was first published in English in 1926, although his work did not become widely known until the late 1950s and 1960s (see below). Nevertheless, the notion of the primary school as embracing recognisable and significant stages of intellectual development is clearly evident.

Why, in the early years of the century, when the elementary school curriculum was still dominated by the 3Rs, as it had been for many years, did such a wealth of progressive ideas emerge? Those who were stressing freedom believed that by granting it to a child, the child would respond in a responsible manner derived from its natural instincts. However, the reasoning transcended the individual to more communal factors. It was an era of great change, where the future was uncertain. It was thought that only by future generations acting in a responsible way would things improve. This view was strengthened by the experience of the First World War. Nunn believed in the freedom and consequent responsibility of the individual,[56] and more importantly that through educational freedom things might change.

> We stand at an hour when the civilization that bred us is sick – some fear to death. We cannot escape from the duty of seeking a cure for its distemper, any more than from the responsibility that lies, in some measure, upon us all of having brought it to its present pass. But however good our will, however happy our inspiration, the problems we and those who came before us have created are problems we cannot hope ourselves to solve; they must be solved, if at all, by the generations that will take up our work when our place knows us no more. Thus the question we have debated is of no mere academic interest. It concerns all who would fain believe that men are not wholly the sport of circumstance or the puppets of fate, but that their own wills shape the decrees which determine, slowly yet inevitably, 'the doubtful doom of mankind.[57]

Nunn's *Education: Its Data and First Principles* was written and Caldwell Cook's *Play Way* and A.S. Neill's *A Dominie's Log* were published during the First World War.[58]

In the years following the end of that war, progressive ideas, which emphasised greater freedom and informality in education, were most influential on the nursery and infant stages of schooling. Weber describes how in response to Montessorian ideas of children working on an individual basis and the need to create an environment supportive of this approach, the physical nature of these schools was changing, with more attention being given to beauty and space. Furthermore, individual and group learning evolved earlier for younger children, as did specific methods such as Dewey's project method, with its integration of subject areas.[59]

From 1907 onwards, the system of 'free places' introduced by the Liberal government enabled a quarter of places in secondary schools to be filled by pupils from elementary schools. Determining who should benefit from these free places involved a series of tests which became known as the eleven-plus examination. This examination and the psychometric view which underpinned it were to have a restricting influence on elementary education until well after the Second World War. The work of the psychometrists helped to ensure that the fundamental aim of the elementary school was preparation for secondary education, a view which came to be anathema to the progressives. Leading psychometrists, notably Cyril Burt and P.B. Ballard, both firmly believed that intelligence was innate. The fundamental shift that had occurred since Herbart's view had been in ascendancy should be noted. Herbart had claimed that all children were born without innate qualities and *equal*, and that education was the cause of any differences which arose.[60] Mental testing had first appeared in the work of Binet[61] in 1908 and was to have a number of consequences for elementary education. Again in contrast to Herbartianism, it gave education and the elementary teacher a limited and less valuable role in society. It implied that each child's future was pre-ordained by a given, fixed level of intelligence, and that those who would benefit by secondary education (a pre-ordained group) could be determined at an early age. The method of selection used was almost invariably a test given in the 3Rs[62] at age 11. The consequence was that the curriculum of many elementary schools concentrated on these subjects to the neglect of others, including science.

Brian Simon has attributed the popularity of psychometry in the inter-war years to the economic stagnation of the period,[63] and the resultant decline in confidence about what could be achieved, which spread from the economy to education. At this time, 'Differentiation of ability was the key to teaching and learning, with diagnostic measures to identify defects and prescribe remedial teaching, with intelligence as the central concept to explain human learning and failures in learning.'[64] However, an alternative and more positive interpretation presents the popularity of psychometry as supportive of a move away from the methods of mass education of the late nineteenth century towards a pedagogy which encouraged attention to the different needs of individual pupils, the relevant differences having been exposed by the mental testing movement. To this extent, the mental testing of pupils might also be labelled progressive. Indeed, as Walkerdine has commented,[65]

> ... those twin techniques of mental measurement and child development were not formulated in the opposition in which they have been placed pedagogically and psychologically, in the liberal and radical discourses of the 1960s and 1970s.

Although the 11+ examination had a restricting influence on the work of public elementary schools, progressive ideas were not abandoned and the period from the mid-1920s to the Second World War saw their ideas and methods gain a degree of official acceptance.

> In the 1920s and 1930s the 'progressive' tradition was restricted to a relatively small circle of independent schools, but gained steady influence on elementary education.[66]

During this period the work of psychologist William McDougall,[67] who claimed that a child's development and behaviour were derived from its instincts,[68] was also used to give support to progressive views, as were some aspects of Freud's work, in particular his opposition to punishment.[69] Progressive methods were also gaining legitimacy from the scientific study of education, although research of this kind carried out in England in the inter-war period was limited. Susan Isaacs' observation of pupils at the Malting House School, as part of the child study movement, was, however, an important exception (see below).

By the beginning of the Second World War, claims Selleck, the broad principles encompassed in progressive thinking had been accepted as the established educational theory, and 'it was in the primary school that progressives most notably triumphed ...'.[70] Their influence was apparent in works on education, conference speeches, in official reports, most notably the two Hadow reports of 1931 and 1933,[71] and in the training colleges.[72] During the Second World War, the progressive philosophy was further strengthened. A number of important works appeared supporting progressive methods, and the educational press supported developments in this direction.[73] For example, in a report published in 1942, Dorothy Gardner claimed that children taught by progressive methods achieved higher attainments than those taught by traditional methods; and the Board of Education's *Suggestions for Teachers in Elementary Schools*, reprinted in 1944, was influenced by progressive ideas, restating the celebrated phrase of the 1931 Hadow report advocating activity methods in the primary school.[74] Brian Simon asserts that the disruption caused to education by the War and evacuation had forced primary school teachers to improvise with apparatus, personally experience the value of informal methods, and take their pupils out into the countryside. He suggests that, in consequence, 'Many of the more advanced techniques in our primary schools were worked out at this time.'[75]

The acceptance of informal methods in the primary school was further encouraged by a number of post-war developments.[76] The end of the War brought, in 1918, a determination to rebuild a better society, a task in which education necessarily had a central role. Smaller family size, and the further increased proportion of children in the total population, raised the relative political importance of education, and encouraged the view that education should focus on the needs of the child. An optimistic account claimed that 'a great emphasis is now laid on practical activities ... we see a school no longer as a mere machine for giving lessons, but as a social unit concerned with the all-round development of boys and girls'.[77] The first report of the newly-formed (by the 1944 Education Act) Central Advisory Council advocated the improvement of primary school buildings, parental co-operation and attention to a school's environment when determining the curriculum.[78] The NUT's Consultative Committee, which met from 1946 to 1949, considered the question of nursery and infant education and came out in support of activity methods.[79]

The implementation of progressive methods in the classroom was uneven. Purely in geographical terms, certain areas, in particular, the West Riding of Yorkshire under the influence of Alec Clegg, Leicestershire (under Stuart Mason), Oxfordshire and Hertfordshire (which, under J. Newsom planned the building of 30 primary schools by 1948, built the first RIBA-recognised prefabricated school in 1951, and whose architects were subsequently engaged by the Ministry of Education to build schools which favoured modern teaching methods),[80] all had reputations for implementing progressive methods in their primary schools to a greater degree than elsewhere.[81] It is, of course, the case that for many years after 1944 the overwhelming majority of primary school teachers in England and Wales had been trained in the subject-based, class-oriented elementary school tradition. However, Lowe has identified a number of other obstacles to the rapid development of progressive methods in the primary classroom. The post-war birth-rate surge caused a shortage of both teachers and school places. A school-building programme did take place (see Table 6.1) and an Emergency Training Scheme recruited an extra 34,000 teachers by 1951, 'but the very brief and frenetic training offered to these recruits made it difficult for them to absorb fully the practical implications of the new progressivism'.[82] Teacher–pupil ratios had improved little from 31.02 in 1951 to 30.59 in 1964, and teaching space fell back to its 1936 position.[83] Furthermore, in 1951 there were still a million children in unreorganised all-age schools.[84] The raising of the school-leaving age to 15 as part of the 1944 Education Act encouraged the allocation of resources to secondary rather than primary education.[85] At the same time, the 11+ examination and streaming continued to influence the curriculum of the primary school, focusing at least the later years of the primary school on the needs of the 11+ which would determine which kind of secondary school pupils attended. Leo Abse, writing of the primary school in 1959, commented that 'their whole curriculum is hopelessly distorted because of the 11+ exam'.[86]

TABLE 6.1
NEW POST-WAR PRIMARY SCHOOLS COMPLETED IN ENGLAND AND WALES 1947–70

Year	No. of schools
1947–1949	119
1950–1952	918
1953–1955	1,104
1956–1958	724
1959–1961	700
1962–1964	970
1965–1967	1,418
1968–1970	1,918
Total	7,871

Source: M. Seaborne and R. Lowe, *The English School, its Architecture and Organization, Volume II 1870–1970* (London, 1977), 155.

Table 6.1 shows the scale of the primary school building programme which occurred after the Second World War, principally to provide school accommodation demanded as a result of the rapidly increased post-war birth rate, and to a lesser extent until the 1970s, to replace the poor accommodation within which many primary school children were taught, much of it dating back to the nineteenth century. The important point in this context is that although many of the old unsuitable schools remained, the building of new schools allowed for design to be updated, and, as Seaborne and Lowe observe, 'The radical changes in primary-school design which have taken place since the war ... have been the result of changes in teaching methods and building techniques ...'[87] They further note that

> The educational ideas which most influenced the central and local-government officials who were initially responsible for the design of the new primary schools may in fact be traced back to the Hadow Reports on *The primary school* (1931) and on *Infant and nursery schools* (1933) ...[88]

The 'progressive' ideas in these reports and those mentioned earlier encouraged the designing of schools with more spacious classrooms, halls and corridors, and their construction on open, southern-facing sites.[89] However, the Hadow reports, whilst advocating progressive methods of teaching also advocated streaming, and, in the early years after the war, this led most Local Education Authorities to build schools with separate internal classrooms.[90] It was mainly in the 1960s that more open-plan schools were built, although as Seaborne and Lowe discovered, schools designed to facilitate more flexible teaching methods 'were still relatively rare in the late 1960s'.[91] Even by 1978, an HMI report noted that only one in ten classrooms in their survey was open-plan.[92]

Gardner's research from the 1940s through to the 1960s gives a good overview of changes in infant and junior schools during this period. She carried out research into the effects of informal methods on pupils' attainment and attitudes, and compared the outcomes with those from the methods used in 'good traditional' schools. Her findings are mentioned above. However, an interesting aside are her comments that in the 1940s 'the "experimental" Infant Schools ... were very much in a minority ...', and that, during the 1950s, most Junior Schools 'were still at that time on the whole traditional'.[93] But of infant schools in the 1960s she stated 'methods in primary schools have developed and now very large numbers of Infant Schools give part of their time to periods of "free choice" or "creative activities"'. Furthermore, junior schools in the 1960s were the scene of 'major change'. '... there are now a number of schools (which at one time would have been very rare) in which the purposes and interests of the children themselves are permitted to have a considerable influence on the curriculum'.[94]

The late 1950s and early 1960s saw an upsurge in interest in science in the primary and junior school. A number of educational organisations issued statements advocating the increased profile of science at the primary stage.[95] A number of conferences on this subject were held,[96] and projects were established which investigated aspects of primary science in particular. For example, the Oxford Primary Science Project, the aim of which was to 'discover which scientific concepts children can form and to identify the experiences which are fruitful in helping children to form (them)', set out to establish 'the work in science which it is profitable for children to do in primary school'.[97] The National Froebel Foundation carried out a Co-operative Study Scheme project (funded by the British Association for the Advancement of Science and directed by Nathan Isaacs) to assess the value of using 'finding-out' activities in science in the primary school.

Why and how did concern over this area of the curriculum arise? Contemporary rhetoric identified the importance of the value of science, and, in particular, of scientific method, in promoting competence at problem solving. Also identified were a set of claims that, for convenience, might be summed in the phrase 'scientific literacy', and which presented such literacy as intimately linked to economic prosperity and military security: a population well-educated in, and familiar with, scientific concepts would be of benefit both to the economy and to national defence capability.[98] It is perhaps important to recall that the 1950s were marked by considerable tension in the 'Cold War' between East and West and by a range of technological advances including television, space travel and atomic power said to characterise the 'scientific age'.

The methodological value of scientific education, associated earlier in the century with the views of Henry Armstrong, was reclaimed in the 1960s, with, for example, the 'Finding Out' project undertaken by the National Froebel Foundation. The term 'neo-heurism' appeared in the science education literature and the teaching of scientific 'processes' received the support of a number of leading educationists and of the Association of Science Education's (ASE) Primary Schools' Science Committee, as well as being influential in the work of the Nuffield Junior Science Project (NJSP).[99]

Some science educators, however, chose to emphasise economic considerations, even within the context of primary education. Miss E.M. Tuke, in a lecture to the School Nature Study Union, argued that 'this country of ours cries out for more Scientists, Technologists, Technicians. They are necessary for its economic existence and, it believes, desirable for prestige value as well.'[100] F.F. Blackwell (a member of the NJSP team in 1964) acknowledged the influence of technological advances, stating 'It is not surprising ... in view of the scientific background of the twentieth century, that there is an increasing bias towards simple physics, mechanics, chemistry and electricity'.[101]

Concern about, and interest in, primary science education stemmed, therefore, both from a desire to advance the scientific literacy of the population in an increasingly technological age, and from a belief in the value of the scientific method. At government level, this concern was reflected in two pamphlets offering advice to teachers about science education in primary and secondary schools respectively.[102] Using a non-authoritarian, collaborative style characteristic of much writing about progressive primary education, the former suggested to teachers that in primary schools 'we are using science more for its educational value than for its material utility', and emphasised that since 'the pursuit of science at the primary stage encourages qualities that we are already seeking to foster in the child, it links closely with the rest of the curriculum'.[103] Beyond government, the concern led to the establishment of a Primary Schools' Science Committee by the Association for Science Education in 1963, to which reference has already been made.[104] The interest of the Committee lay with teachers' lack of a suitable scientific background and it claimed that there was 'a need for all teachers in primary schools to be given a basic course in science ... We are dealing with the country's scientific illiteracy and its elimination is as important as the elimination of illiteracy in English or mathematics.'[105] The Committee also stated that 'we are more concerned with the developing of an enquiring attitude of mind than with the learning of facts', adding, lest its position be misunderstood, that 'at no time is the imparting of factual knowledge to be regarded as an end in itself'.[106] In the opinion of Roy Richards, a leading figure in primary science curriculum development in the 1960s, '... it's true to say that in the sixties ... process ruled supreme'.[107]

There had, of course, to 'be *some* content' for the children to study,[108] but, as Richards comments,

> No-one said that content wasn't important but I think what they said was that it didn't matter greatly what content you chose. You had to have content as a vehicle in order to do it, but ... you could choose what content you wanted ...[109]

This interplay of 'content' and 'process' found particular expression in a number of primary science curriculum initiatives in the 1960s and 1970s, most significantly in the *Nuffield Junior Science Project* (NJSP) (1964–66) and the *Schools Council Science 5–13 Project* (1967–75) discussed above in Chapter 4.

By the early 1970s, the accommodation of science within at least the rhetoric of progressive primary education was complete and the parallel drawn a generation earlier by Nunn between the 'rhythm' of childhood and that of science itself proved to be alive and well. As part of a commitment to describing 'the way that British primary schools work', undertaken as part of an Anglo-American Primary Education Project, readers were advised that 'In many ways, the development of scientific knowledge and abilities in children mirrors the historical evolution of scientific progress.' They were also left in no doubt of some of the '*working assumptions*' (either stated or merely implied) which are made by 'progressive educators in science', the latter being defined as 'those who build up the learning framework from studies of the child and his (*sic*) behaviour'. These assumptions were listed as follows.

1. A child is very interested in his environment.
2. Observation is the primary way of increasing understanding of the world.

3. Related observations are progressively linked together to give greater understanding.
4. Attempts to assimilate information give rise to problems – a child may want (indeed *need*) to know the answers to these, and intense learning may be provoked.
5. As it is impossible to predict which experiences will provoke interest and encourage observations in any particular child at any specific time, a wide variety of stimuli (provision) is necessary.
6. Children have a need (and often a desire) to communicate the results of their observations and the ideas which develop from them.
7. Free discussion ... aids understanding, and provides a stimulus for further enquiry.
8. Problems are best tackled by practical investigation.
9. The most effective learning is obtained when children's investigations are aided, rather than directed, by the teacher.
10. Second-hand information is of greatest value when it can be integrated with recently acquired (or possibly, recently considered) first-hand experiences.
11. Although the *integrated* body of knowledge built up by a child is important, it is not necessary ... to define which particular pieces of scientific information should be acquired, although some *concepts* may be considered necessary. There are many topics in which children are very likely to be interested.[110]

This progressive stance towards primary school science education was underpinned by the interaction between a set of assumptions about the nature of science and about how children learn and can best be taught. As far as science was concerned, progressive science educators seem to have regarded science as essentially the application of 'scientific method' to the solution of problems. Whereas for Armstrong at the beginning of the century, science had much in common with criminal detective work that depended upon the methodical, logical use of systematised knowledge, the favoured analogy of the progressives some sixty years later was altogether more homely and comforting.

> Science as we know it today is an uncompleted jigsaw puzzle, the pieces (large and small) which have been put together being the work of countless observers and investigators.[111]

Much follows from this view of science. The perception that science is complicated or difficult is challenged and the idea that 'doing science' requires specialised training is denied.

> All too often the popular view of science is of a complicated activity, reserved for specially qualified and trained personnel. Nothing could be further from the truth. Science should be seen as a way of looking at the environment and building up a store of information about it. Every individual continually explores his surroundings in a scientific way whether he (*sic*) is aware of it or not.[112]

Such exploration, however, is rarely the straightforward undertaking portrayed by the primary science curriculum initiatives (and their secondary counterparts) of the 1960s and 1970s. The relationships between scientific observation and explanation are often complex, and the notion of experimental replication is highly problematic. By the 1970s, the essentially positivist philosophy of science that underpinned both primary and secondary school science curriculum reform was already obsolete. Subsequent work by historians, philosophers and sociologists of science has, in Ravetz's phrase, rendered it 'antique'.[113]

Why, therefore, did such a defective understanding of the scientific endeavour play such a significant role in the primary and secondary science projects of the 1960s and 1970s? Part of the answer lies in the absence of an agreed, or at least a widely accepted, alternative. The scholarly work of historians, philosophers and sociologists of science during the last thirty or so years has compounded, rather than eased this position. As Laudan and his colleagues observed in 1986, we now have

> no well-confirmed general picture of how science works, no theory of science worthy of general assent. We did once have a well developed and historically influential philosophical position, that of positivism or logical empiricism, which has by now been completely refuted ... If any extant position does provide a viable understanding of how science operates, we are far from being able to identify what it is.[114]

Also important in the retention and promotion of a defective understanding of the nature of science in the 1960s and 1970s was the enduring influence of the terms upon which science was first schooled in the nineteenth century in England and Wales and, in particular, the emphasis to be given to science's greatest mystery, its method. Such an emphasis had allowed those originally advocating a place for science in the school curriculum to rebut the claims of their opponents that scientific education was concerned merely with the acquisition of facts, rather than the training and disciplining of the mind. Sometimes, as in the 1960s, this commitment to helping pupils develop 'scientific method' has been expressed in terms of so-called processes such as observing or hypothesising. At other times, notably in the 1980s and 1990s, the language has been that of 'skills' (for example, measurement, recording or estimating 'skills') or, occasionally, even of 'process skills'. Nonetheless, such differences of language fail to disguise an underlying, common and enduring rationale.[115]

> Although the actual body of information is central to science and clearly important in its own right, it is the *method* which is so distinctive to science.

Then, as now, the fact that this method has so far evaded agreed characterisation proved no obstacle to curriculum developers seeking to mimic, if not to replicate, it within school classrooms and laboratories.

The primary science curriculum reforms of the 1960s and 1970s reduced scientific method to a pedagogical strategy (for example, teaching processes) and characterised young children, naturally curious about the social and natural worlds, as 'instinctive' scientists. However, as a practical and experience-based activity, science had one more claim upon the progressive primary curriculum. It could readily be taught in a manner that was not only consonant with, but fundamentally supportive of, the ways in which young children were presumed to learn, namely, by *doing*. Although the following quotation comes from the frontispiece of the first teachers' guide produced by the Nuffield Mathematics Project of the 1960s, it applies equally well to the contemporaneous primary science initiatives, and, indeed, was often quoted approvingly at both primary and secondary science in-service courses throughout the 1960s and beyond.

> I hear and I forget
> I see and I remember
> I do and I understand

This, of course, raises the question of why *learning by doing* and pupil activity in general came to be such a prominent feature of the discourse of primary education from the 1960s onwards. As noted earlier in this chapter, progressive ideas had made considerable headway in the 1920s and 1930s, although their influence had been greatest in the education of young children. By the 1950s and 1960s, however, other influences, notably the ideas of Piaget and Susan Isaacs, had come to play a significant role in debates about the education of young children, and to some of these ideas attention is now turned.

THE INFLUENCE OF SUSAN ISAACS AND JEAN PIAGET

The primary science curriculum projects of the 1960s and 1970s were much more influenced by ideas about children's intellectual development than their secondary counterparts which, with the exception of the Schools Council Integrated Science Project (SCISP), derived their programmes directly from the conceptual framework of the established academic scientific disciplines of chemistry, physics and biology. This greater influence at the primary level is not difficult to understand. Progressive primary discourse was strongly marked by ideas and assumptions about how children could best learn and be taught, and experience of teaching scientific ideas to young children was limited. In addition, if the primary science curriculum initiatives were to succeed, the majority of primary teachers would need to be convinced that their pupils were capable of understanding ideas relating to such scientific concepts as force, energy, the reflection of light or current electricity. Perhaps for this reason, the leaders of the Nuffield Junior Science Project argued that:

> We must be able to justify all that we advocate on psychological grounds. More than this; we need to look at all we plan to do in relation to what is known of children's learning processes. No one who is not prepared to accept this idea should be involved in the scheme![116]

Those 'psychological grounds' were derived in large measure from the writings of Susan Isaacs and Jean Piaget, although the work of the latter received by far the more explicit attention.

Born in 1885 near Bolton in Lancashire, Susan Isaacs graduated with a first-class honours degree in philosophy from the Victoria University of Manchester, having abandoned the teacher training course for which she had originally enrolled. After studying psychology for a year at Cambridge, she became a lecturer in infant school education at Darlington Training College, before eventually lecturing in psychology in London. Her first book, *An Introduction to Psychology*, was published in 1922, the year in which she became secretary of the newly-formed Committee for Research in Education established by the British Psychological Society. In 1924, she responded to an advertisement for 'an Educated Young woman with honours degree – preferably first class

– or the equivalent, to conduct the education of a small group of children aged 2½–7, as a piece of scientific work and research'.[117] The 'small group of children' constituted the Malting House School, financed by Geoffrey Pike, a former metallurgist and his wife, Margaret. In 1926, Susan Isaacs was joined by her husband, Nathan, whom she had married after eloping with him to Austria and divorcing her first husband. The Isaacs remained at the Malting House School until 1927. In London, Susan Isaacs drew upon her work at the school to write several books of seminal importance, notably: *The Nursery Years: Birth to Six Years* (1929), *Intellectual Growth in Young Children, with an Appendix on Children's 'Why' Questions by Nathan Isaacs* (1930), *The Children We Teach: Seven to Eleven Years* (1932), and *Social Development in Young Children* (1933). In 1933, she was appointed to the headship of the newly founded Department of Child Development at the University of London Institute of Education to

> supply the demands of an increasing number of progressive training colleges for well-qualified lecturers with the latest knowledge in the field of child development; and to establish a centre for research into human development in general and sound teaching methods in particular.[118]

In presenting her views about the teaching of young children, Susan Isaacs drew heavily upon the ideas of Dewey, Montessori, Freud and Piaget which had so influenced her work at the Malting House School. An American biographer has described her achievements in the field of child development in the following terms.

> Gesell used one-way glass, Burt administered mental tests, Charlotte Bühler described the minute-by-minute behavior of infants, Piaget talked with and asked questions of children one by one, and Bridges devised a developmental rating scale. But only at the Malting House School were extended observations made of children interacting within an environment specifically designed to stimulate their powers of inquiry and imagination, to provide considerable verbal freedom and the company of other children, and to include adults who dealt with them according to a deliberately planned technique.[119]

Susan Isaacs was not, of course, alone in conferring upon children the status of active participants in the learning process. The Swiss psychologist, Jean Piaget, in particular, had developed a stage theory of cognitive development which stressed the importance of interaction with the environment in promoting intellectual growth through processes of accommodation and assimilation. Isaacs, however, was hostile to several aspects of Piaget's work and her book, *Intellectual Growth in Young Children*, was written to expose what she regarded as the untenable features of Piagetian stage theory. For her, Piaget's emphasis upon the role of logical thinking in cognitive development was too rigid and formal. In appropriate circumstances, notably when children's interests and enthusiasm were aroused, they could, she claimed, make sense of, that is, intellectually organise, their experience in ways that Piagetian stage theory did not allow. For Isaacs, the pace and shape of intellectual maturation was strongly related to interest and experience, and, contrary to Piaget, she argued that even at the young age of seven, children possessed the capacity to engage in formal reasoning. She drew extensively upon her Malting House experience to justify her position, and many of her examples were drawn from children's encounters with natural phenomena such as the melting of snow or the resistance of common fabrics to burning. Isaacs was also critical of the clinical methodology used by Piaget in his study of children's understanding of such concepts as space, time and number. For her, a one-to-one conversation between a child and an investigating adult could not provide the 'circumstances which would provoke questions demanding causal explanation or inquiries about inanimate objects. ... These occur rather in the course of free practical activity in a varied setting and in the play with other children and adults who share in the practical pursuits.'[120] While she acknowledged that children did exhibit the egocentrism and syncretism identified by Piaget, she rejected the idea that these cognitive behaviours were 'hard and fast', stressing instead the flexibility and variability of children's thinking.

> ... on the day (children) would pass easily between the realms of pure phantasy and occasionally of magic, and those of practical insight and resource, and of verbal argument and reasoning.[121]

Until the later 1950s, Susan Isaacs's ideas about child development were much more widely known in England and Wales than those of Piaget. There are perhaps several reasons for this. Isaacs's own intellectual authority and influence were considerable and the examples which she was able to provide for teachers and training college staff were drawn from classroom experience with which they could identify. In contrast, Piaget's work was based on clinical interviews conducted in another country, he was not himself primarily interested in education, and much of his writing, not always easy to understand in the original

French, did not become available in English until after the Second World War. What is important in the present context, however, is that, in different ways, the work of both Susan Isaacs and Jean Piaget served to draw attention to the importance of activity and experience in the intellectual growth of young children. If Isaacs's ideas were more generous in rejecting the genetic epistemology that supported Piagetian stage theory, that stage theory eventually constituted an important framework for the identifying and sequencing of curriculum content. In the 1930s and 1940s, Susan Isaacs's ideas, widely promoted in lectures, pamphlets and books, came to provide an intellectual justification for progressive teaching methods. During the 1950s and 1960s, by which time Isaacs was dead, it was Piagetian ideas which came into prominence. Ironically, one of the key figures in making those ideas more widely known in England and Wales was Susan Isaacs's husband, Nathan.

NATHAN ISAACS AND THE PRIMARY SCIENCE CURRICULUM

As early as 1927, Nathan Isaacs had argued the case for science in the education of young children in an article he contributed to the leading scientific journal, *Nature*.

> ... the world of science is only the common world greatly enlarged and much more adequately known, and if its methods are the methods by which such adequate knowledge is achieved, then guidance to some understanding of this would clearly need to be recognised as a major aim for any humane education.[122]

The terms in which this case for science in education are presented are important, not least because they were to become part of the established rhetoric of the movement, a generation later, to establish science within primary schools. Science is reduced to 'the common world greatly enlarged and much more adequately known'. Even by 1927, thermodynamics, relativity and quantum mechanics would have made it difficult to sustain such a position, redolent as it is of T.H. Huxley's nineteenth-century notion of science as 'organised common sense'. In addition, there is something of a premium upon the teaching of 'scientific method', another feature that was to return to prominence in the 1960s and 1970s.

Drawing upon the science education that had been provided at the Malting House School, the work undertaken at the Institut Rousseau in Geneva and at the Walden School in New York, Nathan Isaacs argued for a teaching approach which exploited fully children's natural curiosity about the natural world. For him, children's 'Why?' questions and their responses to them (for example, Why is there no shadow when there is no light? Why does light pass through glass but not wood?) were evidence of their active concern to impose intellectual order upon their experience. Like Susan Isaacs, he was critical of the interpretation given to children's responses to Piagetian tests conducted by adults, since those tested had not experienced any shock, stimulus or puzzlement that could engage their interest.

After the death of Susan Isaacs in 1948, Nathan Isaacs eventually married Evelyn Lawrence, a former teacher at the Malting House School and, from 1943 to 1963, Director of the National Froebel Foundation. During the 1950s and 1960s, the Foundation published a number of influential articles by Isaacs and it was he who prepared the memorandum submitted by the Foundation to the Plowden Committee. Isaacs also wrote a number of books and articles intended to make the work of Piaget known to a wider readership[123] and took every opportunity to promote the case for the inclusion of science within primary education.[124] Arguably, it is to him that the emphasis upon 'process' which came to characterise primary school science education can be attributed. Speaking in 1962, Isaacs argued that since scientific knowledge continued to increase and there were obvious limits on the amount an individual might acquire, the emphasis within education should be upon 'the distinctive set of processes' whereby such knowledge was acquired. For Isaacs, as for Huxley, a hundred years earlier, 'the different specific sciences (were) ... the result of the successful application of (these processes) to one sector after another of our world'.[125] Moreover, these processes were the ones which children used in making sense of the world around them, that is, 'exploring, manipulating, experimenting, comparing, trying to discover causes or think up the right explanations, discussing and putting to the test'.

By the mid-1960s, 'children's questions' and 'scientific processes' had become established within the small community of primary science educators and the stage was set for their incorporation within the work of the Nuffield Junior Science Project. Ron Wastnedge, the Organiser of the Project and the strongest influence on its philosophical direction, was familiar with the ideas both of Nathan Isaacs and Jean Piaget. The extent and nature of the Project's debt to Nathan Isaacs is acknowledged[126] explicitly in the Teacher's Guide to the curriculum materials published in 1967 and they are most evident in the importance attached to children's questions as they engaged in inquiry about the world about them. The first paragraph of Teacher's Guide 1 refers to children's 'love of asking questions' and Wastnedge has indicated how his own initial ideas about primary science were shaped by his contact with Isaacs.[127] In particular, Wastnedge became convinced of the importance of the distinction between *children's* questions and those posed by their teacher.

> They really do ask questions, although I have been contradicted by a number of teachers on this. They say children don't ask questions. I don't believe this ... My colleague in Kent sent me a considerable list of the children's questions which arose during two 10-minute conversation periods in a junior mixed school.[128]

The asking of questions and the pursuit of answers necessarily involved children in reasoning in some way and Wastnedge's concern to explore the nature and quality of this reasoning inevitably led him towards Piagetian ideas. In 1964, although there is some uncertainty about the date, he had been sent a paper by Isaacs, entitled *Piaget and the Development of Children's Thought*.[129] In this paper, Isaacs ignored his own reservations about some of Piaget's work and argued that Piagetian stage theory should be accepted conditionally. Wastnedge was already familiar with Piaget's writings but a number of others associated with the Project were more wary. J.F. Kerr argued that Piaget's ideas were largely untested and that some American studies seemed to call into question the idea that cognitive development took place in distinct stages.[130] Other members of the Consultative Committee to the Project voiced their concern about associating Piagetian ideas too strongly with their work, since such ideas were not well-known among primary teachers who might, in consequence, feel somewhat alienated from the Project.[131] Writing in 1965, Wastnedge claimed in a reply to criticisms of the project's ideological stance that

> It has been made very clear to me over the past three or four years that the majority of teachers attending courses, and certainly all lecturers with whom I have spoken, are very much *au fait* with the various Piagetian operational stages.[132]

A somewhat detached opinion was offered by Frank Halliwell, the Organiser of Nuffield 'O' level Chemistry Project. He supported the reference to Piagetian ideas in the Junior Science Project, claiming, more than a little simplistically, that

> Piaget was being quoted because what he says is what many of us have thought for a number of years and he is a mouthpiece for

> what we want to express, rather than an authority who makes us think like this.[133]

In the event, Piagetian ideas about the development of logical thinking formed an appendix in the Teacher's Guide 1 to the Junior Science Project. Reading this appendix and examining the curriculum materials produced by the Project, it is difficult to avoid the impression that, for all its intellectual authority, Piagetian stage theory was not a strong operational influence upon the work of Wastnedge and his team. Rather, it offered a degree of respectability to, and support for, the kinds of science-based activities that the Project suggested might be undertaken in primary classrooms. Little, it was said, was known about concepts and their formation, and the evidence suggested that 'it is not possible to hasten (this formation, although) schools can make it easier by providing suitable materials and situations'.[134] Encouraging and helping primary teachers to provide 'suitable materials and situations' within which children could ask questions and engage in reasoned activity was ultimately what the Project was about. To this extent, it was simply an example of the application of progressive educational ideas to primary science education.

Piagetian ideas played a much more substantial role in the work of the Science 5–13 Project, sponsored jointly by the Schools Council, the Nuffield Foundation and the Scottish Education Department (see Chapter 4). This joint Project sought to move beyond individual or small group investigations undertaken by children in response to their own questions and interests towards a programme of primary science activities that could be structured and sequenced by teachers in accordance with Piagetian principles. The Project described children's intellectual development as occurring in three stages, which 'follow quite closely Piaget's ideas ... (and) have similar properties to Piaget's stages'.[135] The Project also drew upon behaviourist ideas and the Tyler–Bloom model of curriculum development by specifying behavioural objectives, and teachers were eventually offered over 150 objectives grouped in terms of the Project's three (Piagetian-derived) stages. Wynne Harlen, the main architect of this approach, has acknowledged her familiarity with the seminal work of Benjamin Bloom;

> the Taxonomy ... was one of the things that I ... had been looking at earlier for my Master's degree.[136]

The objectives of the Science 5–13 Project, however, were not classified as in Bloom's Original Taxonomy and, according to Harlen, 'they were nothing like the behavioural objectives that were being promoted in the United States at that time'. Although most primary teachers readily recognised the Piagetian impulse behind the Project ('Someone's been reading Piaget'),[137] many had difficulty in matching science-based activities with the level of intellectual development of their pupils. The Project offered assistance in the form of diagnostic statements intended to 'help direct teachers' observation to things that children may or may not do which would be indicative of the stages reached by the children'. The Science 5–13 Project is significant in the emphasis it placed upon research into children's intellectual development as a basis for constructing a science curriculum. Such an emphasis reflected both the lack of an experiential base that might have derived from an established tradition of teaching scientific ideas to young children, and a confidence that empirical research, conducted in settings far removed from the primary classroom, could be applied in a relatively unproblematic way to curriculum construction and pedagogy. As subsequent work was to confirm, there were both significant gaps in that research and with the underpinning notion of application. Important among this subsequent work was the *Match and Mismatch* study, prompted by 'teachers' requests for help in selecting from the wide range of suggestions for activities' in primary science which had emerged during the 1960s and 1970s. The principal aim of the four-year study ending in 1977 was the '*matching* (of) activities to development' and much of its output was directed at in-service programmes for primary school teachers.[138] Also important and of current significance is the rise of constructivism and the insights from research into the understanding of scientific ideas which children construct from their everyday experience and bring with them to their primary science education. These ideas are known by a variety of names, the most common of which are children's science, informal science, alternative conceptions, and misconceptions. Although many variants of constructivism have developed,[139] marked by considerable tension and controversy between the various positions, the common tenet, now widely accepted, is that all human knowledge, including scientific knowledge of the natural world, is 'constructed'.

As far as science education is concerned, the teaching of science becomes one of facilitating and promoting conceptual change. To the extent that science educators committed to a constructivist approach to teaching and learning respect children's 'informal' scientific ideas and see it as their task to provide learning experiences likely to refine or change these, constructivism is firmly in the progressive mould.

Curiously, however, it has escaped much of the criticism levelled at progressive education in the last quarter of a century. The influence of constructivist ideas on the science component of the national curriculum in England and Wales is evident in the advice offered to primary school teachers by the former National Curriculum Council. Commenting that:

> Children arrive at school with ideas about natural phenomena and events in the world around them. ... Children do not necessarily change their ideas as a result of being taught the 'true explanation'; ... It is very important to appreciate that children's preconceptions affect their thinking and interpretation of scientific events,[140]

teachers were advised that:

> as well as planning science lessons on the basis of skills, knowledge and understanding in the National Curriculum, it is essential to consider the children's starting points. ... Listening carefully to what children have to say on a subject helps us to identify what their existing understanding is. ... The language is also very important.[141]

Despite its attachment to behavioural outcomes, the Science 5–13 Project was firmly in the progressive mould. As one of the Project's publications made clear, children 'work best when trying to find answers to problems that they have themselves chosen to investigate'.[142] Progressive educational ideas of this kind were strongly endorsed in the report of the Plowden Committee, published in 1967, which attempted to develop and promote some of the recommendations of the three Hadow reports of the interwar period.[143] Part two of the Plowden report, 'The Growth of the Child', begins with the assertion that 'At the heart of the educational process lies the child'.[144] It espoused the Piagetian view that children learn in stages and drew attention to the need to ascertain the level of a child's intellectual development if appropriate educational experiences and learning activities were to be provided. As far as science education was concerned, the report advocated 'learning by discovery'[145] and stressed that both biological and physical aspects of science should be studied. It added that account should be taken of a school's immediate environment, of teachers' individual strengths, and of children's own interests. The value of teaching science in this way would bring benefits, not only to primary science but to the primary curriculum as a whole.[146]

Although the Plowden recommendations for science in the primary school gave official sanction to the methods and approach advocated by the Nuffield Junior Science Project and Science 5–13, both of which were mentioned in the report, the attention given to science, as with all specific subject areas, was limited. The chapter 'Aspects of the Curriculum' which covered all the subject areas, accounted for around only ten per cent of the first volume of the report. Of these 59 pages, science accounted for just eight. Two questionnaires were sent out, one to teacher and local authority associations, and several hundred individual witnesses, and the other to 2,500 primary and secondary school teachers. Neither of these questionnaires mentioned science. Nor were leading science education organisations approached to give evidence. The Association for Science Education submitted no evidence and the School Natural Science Society gave evidence only after it had requested to do so. In an era when 'process' reigned supreme, the report's lack of attention towards the content of particular areas of the curriculum is, of course, only to be expected.

For all its rhetoric, the Plowden report revealed that the progressive/informal approach which it advocated so strongly was not one that reflected the reality of most primary teachers' work. HMI surveyed, for the report, all 20,644 primary schools in England, except for 676. The schools were assessed and placed in one of nine categories ranging from 'outstanding quality' to 'bad'. Those in category one, the best, were described as 'outstanding in their work, personal relationships and awareness of current thinking on children's educational needs. They are the pacemakers and leaders of educational advance.'[147] However, only 109 schools fell into this category, which represented just one per cent of the primary school population. Schools in the three best categories, described in the report as 'quite clearly good' comprised 5,802 schools, which represented 33 per cent of the primary school population.[148]

Bennett's survey of teaching styles in primary schools in Lancashire and Cumbria almost a decade later (1976) concluded that informal teaching was not even as widespread as Plowden had claimed. From the responses of 88 per cent of the 871 schools sampled, a fairly generous estimate is that only some 17 per cent of teachers taught in the manner prescribed by Plowden, while at the other end of the teaching continuum approximately one in four taught formally. The majority of teachers used what has been termed a mixed style, incorporating elements of both formal and informal practice.[149] Examining particular elements of teachers' style, he found that group work was considerably less popular than individual work, and that, in general, pupil work was teacher-directed for 77 per cent of the time and child-directed for the remainder.

Pupils' freedom to move around, talk and leave the classroom was not very common, with two-thirds of teachers restricting these activities. Furthermore a subject-centred timetable predominated.[150] The 1978 HMI report on the primary school reported the results of inspecting 1,127 classes in 542 schools between Autumn 1975 and Spring 1977.[151] It denied that informal, or what it called 'mainly exploratory' methods, were the norm and established that 'mainly didactic' methods were present in about three-quarters of the survey classes, while less than one in twenty used a 'mainly exploratory' approach.[152] It also denied that primary schools were neglecting the 3Rs, or that standards were falling.[153] The HMI's document, *A View of the Curriculum* (1980), advocated the retention of a wide, varied curriculum and saw no need to divert extra time and resources to the 3Rs[154] as many of the critics of primary education were advocating.

The national curriculum introduced following the Education Reform Act 1988 is commonly seen as a reassertion of subject-centredness within primary schooling and a rejection of the progressivism which had so marked reform a generation earlier. Six years after the passage of this Act, however, primary teachers described their 'overwhelming impression' as one of 'continuity with the past'.[155]

Even so, it would be a mistake to underestimate the contribution of the various primary science curriculum initiatives of the last thirty or so years. Much was learnt about the teaching of science to young children, and the importance attached to 'learning by doing' has remained largely undiminished, despite a marked decline in the wider political fortune of progressive educational ideas that began with the publication of the various Black papers, received wider prominence in Prime Minister Callaghan's speech at Ruskin College in 1976 and drew ongoing support from difficulties in the economy and in a number of areas of social policy such as unemployment and law and order. In Wynne Harlen's judgement, the work of the various primary science projects

> ... had a very considerable impact ... on thinking ... and without that ... a very important step in the various things that have happened since ... would have been missing.[156]

Reflecting on the Science 5–13 initiative, Roy Richards has commented as follows.

> I don't think I can emphasise too much ... the fact that if you're going to teach science, you need to know what to teach, what

> activities, and there is a whole repertoire of activities which has profoundly influenced all the succeeding projects and all the ... publishers' projects that have come since. If you look, you can trace them all back to these books.[157]

Although both these judgements are those of 'insiders', it is almost certainly the case that the work of the 1960s and 1970s made possible the introduction in 1988 of science as a compulsory component of the education of children between the ages of 5 and 11 in maintained schools in England and Wales. It also helped to shape both the form of that component and the practice and rationale that underpins its 'delivery'.

NOTES

1 R.J. Alexander, *Primary Teaching* (London, 1984), 9.
2 Central Advisory Council, *Children and Their Primary Schools* (London, HMSO, 1967), Vol. 1, 189–90.
3 P. Cunningham, *Curriculum Change in the Primary School since 1945* (London, 1987), 12.
4 D. Layton, *Science for the People. The origins of the school science curriculum in England* (London, 1973), 23.
5 Board of Education, *Report for the Year 1909–10* (London, HMSO, 1911), 79.
6 *Report on the Teaching of Science in London Elementary Schools* (1909), PRO Ed. 14/95, dated 21/1/08 and signed E.D.F. Bloom.
7 W.H. Brock (ed.), *H.E. Armstrong and the Teaching of Science* (Cambridge, 1973), 51. The Thomson Committee noted in 1918 that much of the science taught in the training colleges ought to have been done in the secondary schools or in a pupil-teacher centre (*Natural Science in Education* (London, HMSO, 1918), para. 89).
8 BAAS, *Report of the Annual Meeting 1908* (London, 1909), 533.
9 David Thompson, 'General Science – its Origin and Growth', *School Science Review* 140 (1958), 110.
10 They included Margaret Macmillan, Maria Montessori, John Dewey and Homer Lane. See R.J.W. Selleck, *The New Education 1870–1914* (London, 1968).
11 R.J.W. Selleck, op. cit., 180.
12 *Report of the Conference on New Ideals in Education*, Aug. 1915, quoted in R.J.W. Selleck, op. cit., 14.
13 Rousseau believed that the child should be left without such direct influence until a much later age.
14 A. Darroch, 'Modern Education. Second Period. From Rousseau to the Present Time', in A.P. Laurie (ed.), *The Teacher's Encyclopaedia of the Theory, Method, Practice, History and Development of Education*, Vol. VII (London, 1912), 173–4.
15 S.J. Curtis and M.E.A. Boultwood, *A Short History of Educational Ideas* (London, 1953), 321.
16 Ibid., ch. XIII, 316–51.
17 Ibid., 349.
18 Froebel opened his first school in 1816. Ibid., 370.
19 Rousseau believed that man is naturally good (as Froebel was to later agree upon) and that evil comes from society. He saw the solution occurring through man returning to nature. A. Darroch, op. cit., 167.

20 R.J.W. Selleck, op. cit., 188; M. Sutherland, *Theory of Education* (London, 1988), 14.
21 M. Sutherland, op. cit., 14.
22 L. Weber, *The English Infant School and Informal Education* (NJ, 1971), 162.
23 S.J. Curtis and M.E.A. Boultwood, *An Introductory History of English Education Since 1800* (London, 1966, 4th edition, first published 1960), 155.
24 S.J. Curtis and M.E.A. Boultwood, *A Short History of Educational Ideas* (London, 1953), 372–3.
25 Herbart's most important book, *The Science of Education*, was published in 1806. R.J.W. Selleck, op. cit., 242.
26 J. Findlay in R.J.W. Selleck, op. cit., 244.
27 Herbart quoted in R.J.W. Selleck, op. cit., 229.
28 The five steps derived from Herbart's followers dividing his first step into two steps. R.J.W. Selleck, op. cit., 236.
29 S.J. Curtis and M.E.A. Boultwood, *A Short History of Educational Ideas* (London, 1953), 361.
30 A. Darroch, op. cit., 190.
31 The five steps, derived from Herbart's original four, were known by a variety of names. M. Fennell, *Notes of Lessons on the Herbartian Method* (London, 1902), offered 80 lessons, each complete in itself and lasting 30–45 minutes.
32 Quoted in R.J.W. Selleck, op. cit., 235.
33 F.F. Potter, *Educational Journey* (London, 1949), 26.
34 *Journal of Education*, XXXIII, Jan. 1911, 39.
35 J.R. Seeley, *Ethics and Religion*, Society of Ethical Propagandists (London, 1900), 12, and R.J.W. Selleck, op. cit., 301.
36 J. Lawson and H. Silver, op. cit., 366.
37 *Report of Interdepartmental Committee on Physical Deterioration* (London, HMSO, 1904).
38 F.H. Hayward, *The Secret of Herbart* (London, 1904), 76.
39 W.H. Brock, op. cit., 39.
40 R.J.W. Selleck, *English Primary Education and the Progressives, 1914–1939* (London, 1972), 25–6.
41 Ibid., 40–41.
42 E.M. Standing, *Maria Montessori, Her Life and Work* (London, 1957), 36.
43 S.J. Curtis and M.E.A. Boultwood, *A Short History of Educational Ideas*, 498.
44 R.J.W. Selleck, *English Primary Education and the Progressives*, 31.
45 S.J. Curtis and M.E.A. Boultwood, *A Short History of Educational Ideas*, 513–14.
46 From Homer Lane, *Talks to Parents and Teachers* (London, 1928), quoted in S.J. Curtis and M.E.A. Boultwood, *A Short History of Educational Ideas*, 516.
47 A.S. Neill, *Summerhill* (London, 1971), 20.
48 S.J. Curtis and M.E.A. Boultwood, *A Short History of Educational Ideas*, 518.
49 R.J.W. Selleck, *English Primary Education and the Progressives*, 45.
50 Ibid., 46–7.
51 Clothilde von Wyss, born in 1871, trained as a teacher at Maria Grey College, and taught in schools and training colleges, finally settling at the London Day Training College in 1903 where she taught for 33 years. During the late 1890s she encountered the naturalist J.A. Thomson and became greatly interested in nature study and natural history. She was a founding member of the School Nature Study Union, and remained extremely active in the Union, and amongst other things, edited its journal for 30 years. Obituary of C. von Wyss, *School Nature Study*, 34, 134 (1939), 4.
52 British Association for the Advancement of Science, *Report* (London, 1917), 135–6.
53 S.J. Curtis and M.E.A. Boultwood, *A Short History of Educational Ideas*, 515–16.
54 Quoted in ibid., 540.
55 C. von Wyss, 'The Teaching of Nature Study', in F. Hodson (ed.), *Broad Lines in Science Teaching* (London, 1909), 30–36.

56 S.J. Curtis and M.E.A. Boultwood, *A Short History of Educational Ideas*, 528.
57 T. Percy Nunn, *Education. Its Data and First Principles* (London, 1925), 219.
58 S.J. Curtis and M.E.A. Boultwood, *A Short History of Educational Ideas*, 518.
59 L. Weber, op. cit., 164–5.
60 A. Darroch, op. cit., 193.
61 Binet's original interest in mental testing was prompted by its potential for remedial work. It was not until a link with work in the USA was established that Binet's ideas became linked with mental testing for the purposes of selection/exclusion, and mental measurement came to be associated with a view of intelligence as innate.
62 There were a few cases in which tests included subjects other than the 3Rs.
63 B. Simon, 'The History of Education', in P.H. Hirst (ed.), *Educational Theory and Its Foundation Disciplines* (London, 1983), 79.
64 J. Nisbet, 'Educational Psychology', in P.H. Hirst, op. cit., 84–5.
65 V. Walkerdine, 'Developmental Psychology and the Child-centred Pedagogy: the insertion of Piaget into early education', in J. Henriques *et al.*, *Changing the Subject: Psychology, Social Regulation and Subjectivity* (London, 1984), 171–2.
66 J. Lawson and H. Silver, op. cit., 401.
67 His most influential work was *An Introduction to Social Psychology* (London, 1908).
68 R.J.W. Selleck, *English Primary Education and the Progressives*, 102.
69 Ibid., 106.
70 Ibid., 32.
71 Board of Education Consultative Committee, *The Primary School* (London, HMSO, 1931) and *Infant and Nursery Schools* (London, HMSO, 1933).
72 R.J.W. Selleck, *English Primary Education and the Progressives*, 120.
73 For example, M.V. Daniels, *Activity in the Primary School* (Oxford, 1947), in Roy Lowe, *Education in the Post-War Years: A Social History* (London, 1988), 24.
74 R. Lowe, ibid., 23.
75 Brian Simon, *Education and the Social Order 1940–1990* (London, 1991), 35.
76 Peter Cunningham, *Curriculum Change in the Primary School since 1945. Dissemination of the Progressive Ideal* (London, 1988), 13.
77 Ministry of Education, 'The Story of Post-war School Building', in R. Lowe, *Education in the Post-War Years*, 102
78 P. Cunningham, op. cit., 40–41.
79 R. Lowe, *Education in the Post-War Years*, 24.
80 Ibid., 26.
81 M. Kogan, 'The Plowden Report Twenty Years On', *Oxford Review of Education*, 13, 1 (1987), 18; M. Galton, 'Change and Continuity in the Primary Schools: the research evidence', *Oxford Review of Education*, 13, 1 (1987), 82.
82 R. Lowe, 'Primary Education since the Second World War', in R. Lowe (ed.), *The Changing Primary School* (East Sussex, 1987), 8.
83 R. Lowe, *Education in the Post-War Years*, 96, 99.
84 R. Lowe, *Primary Education since the Second World War*, 9.
85 R. Lowe, *Education in the Post-War Years*, 27–8.
86 Ibid., 105.
87 M. Seaborne and R. Lowe, *The English School, its Architecture and Organization*, Vol. II, 1870–1970 (London, 1977), 156.
88 Ibid., 170.
89 Ibid., 171.
90 Ibid., 170.
91 Ibid., 177.
92 P. Cunningham, 'Open Plan Schooling: Last Stand of the Progressives', in R. Lowe (ed.), *The Changing Primary School*, 64
93 D.E.M. Gardner, *Experiment and Tradition in Primary Schools* (London, 1966), 5–6.
94 Ibid., 6–7.

95 The Association of Teachers in Colleges and Departments of Education, The Association of Women Science Teachers, The London Association of Science Teachers, The Science Masters' Association, *Science in the Primary School* (London, 1959); Ministry of Education, *Science in Primary Schools*, Pamphlet No. 42 (London, HMSO, 1961); ASE Primary Schools' Science Committee, 'Policy Statement', *ASE Bulletin* (Nov. 1963).

96 For example, a one-day conference on the teaching of science in the junior school held at the University of Leicester, 23 April 1959, and a weekend conference on 'Scientific Exploration in the Primary School', held at the University of Reading, Institute of Education, 24–25 April 1959. The University of Leicester, Institute of Education held lectures on 'Natural Science in Primary Schools' in the summer and autumn of 1961. *JSP 1*; British Association for the Advancement of Science (BAAS) held a conference on 'Approaches to Science in the Primary School' in Sept. 1961.

97 S. Redman *et al.*, 'Young Children and Science: The Oxford Primary Science Project', (First published in *Trends in Education*, 12, 1968, 17–25), Reprinted in C. Richards and D. Holford (eds), *The Teaching of Primary Science: Policy and Practice* (London, 1983), 131–2.

98 M. Waring, *Social Pressures and Curriculum Innovation. A Study of the Nuffield Foundation Science Teaching Project* (London, 1979), 8–9. The findings of this research were published by The Froebel Foundation in 1966 under the title *Children Learning through Scientific Interests*. Ron Wastnedge, 'Nuffield Junior Science: The End of a Beginning?', in C. Richards and D. Holford (eds) op. cit., 140.

99 Both J.F. Kerr and Nathan Isaacs advocated the use of 'finding out' methods in their speeches to the BAAS Conference on Approaches to Science in the Primary School, 29–30 September 1961. *JSP 1*, Rough Draft of Kerr's speech to the conference, 1; The ASE Primary Schools' Science Committee advocated the use of finding out methods, 'Policy Statement', *ASE Bulletin* (Nov. 1963), 19.

100 E.M. Tuke, 'Autumn Meeting', *School Nature Study*, 53, 210, Jan. 1958, 13.

101 F.F. Blackwell, 'Possibilities and Limitations', in The Association of Teachers in Colleges and Departments of Education, The Association of Women Science Teachers, The London Association of Science Teachers, The Science Masters' Association, *Science in the Primary School* (London, 1959), 25.

102 Ministry of Education, *Science in Secondary Schools*, Pamphlet No. 38 (London, HMSO, 1961) and *Science in Primary Schools*, Pamphlet No. 42 (London, HMSO, 1961).

103 Ministry of Education, *Science in Primary Schools* (1961), 5 and 6.

104 The ASE was formed in 1963 by the merging together of the Science Masters' Association and the Association of Women Science Teachers. Waring, op. cit., 12.

105 Primary Schools' Science Committee, 'Policy Statement', *ASE Bulletin*, 21.

106 Ibid., 19.

107 Roy Richards, interview with BS, 2 May 1995.

108 W. Harlen, 'Does Content Matter in Primary Science?', in C. Richards and D. Holford, op. cit., 60. Harlen is actually referring to NJSP but it also held true for Science 5–13 that it was impossible for it to be content-free.

109 Roy Richards, interview with BS, 2 May 1995, London.

110 P. Shaw, *Science* (London, 1972), 10–11.

111 Ibid., 8.

112 Ibid., 7.

113 J.R. Ravetz, 'Some New Ideas about Science Relevant to Education', in E.W. Jenkins, *Policy Issues and School Science Education*, Centre for Studies in Science and Mathematics Education, University of Leeds (Leeds, 1989), 20.

114 L. Laudan *et al.*, 'Scientific Change: Philosophical Models and Historical Research', *Synthese*, 69 (10), 1986, 141–223.

115 For some discussion of this point with reference to secondary schooling, see E.W. Jenkins, 'Processes in Science Education: an historical perspective', in J.J. Wellington (ed.), *Skills and Processes in Science Education: A Critical Analysis* (London, 1989), ch. 2.
116 *JSP 10*, 'Team Leaders Meeting', 5 Dec. 1965, 3.
117 Quoted in D.E.M. Gardner, Susan Isaacs (London, 1969), 54–5.
118 L.A.H. Smith, *To Understand and to Help: The Life and Work of Susan Isaacs (1885–1948)* (NJ, 1985), 131.
119 Ibid., 76.
120 S. Isaacs, *Intellectual Growth in Young Children* (London, 1930), 83.
121 Ibid., 92.
122 N. Isaacs, 'Education and Science', *Nature*, 120 (1927), 23 July, 105.
123 For example, N. Isaacs, *The Growth of Understanding in the Young Child: A Brief Introduction to Piaget's Work* (London, 1961).
124 He was a speaker, for example, at the BAAS Conference on Primary Science held in 1962. See W.H. Perkins (ed.), *The Place of Science in Primary Education* (London, 1962), 4–23.
125 Ibid., 6.
126 Nuffield Foundation, *Nuffield Junior Science: Teacher's Guide 1* (London, 1967), 317.
127 J.S. Hall, *Experience, Experiment and Research: English Primary Science 1959–1967*, Unpublished Ph.D. thesis, University of Liverpool, 1993, 224.
128 E.R. Wastnedge, 'Science in Primary Schools', *Visual Education*, Aug./Sept. 1964, 20, quoted in J.S. Hall, op. cit., 224.
129 Ibid., 222 and 292.
130 *JSP 1*, Letter from J.F. Kerr to D.H.J. Marchant (Head of Science Department at Kesteven Training College, Lincolnshire) Re: Policy Statement of the ASE Primary Science Committee, 13 May 1963, 1.
131 *JSP 4*, 'Consultative Committee Meeting 2 Dec. 1964, Discussion of Teacher's Guide Chapter 1', 1.
132 *JSP 7*, E.R. Wastnedge, 'Reply to Irene Finch', 29 Oct. 1965, 5.
133 *JSP 4*, 'Consultative Committee Meeting 2 Dec. 1964, Discussion of Teacher's Guide Chapter 1', 2.
134 Nuffield Junior Science Project, *Teacher's Guide 1*, 294.
135 L. Ennever and W. Harlen, *With Objectives in Mind: Guide to Science 5–13* (London, 1972), 10.
136 W. Harlen, Interview with BS, 9 May 1995, Edinburgh.
137 Schools Council Science 5–13, *Getting to Know the Science 5–13 Project*, Students' Guide and Tutors' Notes prepared for the Science Teacher Education Project, Trial copy, Jan. 1973. Archives held at King's College London, File C/SCION-13/PUB25.
138 W. Harlen, Sr., A. Darwin and M. Murphy, *Match and Mismatch: Raising Questions: Leader's Guide* (Edinburgh/London, 1977).
139 See, for example, D.C. Phillips, 'The Good, the Bad and the Ugly: The Many Faces of Constructivism', *Educational Researcher*, Oct. 1995, 24 (7), 5–12.
140 National Curriculum Council, *Teaching Science at Key Stages 1 and 2* (York, 1991), 36.
141 Idem.
142 L. Ennever and W. Harlen, op. cit., 4.
143 R.F. Dearden, 'The Plowden Philosophy in Retrospect', in R. Lowe (ed.), *The Changing Primary School*, 69.
144 Central Advisory Council, *Children and Their Primary Schools* (London, HMSO, 1967), Vol. 1, 7.
145 Ibid., Vol. 1, 242.
146 Ibid., Vol. 1, 241–5

147 Ibid., 101–2.
148 Ibid., 101.
149 N. Bennett, *Teaching Styles and Pupil Progress* (London, 1976), 149.
150 Ibid., 43.
151 DES, *Primary Education in England. A Survey by HM Inspectors of Schools* (London, HMSO, 1978), 1–2.
152 Ibid., 26–7.
153 Ibid., 47, 52–3, 95.
154 G.M. Blenkin and A.V. Kelly, *The Primary Curriculum* (London, 1981), 166.
155 J. Campbell and S. Neill, *Curriculum Reform at Key Stage 1: Teacher Commitment and Policy Failure* (London, 1994), 96.
156 Wynne Harlen, Interview with BS, 9 May 1995.
157 Roy Richards, Interview with BS, 2 May 1995.

7

Afterword

This concluding afterword is structured around two broad questions. First, why was it not until almost the end of the twentieth century that science secured a place in the curriculum of the primary school, and why did it do so when earlier attempts at reform met with, at best, only a modest degree of success? Second, on what terms has primary science been schooled in England and Wales in the 1990s? Or, to put this second question in a more elaborate form, what assumptions about science, about learning and teaching, and about primary education currently underpin the scientific education of 5–11-year-old pupils, and how do these assumptions articulate with the realities of primary school practice?

WHY SO LATE?

Until the final decade of the twentieth century, the scientific education of the majority of children of primary school age was largely confined to work derived from the biological sciences which, for convenience, can be described as nature study. As noted in Chapter 3, attempts during the 1950s to broaden the scheme of work encompassed by nature study to include topics drawn from the physical sciences were not only unsuccessful but, to some degree, opposed as inappropriate for the education of young children. The kind of work undertaken in this period has been described in the following terms by Conran, a Froebel-trained teacher.[1]

> We started with a 'Seaside Room'. Ready beforehand were displays of shells, pebbles, and sand; aquaria with live crabs and sea anemones; seaweeds; boxes and tables for collections made during the summer holidays; drawing material, paper for labelling and selection of named specimens, reference books and pictures. We then followed the seasons with an ever-changing set of exhibits, a growing family of resident plants and animals, and a flow of temporary visitors brought in by the children ... I spent two hours

> per week in each classroom, was in the Nature Room before school and at playtimes, and ran a weekly club.

In 1978, a survey[2] by HMI of the work of a representative sample of 1,127 classes in 542 primary schools in England suggested how little had changed.

> In about two-thirds of all the classes a nature table or 'interest' table was kept, where objects such as pieces of wood, sea shells, building materials, old clocks or radios were collected or displayed. In a similar number of classes plants were either grown in school or brought in for study. About half the classes kept small animals such as hamsters or gerbils and a similar proportion undertook some work arising from outdoor activities such as a nature walk, a visit to a local park or the study of a local habitat such as a canal or pond.

The survey also indicated[3] the limited use made by the pupils of some of the materials collected as part of their nature study work.

> ... although children in a fair proportion of the classes were introduced to plants, animals and objects intended to stimulate scientific enquiry, in very few cases were opportunities taken to teach children how to make careful observations or to plan and carry out investigations of a scientific nature. For example, collections of autumn leaves were commonly used for decorative purposes or to stimulate work with pattern and colour; they were seldom used to help children to recognize similarities and differences in formation, such as the different forms of multiple leaf in ash and horse-chestnut trees, or notions of stability and change in living things.

Findings such as these are perhaps the more surprising given the attempts during the 1960s and 1970s to introduce science into primary education by means of large-scale investment in programmes of curriculum reform, notably the Nuffield Junior Science Project and the Schools Council Science 5–13 Project. As noted in Chapter 4, these attempts to secure a place for science in the education of young children were much less successful than had been hoped,

> ... the progress of science teaching in primary schools has been disappointing; the ideas and materials produced by curriculum development projects have had little impact in the majority of schools.[4]

although the longer-term significance of these and other projects, not least in promoting the notion of a broadly-based 'primary science', should not be underestimated.

Reference has already been made in Chapter 6 to the failure, until the second half of the twentieth century, of any professional organisation or group to articulate and promote the case for science within the education of young children. The British Association for the Advancement of Science, an important and influential contributor to debates about the form and content of elementary education during and beyond the nineteenth century, declined in influence in the years after the end of the First World War. The School Nature Study Union, with a relatively small membership and never really a national organisation, was divided over the issue of broadening the scope of nature study to include topics drawn from the physical sciences. By the time the organisation resolved this policy issue and transformed itself into the School Natural Science Society, the initiative in primary science education had passed elsewhere, notably to the Nuffield Foundation, the Schools Council and the Association for Science Education (ASE). However, as far as the ASE and, more particularly, its predecessors[5] were concerned, the traditional field of interest was science education in grammar and public, rather than elementary or primary schools, an interest which enabled the Association to find natural and powerful allies in the Royal Society and the professional scientific institutes established to promote the cause of science itself. Not surprisingly, therefore, the eventual involvement of the Association with primary science and the recruitment of a significant number of primary teachers into membership were part of much wider and profound changes in the Association, made, not without difficulty, in response to the expansion of comprehensive education and a commitment to science education for all.[6]

For most of the twentieth century, promoting the cause of science at school level necessarily focused attention on the work of grammar and public schools, rather than on that of the elementary, senior and secondary modern schools which provided the formal education available to the majority of young people. The curricula, including the science curricula, and the resources provided in these latter, non-selective schools reflected the social purposes which they were intended to serve. That purpose was, for the most part, captured by the notion of education for 'followership', rather than the leadership associated with grammar and public schools. Elementary, senior and secondary modern schools were not concerned with the pre-professional training of scientists. Their courses sometimes had 'a bearing on future employment', commonly of a local nature, and they were frequently, although not always, structured on a topic, rather than a disciplinary, basis. In the 1930s, the Board of Education claimed[7] that achieving the aims of science in the senior school was difficult because 'it implies an abandonment of the academic tradition in which its own teachers were nurtured'. In the secondary modern schools set up after 1945 to cater 'for the rank and file',[8] schemes of work in science were often organised under such titles as Science in the Home, Science and Health and The Science of Common Things. Even as late as the 1960s, gender and social differentiation in science education found expression both in government reports, notably the Newsom report[9] of 1963, and in curriculum initiatives such as the Nuffield Secondary Science Project[10] in which the structure of the individual scientific disciplines was sacrificed to broad themes such as Movement, Using Materials and the Interdependence of Living Things. The reality is, therefore, that the historic neglect of science within the education of young children is not unique, but part of a wider disregard of science within the schooling of the majority of the population that was not to be rectified until the closing decade of the twentieth century.

This wider neglect can probably be understood only in terms of the educational function attributed to science and, beyond this, of the perception and standing of science itself within the wider community. Although it has fluctuated considerably, the cultural esteem of science has remained contested territory, not just throughout the twentieth century but arguably since at least the seventeenth century when wits like Addison and Pope poured scorn on the work of some members of the newly-founded Royal Society.[11] Desmond, reviewing the life of T.H. Huxley, notes[12] that by the time of Huxley's death in 1895,

> The years of science's heady excitement were over ... On the eve of the twentieth century science was specialized and esoteric; it shut itself away in the laboratory and lost its public appeal. Its radicalism passed to politics, its moral drive to humanism; and the poison bombs raining death in the Great War finally killed its nineteenth-century promise.

By 1929, A.N. Whitehead, writing of science and the modern world, was warning[13] of the 'celibacy' of an intellect which is 'divorced from the concrete contemplation of the complete facts', and, a generation later in 1959, C.P. Snow reinvigorated the long-standing two cultures debate with his Rede lecture[14] at Cambridge. It is inappropriate in the present context to rehearse the complex issues that surround the distinction drawn between science and the wider culture in England and

Wales, although the separation has been studied by a number of scholars and can be dated with some precision. Shapin and Thackray, for example, have concluded[15] that 'it was in the years from 1870 to 1900 that the divorce was effected between natural knowledge and general culture'. What is important to note here is that the securing, by statute, of a broad and balanced science education for all pupils of compulsory school age in maintained schools may owe less to any bridging of this cultural divide than to the economic and instrumental concerns that have recast educational provision in the United Kingdom as a part of the commercial market place and underpinned a variety of related educational initiatives – for example, the Technical and Vocational Education Initiative, the rise of technology as a school subject and the national curriculum itself.[16]

Conventional wisdom attributes the failure of science to secure a place in the primary curriculum to teachers' lack of knowledge of elementary science appropriate to the education of young children. However, when the Education Reform Act 1988 established science as a compulsory component of the education of all children in maintained primary schools, primary teachers' response to the challenge was such that, by 1990–91, two-thirds of the lessons in science with 5–7-year-olds were judged[17] by HMI to be 'satisfactory or better'. At Key Stage 2, the national curriculum was said to have broadened pupils' scientific experience, although the standards of work were less satisfactory than at Key Stage 1. By 1993–94, the standards of achievement in science were reported as 'at least satisfactory in relation to pupils' capabilities in 79 per cent of the Key Stage 1 lessons', with standards described as 'good or very good in 21 per cent of lessons'. In the same year at Key Stage 2, although standards of achievement remained slightly less satisfactory than at Key Stage 1, 73 per cent of lessons were judged to be satisfactory or better, with 20 per cent identified as good or very good.[18] While both surveys commented upon the restricting influence of some teachers' scientific knowledge on the work done with pupils in years 5 and 6, it is difficult to avoid the impression that, during a period of turmoil and major changes to the statutory curriculum, primary teachers had responded with considerable success to the demands placed upon them. In 1994, a review of school science and mathematics education by the Office for Standards in Education,[19] while acknowledging areas where improvement was still needed, commented as follows.

> In primary schools science and technology have been the most significant areas of curricular growth during the last decade. ...

> Inspection reveals that science in Key Stages 1 and 2 has intellectual substance and involves the study of topics as diverse as electricity and electronic circuitry, local habitats and ecology and the properties of materials.

By 1995–96, Her Majesty's Chief Inspector of schools reported that, despite weaknesses in Years 3 and 4, pupils' knowledge and understanding of science was 'good in half of the schools' inspected in that year.[20]

A survey[21] by the National Foundation for Educational Research, conducted in the autumn of 1995, revealed that 94 per cent of the mainly primary schools sampled (n = 426) had a curriculum plan for science either prepared or in preparation, and that the majority of the schools allocated time for science each week which was in line with, or greater than, the Dearing recommendations of 54 and 72 hours per year at Key Stages 1 and 2 respectively.[22] When asked to identify particular challenges or difficulties in implementing the post-Dearing national curriculum in science, a lack of resources (equipment, time, etc.) was cited by over twice as many headteachers as staff-related issues, including teachers' lack of confidence in teaching science. At both Key Stages 1 and 2, the science was taught overwhelmingly on a topic basis, although the evidence 'suggested that even when a topic-based approach predominated, teachers recognised that it was preferable to teach some aspects of science as a separate subject'.[23] The teaching of at least some science as a separate subject became increasingly common in the later years of Key Stage 2.

An international perspective on the quality of primary school science education in England and Wales is available from the results of the Third International Mathematics and Science Survey (TIMSS). In a study of the achievement in science of nine-year-olds involving 26 countries, carried out in 1995, no Western European country achieved higher overall mean scores than England, and Year 5 pupils in England performed at a level bettered only by Korea, Japan, the Czech Republic and the USA. While this level of achievement compared favourably with pupils' performance in mathematics, it needs to be remembered that, in a number of the countries surveyed, science receives little or no attention in the primary curriculum and that, in most cases, formal schooling begins later than in England.[24]

This seemingly rapid progress in the accommodation of primary science in England and Wales is not only a testament to the commitment and professionalism of primary teachers. It suggests that the long-standing scientific shortcomings in the scientific education of those who teach young children may have been over-emphasised, at the expense of wider cultural factors,[25] in seeking to explain the hitherto inhospitable response of the primary schools to the introduction of science into the primary curriculum. This is not, of course, to suggest that all is necessarily well with the teaching of science in primary schools in the 1990s. There is some evidence that standards of work in some aspects of primary science, such as planning investigations, are lower than for other aspects of the national curriculum.[26] It would also be a mistake to ignore such issues as the provision of equipment and other resources, the role of science coordinators, and the monitoring and assessment of pupils' progress, or to deny that problems remain with teachers' subject knowledge, especially when teaching science to pupils in the last two years of primary schooling.

The problem of teachers' scientific knowledge, however, is more subtle and complex than a simple lack of understanding of scientific ideas. The teaching of science to pupils requires the teacher to transform scientific knowledge into programmes and activities from which children might learn, that is, scientific knowledge of the topics to be taught is a necessary, but not a sufficient, condition for promoting the effective learning of scientific concepts. Shulman has captured this issue in his notion[27] of pedagogical content knowledge, the 'special amalgam of content and pedagogy that is uniquely the province of teachers'.

What seems clear, however, is that, when allied with a lack of confidence, the consequence[28] of teachers' lack of subject expertise is that

> primary teachers tend not to be sufficiently aware of the 'conceptual understanding that they want the children to acquire' ... To put it simply, primary teachers tend to concentrate on 'doing science', rather than drawing out the underlying scientific ideas.

A corollary may be that tasks ostensibly concerned with the learning of science are redirected to serve other purposes. Edwards and Collison have studied[29] what happens when student teachers attempt to apply their knowledge of curriculum subjects to their work in primary classrooms. Using data collected over three years in 30 classrooms, they categorised the tasks undertaken by the student teachers as follows.

1. Tasks which offered pupils experience of the intended subject focus and sustained their engagement with the discourse of the subject.

2. Tasks which engaged with aspects of the intended subject but were less cognitively demanding than was intended and so allowed distortion of intended learning outcomes.
3. Tasks which in their execution became transformed to focus on a subject other than the intended subject.

While the majority of tasks which the researchers observed did focus on the intended subject matter and the intended learning outcome, they also found considerable variation between the subjects that make up the primary curriculum. In particular,

> The subject where focus appeared most difficult was science, where only 17 per cent of tasks were judged to carry the intended feature of the science curriculum (category 1). The most common manifestation of lack of attention to the discourse of the subject (category 3) was the transformation of a task into a craft activity, e.g. cutting and pasting or ... a language activity where the focus was not the discourse of the subject but attention to the correct spelling of more common words. Take, for example, an observed session where the student teacher worked with pairs of Year 2 children to create silhouette, cameo-style, pictures. The activity could have been a suitable vehicle for a transformation of the desired subject knowledge and could therefore have met the original subject intentions of reinforcing the concepts of opacity and transparency. However, the task failed as an opportunity for the pupils to engage with the discourse of the science curriculum because the student teacher attended to the mechanical aspects of task completion, i.e. finishing the silhouette. She did not provide opportunities, for example, for children to engage with the language in which the concepts of opacity and transparency were carried, or to attempt forms of experimentation, or to represent what they had found out about the materials and opacity and transparency in a written form. She did not treat the experience authentically as a science activity.

It would be precipitate to extend these findings beyond students in training, although other work[30] has revealed ways in which even skilled and experienced teachers can fail to implement their intended curriculum demands. Three brief comments, however, are appropriate. First, the findings serve as an important reminder of the distinction to be drawn between an intended and the delivered curriculum, a distinction which is all too easily overlooked, not least in seemingly straightforward surveys of how much time primary schools devote to the teaching of science. Second, by drawing attention to the subtle, complex and time-consuming nature of any worthwhile judgement of lesson quality, the research findings invite scrutiny of the criteria used for this purpose by the Office for Standards in Education. Finally, it is clear from this and many other sources[31] that 'pupil activity' remains central to the professional practice of primary teachers whether they are teaching science or other components of the primary curriculum. In the case of science, this enduring commitment to pupil activity is more than part of the general legacy of progressive ideas in education. It owes much to the emphasis placed upon activity in the science curriculum projects of the 1960s and 1970s, conveniently coupled with the notion that science is essentially a practical subject. Arguably, this emphasis, in turn, derives from a particular reading of Piagetian psychology and the interpretation of 'match and mismatch' that followed from it.

There remains the supplementary question posed at the beginning of this chapter. Why, when earlier attempts at reform were, at best, only moderately successful, did science secure its present place in the primary curriculum? The compelling force of statute is, of course, the most immediate and straightforward answer. Legislation in curriculum matters, however, requires a sense, particularly on the part of a radical government broadly committed to rolling back the boundaries of the state, both that statute offers the best way of achieving its policy objectives and that science can and should be taught to all pupils between the ages of five and 16 in maintained schools. It would have been perfectly possible in principle to construct a statutory national curriculum which did not compel the teaching of science within primary schools. That the government chose not to do so, therefore, suggests that a politically persuasive case for science in primary education had been made, notwithstanding earlier disappointments and enduring problems over the scientific background of primary teachers. It must, at least for the moment, remain an open question whether science secured its place in the primary curriculum principally as a component of a wider legislative curriculum package, or whether, in deciding upon legislation as a means of reform, the failure of earlier curriculum initiatives, including the primary science projects, suggested that there was no other effective way forward in a timescale that would satisfy the government's political priorities.

The elements of that politically persuasive case were already in place by 1981 when the government announced its objective of securing more effective science teaching in primary schools.[32] Following a consultation paper on science education in schools in the following year, a formal statement of government policy for school science education was published[33] by the Department of Education and Science and the Welsh Office in 1985. That policy was formulated on the basis of a 'quickening interest' in primary science at both national and local level. As evidence of this quickening interest, the Department was able to cite not only the findings of the survey of science at age 11 undertaken by the Assessment of Performance Unit, but also a range of other initiatives, some by government itself, to sustain and promote the teaching of science to young children.[34] The wider policy context, however, was a growing concern about national competitiveness in a global, technology-based economy, and a mounting public suspicion of, even hostility towards, some aspects of the scientific endeavour. Both of these issues were evident in a report[35] on the public understanding of science, published by the Royal Society in the same year as the statement of policy for school science. The Association for Science Education, for its part, published[36] a controversial consultation document in 1979 and its formal policy position two years later in a publication entitled *Education Through Science*.[37] By June 1982, when Sir Keith Joseph, the Secretary of State for Education and Science, visited the ASE he was able to comment that 'All present accept the need to develop science for all'.[38] Initiatives such as the Secondary Science Curriculum Review[39] and, subsequently, the national curriculum, were both, in very different ways, attempts to translate this commitment to science education for all into curriculum practice.

The answer to the subordinate question posed above lies, therefore, at least in part, in the wide political consensus about science education for all which emerged in the 1980s. Such consensus, however, was promoted in the context of a system of comprehensive schooling which accommodated a very different interpretation of equality of opportunity from that which had characterised the selective system of the 1960s. From this perspective, therefore, any growth in the teaching of science in primary schools during the 1980s reflects not only a change in policy for school science education but also wider, and long-standing concerns, about how best to promote scientific and technological excellence in the few while seeking to satisfy the educational needs of the majority. How far such growth might, of its own, have led to a broad and balanced science education for all in primary schools must remain an open question. Perhaps, however, it is also an unimportant question since, with the introduction of the national curriculum, attention has necessarily turned to the manner in which science has been schooled in the education of children between the ages of five and 11.

THE SCHOOLING OF PRIMARY SCIENCE UNDER THE EDUCATION REFORM ACT 1988

The national curriculum introduced under the Education Reform Act 1988 was an ambitious undertaking and one which required urgent and major changes in the early 1990s before it could be said to be working at all effectively in schools. These changes, however, have not altered the specification of the statutory requirements in terms of a range of subjects, of which science is one. Although parallels have been drawn[40] between the government's intervention in the curriculum in 1988 and the Secondary School Regulations issued by the Board of Education in 1904, both the subject basis of the present national curriculum, and much of its underlying philosophy, are of more recent origin. In particular, they stem from the debates about the form, content and purpose of the school curriculum that had taken place throughout the 1970s and early 1980s. According to Bolton,[41] Her Majesty's Chief Inspector of Schools from 1983 to 1991, the work of HMI and others led to the development of a particular model of the curriculum based on eight (later extended to nine to include technology) areas of experience.[42] By the time the government's White Paper, *Better Schools*,[43] was published in 1985, the government's curriculum policy was set out in terms almost identical with those that were to emerge in the Education Reform Act 1988. The shift from 'areas of experience' to subjects, sometimes regarded as profound, is explained by Bolton as no more than the need to satisfy the requirements of Parliamentary draftsmen.

> ... the drafting of legislation, because it is to become law, needs to be commonly understood and as unambiguous as possible. This requirement calls for precision and specificity in the drafting of the Bill. Consequently, even if areas of experience, or indeed any other sort of description of a school curriculum, had been possible in practice, they would create severe difficulties for the Parliamentary draftsmen when setting out the legislation. It is possible to be clear about what is commonly meant and understood by the terms 'mathematics' and 'history' to a degree that is not possible with terms such as 'humanities' or 'social studies'.[44]

Whatever the validity of Bolton's explanation, the specification of the national curriculum in terms of subjects has had a number of consequences. It has aligned primary schools more closely with their secondary counterparts. Both now 'teach subjects', and both are held to public account for pupils' knowledge and understanding of them. It has also clarified the relationship between primary and secondary schooling, since the statutory curriculum is meant to provide for continuity and progress in pupils' learning between, as well as within, these two stages of education.

More fundamentally, however, the emphasis upon subjects in the national curriculum has challenged several of the assumptions that have underpinned the work of many primary schools in the post-Plowden era. Subject expertise is not easily reconciled with the work and training of the generalist class teacher whose expertise is said to lie in managing children's learning as a coherent whole. The teaching of individual subjects does not sit comfortably alongside the integrated timetable, and it undermines a primary culture which accords centrality to the child and the learning process. The extent of the challenge is indicated by Alexander's comment,[45] made in 1984, that

> The word 'knowledge' itself, and certainly 'subjects', can be taboo in professional circles: introduced in embarrassed terms they are hedged around with apologies and qualifications such as 'I don't mean of course that subjects should be taught separately, I'm just using the word for the sake of convenience'.

The fact that such sentiments continue to be expressed in 1997 is evidence of the enduring tension between a subject-based curriculum 'reminiscent of the ... subject areas taught at secondary school' and an approach to primary science education in which teachers develop 'chance happenings that have intrigued children'.[46]

If, as several commentators have suggested, the national curriculum is in 'fundamental conflict with the values and deeply held beliefs of many primary teachers in England and Wales',[47] it is hardly surprising that their response to its introduction has ranged from the 'protective', 'innovative' or 'collaborative mediation' of policy to conspiratorial subversion intended to 'resist aspects of the National Curriculum that were felt to be particularly inappropriate for the children'.[48] In less dramatic terms, it seems that most primary teachers have responded to the statutory requirement to teach science in ways that allow them to retain a commitment to 'pupil activity', and to use a topic approach where this is judged appropriate, that is, the subject-based prescribed curriculum has been transformed into schemes of work and teaching strategies with which most primary teachers are both familiar and comfortable.

> When science came on the planning agenda, teachers found they could adapt their topic plans accordingly. From 1990 science-

> related topics became the norm ... it would be interesting to know if science has now gone 'off the boil'.[49]

The national curriculum specification of science also conveys a view of the nature of science and of science education. As far as the nature of science is concerned, there has been criticism of the way in which this has been 'delivered' in the classroom and laboratory, principally, but not exclusively, through Attainment Target 1. Black, for example, referred[50] to the 'capture of the agenda by those committed to an over-emphasis on the model of variable handling', a model which arguably sustains the curious notion of a 'fair test' common in the discourse of primary teachers. There is, however, a more fundamental objection to any attempt to prescribe in statutory form the methods whereby science engages with the physical world to establish scientific knowledge. Whether such methods exist, can be described, are indeed employed by practising scientists at an individual level or are the causes of their success have been the subject of debate since science was judged sufficiently distinct and progressive to merit some special account. The issue has been the subject of endless study and from a variety of perspectives derived from the philosophy, history and, more recently, the sociology of science. When set against what is known from these studies about the practice of science, Attainment Target 1 and, arguably, the practice derived from it, must be judged both deficient and, what is perhaps more significant, positively misleading. While professional scientists or others who actually engage in experimental work no doubt undertake the activities specified in this Attainment Target, there is nothing about such activities *per se* which is unique to science. Characterising the practice of natural science requires an altogether more complex framework, if indeed it can be done. In most academic studies of science as an activity, the emphasis has moved away from attempts to generate universal cognitive foundations which guarantee success. The work is more descriptive in character, and focuses on such issues as the meaning of the claim that the practices of science are entirely rational, whether the conceptualisations of the physical world generated within scientific practice are uniquely predetermined, in what sense the entities and regularities described within science can be judged 'real', and whether, and to what degree, scientific practice is independent of, or implicated in, wider social and intellectual processes. All these issues, and many others, are the subject of on-going and lively debate within a field that has come to be known as science studies.[51] The field encompasses such diverse subject matter as the linguistic practices of scientific writing, the ethnomethodology of working laboratories, social histories of scientific institutions and technical studies of the contingencies and difficulties of instrumental work, as well as studies which integrate sociological and philosophical theorising. In these studies, science is seen to address the material world through diverse, loosely-coupled material and intellectual practices, and the working of these practices is seen to be inescapably socially and institutionally situated. 'Doing' science cannot be equated with the work of individuals in the laboratory, nor, like any imaginative and creative activity, can it be readily reduced to a curriculum prescription.

There is the further point that to refer to 'science' as though it were a single set of homogeneous intellectual and material practices is to disguise important differences between individual scientific disciplines. In these circumstances, the national curriculum prescription of science and its translation into practice reflect an account of science which minimises, where it does not ignore, the contingent and social dimensions of science, that is, the extent of the human endeavour of all kinds, individual, directly interpersonal, institutional, material and discursive, which is necessary to create and sustain scientific knowledge. Science is not Huxley's 'clear, cold logic engine', and it is more than a simple matter of 'fair testing'. To present it as such is not only to devalue one of the supreme intellectual achievements of the human race. A depersonalised, even algorithmic, account of scientific practice seems unlikely to appeal in the long term to young people whose encounters with science beyond the world of the laboratory over such issues as BSE or DNA technology will not easily accommodate the model of science promoted at school.

As for AT1, entitled Experimental and Investigative Science in the version of the national curriculum introduced in September 1995, the history of this Attainment Target is complex and has been described in some detail, although with particular reference to secondary schools, by Donnelly *et al.*[52] In the present context, it will be sufficient to make three points. First, the immediate antecedents of the 1995 Attainment Target lie in the revision in 1991 of Attainment Targets 1 and 17 of the 1989 version of the national curriculum, a revision which created a new Attainment Target, Scientific Investigation, commonly referred to as 'Sc1'. Second, the more distant origins of the commitment to experimental and investigative science lie in the schooling of science in the nineteenth century and, more particularly, in the confidence that pupils can, and should, be taught 'scientific method'.[53] Third, the language used to advocate and support the teaching of investigative science was, and remains, redolent of the dichotomies commonly associated with, and central to, progressive, child-centred ideas about teaching and learning. Thus, the teaching of scientific 'processes' is contrasted with scientific content, and 'whole investigations' are favoured over 'atomised' skills. Given dichotomies of this kind and the different histories of primary and secondary school science education, it is not surprising that when primary and secondary school members of the Association for Science Education were asked in 1993 for their views about Sc1, the responses were markedly different. Eighty per cent of the primary teachers surveyed by means of a questionnaire regarded Sc1 as the 'most important of the ATs', a figure that contrasts sharply with that of 25 per cent applicable to their secondary colleagues. The Association was left to comment, rather lamely, that 'it is interesting ... that teachers mostly qualified in core science subjects feel Sc1 to be less important than those with mostly other teaching qualifications who may be having difficulty in delivering this area of the curriculum'.[54]

It is not difficult to understand how Experimental and Investigative Science, as defined in the national curriculum Statutory Order, can be readily accommodated to those activities and pedagogies that primary school teachers continue to value. There are beguiling resonances between scientific investigation, active learning and the currently fashionable 'constructivist' pedagogy. Such accommodation, however, validates neither the educational claims made for engaging pupils in scientific investigations nor the picture of science presented by the Attainment Target and the curriculum practices derived from it. The range of educational benefits and outcomes said to flow from the involvement of pupils with investigative work in science is both extensive and heterogeneous, although many of the claims are cast in terms more directly appropriate to the teaching of laboratory science in secondary schools. Some relate to the alleged effect upon pupils' motivation or interest, and to pupils developing a sense of responsibility for their own work. From this point of view, pupil investigations are essentially a pedagogic device rather than connected directly with educational outcomes. The existence of a range of quite general cognitive outcomes is also frequently asserted, for example, problem-solving skills, logical thought or objectivity, although the last two of these are perhaps now less fashionable than hitherto. There is also a different group of supposed cognitive outcomes, namely those which relate specifically to science. Three groups can be identified. First, pupils may develop intellectual and practical skills similar to those of professional scientists. They may be able to deploy such skills in their everyday life or, later, as lay adults, or the skills may form the foundation for the further study of, and perhaps a career in, science. Second, pupils may gain an understanding, preferably a critical understanding, of the practices of science, and thus, in due course, be able to make an informed judgement when, as citizens and consumers, they are confronted with scientific knowledge claims. Third, pupils may be supported in their learning of substantive scientific ideas. This last claim is more complex than the other two, with several possible bases, of which the following are perhaps the most plausible. It might relate to a largely motivational effect, thus aligning itself with an earlier claim above, or it might be grounded in a pupil's repeated use of scientific concepts and a consequent improvement in their understanding and use. Another possibility is that the claim might derive from some parallels between the means by which pupils learn science and the putative (generic) practices of individual scientists, or between the development of children's understanding of scientific ideas and the history of science.[55] While many of these anticipated cognitive outcomes might carry more immediate weight in the context of secondary rather than primary science education, almost all of them derive from a supposed isomorphism between the practice of scientists and the activities which pupils undertake when learning science at school. Although the empirical basis of this suggested isomorphism is far from established, it continues to sustain some significant claims about both science and science education, for example, '*Learning* science and *doing* science proceed in the same way', and '*The development of understanding in science is ... dependent on the ability to carry out process skills in a scientific manner.*'[56]

The teaching of Attainment Target 1, Experimental and Investigative Science, in the national curriculum, therefore, prompts a number of questions. Is it meant to convey to primary school children a picture of how science is conducted? What importance is to be attached to variable handling and to the associated notion of a 'fair test'? Is it suggested or implied that 'doing' science at school is the best way of learning what science has to say about some aspects of the natural world? What connection is assumed between the nature of scientific knowledge and how that knowledge can be best taught and learned? What are the intended relationships between the first Attainment Target and the remaining three which are much more content-orientated? To what extent is the commitment to experimental and investigative science intended to promote, or be reflective of, a particular (constructivist) view of learning or of pedagogy? All of these questions present difficulties that have not had the attention they deserve, and, together, they hint at some lack of clarity about the purpose and 'delivery' of experimental and investigative science to young pupils. Among the questions, the last has perhaps a particular significance in the context of primary science education given the importance traditionally attached to theories of learning in shaping both the rhetoric and practice of primary schooling.

Black,[57] although referring principally to AT1 and the secondary curriculum, has commented that, in constructing this Attainment Target, 'The aim was a great leap forward in learning – since for pupils to take responsibility for planning and carrying out their own investigations would break the cook-book mould and make possible a *constructivist* approach to experimental work' (emphasis added). Such a comment reflects the dominant position that constructivist ideas have come to occupy in much of contemporary school science education, not just in England and Wales but in many countries of the world. One commentator[58] has described such ideas in education as currently 'something akin to a secular religion' and another has claimed that 'The most conspicuous psychological influence on curriculum thinking since 1980 has been the constructivist view of learning.'[59] Constructivism has many variants,[60] and has obvious resonances with post-modern ideas in fields other than education, but within science education, constructivist ideas have come to be closely allied with a substantial international programme of research into children's understanding of scientific ideas[61] and with the implications sometimes drawn from the findings for how science should be taught and can best be learned. A major research project, the Science Processes and Concepts Exploration (SPACE) Project, resting upon work of this kind, has been developed into another primary science curriculum initiative, funded by the Nuffield Foundation.[62]

Some of the features of constructivism within science education are hardly contentious. Most, for example, are likely to accept that science is a human intellectual construct, that pupils must be actively engaged in thinking if their understanding is to be secured, and that the successful teaching of science requires pupils to make sense of what they are being taught and asked to learn. Other constructivist ideas, however, such as equating the investigating pupil with the research scientist or assuming that because all knowledge is 'constructed' in the mind there can be no external reality, have generated heated and often intemperate debate, the tone of which is captured by Devitt's[63] offering of constructivism as a candidate for '*the* most dangerous contemporary intellectual tendency ... (because it) attacks the immune system that saves us from silliness'. Matthews has adopted[64] much the same tone in his criticism of the national curriculum in New Zealand, although other more balanced critiques of aspects of constructivism are available.[65]

It is inappropriate in this volume to engage in this debate which, for the moment, continues unabated elsewhere. Two brief concluding comments are, however, appropriate. First, as far as science education is concerned, the debate has ranged over a number of fields of human endeavour, from epistemology to psychology and pedagogy. Given this, it is perhaps not surprising that confusion has arisen about the nature of a particular claim and/or the grounds upon which it rests. What, for example, is meant by a 'constructivist' pedagogy? If it is anything, it is presumably a theory of teaching, i.e. of instruction, rather than some naive derivation of a (constructivist) theory of learning. A theory of teaching is necessarily more complex and wide-ranging than any theory of learning, not least because it must accommodate what is known about a range of matters not embraced by studies of how pupils learn. In these circumstances, caution seems necessary in invoking constructivist ideas to support, and more so, to justify, the teaching of experimental and investigative science, and in allying the teaching of primary science with one particular approach to learning. The need for such caution is reinforced by the relative lack of knowledge about the effectiveness of 'constructivist' approaches to teaching and learning and, more particularly, about the best way to promote conceptual change. Second, the debate about constructivism referred to above is not one in which most primary teachers have engaged. For the most part, it has been conducted elsewhere in scholarly journals and academic conferences. In contrast, however, within the primary teaching profession, constructivist ideas have acquired something of the status of a 'given', Harlen claiming that the SPACE Project 'was largely responsible for bringing "constructivism" into common discourse in primary science teaching, although, like many ideas in education, it had roots in earlier work, particularly that of Piaget'.[66] Given this 'common discourse', it seems important to clarify the claims which underpin it, and to be satisfied that 'constructivist' ideas are not simply being raided to sustain classroom practices and activities which, while they may engage children with natural phenomena or be justified on quite other grounds, do not introduce pupils to scientific concepts and ideas in ways that are efficient and economic in promoting learning.

NOTES

1 J. Conran, 'Primary Science 1950–82: A Personal View', in C. Richards and D. Holford, (eds), *The Teaching of Primary Science: Policy and Practice* (Lewes, 1983), 18.

2 Department of Education and Science, *Primary Education in England. A survey by HM Inspectors of Schools* (London, HMSO, 1978), para. 5.71.

3 Ibid., para. 5.72.
4 Ibid., para. 5.83.
5 The Association of Public School Science Masters (APSSM), the Science Masters' Association (SMA) and the Association of Women Science Teachers (AWST).
6 For the ASE, see D. Layton, *Interpreters of Science: A History of the Association for Science Education* (London, 1984).
7 Board of Education, *Science in Senior Schools*, Educational Pamphlet, No. 89 (London, HMSO, 1930), 64.
8 H.J. Bonham, 'Modern School Biology', *Advancement of Science*, VI, 21, (1949), 41.
9 Ministry of Education, Central Advisory Council on Education (England), *Half Our Future* (London, HMSO, 1963). The Newsom Committee claimed that 'the girls may come to the science lesson with a less eager curiosity than a boy'. Ibid., Vol. 1, para. 421.
10 See, for example, H. Misselbrook, *Nuffield Secondary Science, Teacher's Guide* (London, 1970). Misselbrook was the Organiser of the Project.
11 R.H. Syfret, 'Some early critics of the Royal Society', *Notes and Records of the Royal Society of London*, Vol. 8 (1970), 65–7.
12 A. Desmond, *Huxley: Evolution's High Priest* (London, 1997), 248.
13 A.N. Whitehead, *Science and the Modern World* (Cambridge, 1929), 245.
14 C.P. Snow, *The Two Cultures and the Scientific Revolution* (Cambridge, 1959).
15 S. Shapin, and A. Thackray, 'Prosopography as a Research Tool in the History of Science: the British Scientific Community 1700–1900', *History of Science*, XII, 1974, 11. Much the same conclusion is reached by Shen, writing from a different perspective. He comments that 'Between the 1870s and World War I ... the increasing professionalization of scientists ... finally induced them to take on a new attitude towards the lay public ... the explaining of science to the layman (came to be regarded) as something not entirely worthy of the professional.' See B.S. Shen, 'Scientific literacy and the public understanding of science', in S.B. Day (ed.), *The Communication of Scientific Information* (Basel, 1975), 45.
16 For insights into this shift, see D. Lawton and C. Chitty, (eds), *The National Curriculum* (London, 1995) and D. Graham and D. Tytler, *A Lesson for Us All: The Making of the National Curriculum* (London, 1993).
17 Department of Education and Science, *Science: Key Stages 1, 2, and 3, A Report by HM Inspectorate on the Second Year, 1990–91* (London, HMSO, 1992), 9.
18 Office for Standards in Education, *Science: A Review of Inspection Findings 1993/4* (London, HMSO, 1995), 6.
19 Office for Standards in Education, *Science and Mathematics in Schools: A Review* (London, HMSO, 1994), 17.
20 Office for Standards in Education, *The Annual Report of Her Majesty's Chief Inspector of Schools* (London, HMSO, 1996),
21 S. Harris, *Science in Primary Schools* (Slough, 1996). The sample included some independent schools, middle schools (deemed primary) and some first and middle combined schools.
22 Ibid., 56 and 64.
23 Ibid., 71 and 61.
24 W. Keys, S. Harris and C. Fernandes, *Third International Mathematics and Science Study, Second National Report, Part I* (NFER, 1997). The *First National Report* (NFER, 1996) deals with the performance of 13-year-old pupils. Again, the performance of pupils in England is better in science than mathematics. For an overview of international comparisons, see D. Reynolds and S. Farrell, *Worlds Apart: A Review of International Survey of Educational Achievement involving England*, Ofsted Reviews of Research (London, HMSO, 1996).
25 It is perhaps important to note that attempts to promote science in the primary curriculum were by no means confined to the United Kingdom or to the industrialised

nations of the world. See, for example, Unesco, *Meeting of Experts on the Incorporation of Science and Technology in the Primary School Curriculum, Final Report* (Paris, 1980), and *Prospects*, VIII, 1, 1978, 47–109. This latter publication contains (48–57) an account of the Science Curriculum Improvement Study in the USA.

26 Office for Standards in Education, *Annual Report of Her Majesty's Chief Inspector of Schools, 1995–96* (London, HMSO, 1996), 13.

27 L.S. Shulman, 'Knowledge and Teaching: Foundations of the New Reform', *Harvard Educational Review*, 57, 1 (1987), 1–22. Shulman identified seven different forms of knowledge: content knowledge, general pedagogic knowledge, pedagogic content knowledge, curriculum knowledge, knowledge of learners and their characteristics, knowledge of educational contexts, and knowledge of educational goals and values. For some comments on the relevance of teacher subject knowledge to the task of teaching primary science, see J. Osborne and S. Simon, 'Primary Science: Past and Future Directions', *Studies in Science Education*, 27, 1996, 99–147, especially 115 onwards. The comments draw upon the Mathematics and Science Tasks (MAST) Project, funded by the Economic and Social Research Council.

28 House of Commons Education Committee, Fourth Report, *Science and Technology in School*, Vol. I, (HMSO, 1995), para. 80.

29 A. Edwards and J. Collison, *Taking Teacher Education to Task; an examination of primary school subject studies in school-based teacher training*, Paper presented to the Annual Meeting of the American Educational Research Association, New York, 1996.

30 N. Bennett, C. Desforges, A. Cockburn and B. Wilkinson, *The Quality of Pupil Learning Experiences* (London, 1984). This work is not particularly concerned with science. The scientific ideas of primary teachers and their relationship to their professional practice have received considerable attention in recent years. See, for example, C. Holroyd and W. Harlen, 'Teachers' Understanding of Science: a Cause for Concern?', *Primary Science Review*, 39 (1995), 23–5, and the work of the Primary Teachers' Understanding Project.

31 See, for example, Department of Education and Science, *Science: Key Stages 1, 2, and 3* (London, HMSO, 1992), 12 for the comment that 'In most schools science continued to be taught through topics covering a range of subjects such as "Toys" or "Ourselves"'.

32 Department of Education and Science, *The School Curriculum* (London, HMSO, 1981).

33 Department of Education and Science, *Science 5–16: A statement of policy* (London, HMSO, 1985).

34 Ibid., paras. 15–18. As examples of non-governmental initiatives, the statement of policy identified the work of the Association for Science Education (a validating organisation for in-service programmes in primary science) and of the British Association for the Advancement of Science (a scheme of 'Awards for Young Investigators').

35 Royal Society, *The Public Understanding of Science* (London, 1985).

36 Association for Science Education, *Alternatives for Science Education: A Consultative Document* (Hatfield, 1979). The document was not well received by many members of the ASE, the less charitable among whom referred to it as Alternatives *to* Science Education.

37 Association for Science Education, *Education Through Science* (Hatfield, 1981).

38 Comments made during a visit by Sir Keith Joseph to ASE headquarters, 14 June 1982. Joseph went on to comment that 'the DES cannot make things happen'. It is important to note that initiatives in science education to parallel those in maintained primary schools had been underway for some time in the independent sector of education. The objective during the 1970s was to secure a place for science, first as

a 'compulsory supporting', and later as a 'compulsory qualifying' subject in the Common Entrance Examination. See, Joint Standing Committee of HMC and IAPS, *Guide to Science Teaching in Preparatory Schools*, revised edition, 1973.

39 The SSCR and, more particularly, its Director, Dick West, were influential in the shaping of the DES 1985 policy statement on science education. The Review itself ran from 1981 to 1986, with a dissemination phase from 1986 to 1989. It operated under the aegis of the Schools Council and was supported by the ASE. Over the years of its existence, a variety of organisations, including the Department of Education and Science, local education authorities and the Department of Trade and Industry, all helped to support its work.

40 See, for example, I. Goodson, *Studying Curriculum: Cases and Methods* (Buckingham, 1994).

41 E. Bolton, 'Perspectives on the National Curriculum', in A. O'Hear and J. White (eds), *Assessing the National Curriculum* (London, 1993), 46.

42 Department of Education and Science, *Curriculum 11–16* (London, HMSO, 1977).

43 Department of Education and Science, *Better Schools* (London, HMSO, 1985).

44 E. Bolton, op. cit., 47.

45 R.J. Alexander, *Primary Teaching* (London, 1984), 60.

46 This is the distinction drawn by Roy Richards in 1997, reviewing a decade of change in primary science education. R. Richards, 'A Bumpy Ride: the Progress of Primary Science', *Primary Science Review*, 47 (1997), 3–5.

47 M. Osborn *et al.*, 'Policy into Practice and Practice into Policy: Creative Mediation in the Primary Classroom', in G. Helsby and G. McCulloch (eds), *Teachers and the National Curriculum* (London, 1997), 52.

48 Ibid., 63.

49 B. MacGilchrist, 'A Primary Perspective on the National Curriculum', in A. O'Hear and J. White (eds), op. cit., 122.

50 P. Black, *School Science Education: The Past 25 Years*, Paper prepared for Nuffield Foundation Seminar on the National Curriculum, London, January 1997, 9. Black also refers to teachers' confusion about the purpose of Attainment Target 1, 'some thinking investigations were for motivation, others that they were mainly to serve assessment, others again seeing them through "process-only" spectacles and elevating consumer comparison tests to the status of scientific research'.

51 For a review, see S. Jasanoff, G.E. Markle, J.C. Petersen and T. Pinch, *Handbook of Science and Technology Studies* (London, 1995).

52 J.F. Donnelly *et al.*, *Investigations by Order: Policy, curriculum and science teachers' work under the Education Reform Act* (Nafferton, 1996).

53 Although concerned with the secondary curriculum, there is much of relevance in E.W. Jenkins, 'Science for Professionals: Scientific Method and Secondary Education', in M.H. Price (ed.), *The Development of the Secondary Curriculum* (London, 1986), 156–81.

54 Association for Science Education, *The Place of Investigations in Science Education: A Report from the Investigations in Science Task Group* (Hatfield, 1993), 37.

55 Although now coloured by a substantial body of research evidence about children's understanding of natural phenomena (variously referred to as 'children's science', misconceptions, alternative conceptions, etc.), the notion of a parallel between the history of scientific ideas and the way in which those ideas develop in children is far from new. Its significance, however, remains not entirely clear. It is interesting to note that in the 1920s, T.P. Nunn's claim that the interest of children in science exhibited a rhythm corresponding to the rhythm of its history was used to justify both the sequencing of topics within a school science course and the strategy by which they should be taught. See, T.P. Nunn, *Education: Its Data and First Principles* (London, 1920). See also Chapter 3.

56 W. Harlen, *The Teaching of Science in Primary Schools* (London, 1996), 5 and 14.

For a critical commentary on the claims made to justify science education on the basis of goals that transcend the learning of scientific content, see S.P. Norris, 'Intellectual Independence for Non-scientists and Other Content-Transcendent Goals of Science Education', *Educational Researcher*, 81, 2 (1997), 239–58.

57 P.J. Black, op. cit., 9.

58 D.C. Phillips, 'The Good, the Bad and the Ugly: The Many Faces of Constructivism', *Educational Researcher*, 24, 7 (1995), 5.

59 P.J. Fensham, 'Science and Technology', in P.W. Jackson (ed.), *Handbook of Research on Curriculum* (New York, 1992), 801.

60 D.C. Phillips, op. cit., 5–12. Phillips identifies the 'bad' in constructivism as 'the tendency within many forms of constructivist pedagogy ... towards relativism, or towards treating the justification of our knowledge as being entirely a matter of sociopolitical processes or consensus, or toward the jettisoning of any substantial rational justification or warrant at all ...'.

61 Substantial bibliographies and reviews are available. See, for example, R. Duit, *Research on Students' Conceptions: Developments and Trends*, Paper presented at the Third International Conference on Misconceptions in Science and Mathematics Learning, Cornell University, 1993.

62 The SPACE project sought to establish the understanding which primary school children have of particular scientific concepts and to explore ways in which such understanding may be modified. The Project produced a number of research reports covering different concepts, for example, T. Russell and D. Watt, *Evaporation and Condensation* (Liverpool, 1990).

63 M. Devitt, *Realism and Truth* (Oxford, 1991), ix.

64 M.R. Matthews, *Challenging NZ Science Education* (Palmerston North, 1995).

65 See, for example, J. Ogborn, 'Constructivist Metaphors of Science Learning', *Science & Education*, 6, 1–2, 121–33.

66 W. Harlen, 'Ten years on: the Past and the Future of Research in Primary Science', *Primary Science Review*, 47, 1997, 6.

Bibliography

Aldrich, R., The Evolution of Teacher Education, in Graves, N.J., op. cit., 12–24.

Alexander, R.J., *Primary Teaching*, London, Holt, Rinehart and Winston, 1984.

Allen, B.M., *Sir Robert Morant, A Great Public Servant*, London, Macmillan, 1934.

Allen, D.E., *The Naturalist in Britain, A Social History*, London, Allen Lane, 1976.

Association for Science Education, *Alternatives for Science Education*, Hatfield, ASE, 1979.

Association for Science Education, *Education Through Science*, Hatfield, ASE, 1981.

Association for Science Education, *The Place of Investigations in Science Education: A Report from the Investigations in Science Task Group*, Hatfield, ASE, 1993.

Association for Science Education, Primary Schools' Science Committee Policy Statement, *ASE Bulletin*, November 1963, 18–21.

Association of Teachers in Colleges and Departments of Education, Association of Women Science Teachers, The London Association of Science Teachers, the Science Masters' Association, *Science in the Primary School*, London, ATCDE/AWST/ASE, 1959.

Bailey, L.H., *The Nature Study Idea, being an interpretation of the new school movement to put the child in sympathy with nature*, London, Heinemann, 1903.

Bainbridge, J.W., Origins of the Nature Study Movement, *Natural Science in Schools*, 16, 1, 1978, 11–14.

Ballard, P.B., *Group Tests of Intelligence*, London, Hodder and Stoughton, 1923.

Bennett, N., Desforges, C., Cockburn, A. and Wilkinson, B., *The Quality of Pupils' Learning Experiences*, London, Lawrence Erlbaum Associates, 1984.

Bennett, N., *Teaching Styles and Pupil Progress*, London, Open Books Publishing, 1976.

Berry, W.A.C., *The Development of Teacher Training in England and Wales since 1944, with particular reference to the establishment of B. Ed. degree courses for students in Colleges of Education*, Birmingham, University of Birmingham Institute of Education.

Bibby, C., *T.H. Huxley, Scientist, Humanist and Educator*, London, Watts, 1959.

Birchenough, C., *History of Elementary Education in England and Wales from 1800 to the Present Day*, London, University Tutorial Press, 1914.

Black, P.J., School Science Education: The Past 25 Years, paper prepared for a Nuffield Foundation Seminar on the National Curriculum, London, January 1997.

Black, P.J., Why Hasn't It Worked? In Richards, C. and Holford, D. (eds), op. cit., 29–32.

Blenkin, G.M. and Kelly, A.V., *The Primary Curriculum*, London, Harper and Row, 1981.

Board for the Final Examination of Student in Yorkshire Training Colleges, *Regulations and Syllabuses*, Wakefield, The Board, 1936.

Board of Education, *Code of Regulations for Public Elementary Schools with Schedules 1904*, London, HMSO, 1904. Issued annually.

Board of Education, *Regulations and Syllabus for the King's Scholarship Examination 1905*, PP LXXV (1905), 672–3.

Board of Education, *Regulations for the Preliminary Education of Elementary School Teachers*, London, HMSO, 1913.

Board of Education, *Regulations for the Training of Teachers and for the Examination of Students in Training Colleges*, PP LXXV (1904), 611–12.

Board of Education, *Regulations for the Training of Teachers and for the Examination of Students in Training Colleges*, London, HMSO, 1907.

Board of Education, *Regulations for the Training of Teachers for Elementary Schools*, London, HMSO, 1913.

Board of Education, *Teachers and Youth Leaders. Report of the Committee Appointed by the President of the Board of Education to Consider the Supply, Recruitment and Training of Teachers and Youth Leaders*, London, HMSO, 1944.

Board of Education, *A School Week in the Country*, London, HMSO, 1910.

Board of Education, *Annual Reports*, London, HMSO.

Board of Education, Consultative Committee, *Infant and Nursery Schools*, London, HMSO, 1933.

Board of Education, Consultative Committee, *The Education of the Adolescent*, London, HMSO, 1926.

Board of Education, Consultative Committee, *The Primary School*, London, HMSO, 1931.

Board of Education, *Handbook of Suggestions for Teachers and Others concerned in the Work of Public Elementary Schools*, London, HMSO 1927 and 1937, reprinted 1947.

Board of Education, *Memorandum on Examinations for Scholarship and Free Places in Secondary Schools*, Educational Pamphlet No. 63, London, HMSO, 1928.

Board of Education, *Provisional Code of Regulations for Public Elementary Schools with Schedules 1903*, London, HMSO, 1903.

Board of Education, *Regulations for the Training of Teachers for Elementary Schools*, London, HMSO, 1913.

Board of Education, *Report of the Departmental Committee on Scholarships and Free Places*, London, HMSO, 1920.

Board of Education, *Report on the Training of Rural Teachers*, London, HMSO, 1929.

Board of Education, *Rural Education*, Education Pamphlet No. 46, London, HMSO, 1926.

Board of Education, *Science in Senior Schools*, Educational Pamphlet No. 89, London, HMSO, 1930.

Board of Education, *Special Reports on Educational Subjects*, Volume II, London, HMSO, 1898.

Board of Education, *Special Reports on Educational Subjects*, Volume VIII, London, HMSO, 1902.

Board of Education, *The New Prospect in Education*, Educational Pamphlet No. 60, London, HMSO, 1928.

Bolton, E., Perspectives on the National Curriculum, in O'Hear, A. and White, J. (eds), *Assessing the National Curriculum*, Paul Chapman, London, 1993, 45–9.

Bonham, H.J., Modern School Biology, *Advancement of Science*, VI, 21, 1949, 40–42.

Bradbury, J.L., *Chester College and the Training of Teachers 1938–1975*, Chester, Chester College, 1975.

Bradley, H., *A Survey of Science Teaching in Primary Schools, Pointers for INSET*, Nottingham, University of Nottingham Institute of Education, 1976.

Bramwell, R.D., *Elementary School Work 1900–1925*, Durham, University of Durham Institute of Education, 1961.

Branson, J.M., Tea Discussion: College of Preceptors, *School Nature Study*, 52, 206 (1957), 9.

Brehony, K.J., The Schoolmaster's Parliament: The origins and formation of the Consultative Committee of the Board of Education, *History of Education*, 23, 2 (1994), 171–93.

Brehony, K.J., What's Left in Progressive Education? in Rattansi, A. and Reeder, D. (eds), op. cit., 196–221.

Briggs, A., *The Golden Age of Wireless*, London, Oxford University Press, 1965.

British Association for the Advancement of Science, *Report of the Annual Meeting (Dundee) 1867*, London, Murray, 1868.

British Association for the Advancement of Science, *Report of the Annual Meeting 1908*, London, Murray, 1909.

Brock, W.H. (ed.), *H.E. Armstrong and the Teaching of Science, 1880–1930*, London, Cambridge University Press, 1973.

Browne, J.D., *Teachers of Teachers. A History of the Association of Teachers in Colleges and Departments of Education*, London, Hodder and Stoughton, 1979.

Burton, H.M., *The Education of the Countryman*, London, Paul, 1944.

Butterworth, H., *The Development and Influence of the Science and Art Department 1853–1899*, Unpublished Ph.D. thesis, University of Sheffield, 1968.

Campbell, J. and Neill, S., *Curriculum Reform at Key Stage 1: Teacher Commitment and Policy Failure*, London, Longman, 1994.

Cane, B., Inservice Education for Teachers , in Tibble, J.W. (ed.), op. cit., 134–55.

Cardwell, D.S.L., *The Organisation of Science in England, A Retrospect*, London, Heinemann, 1957.

Chard, J., On Circulating Museum Cabinets for Schools and Other Educational Institutions, *Proceedings of the Museums Association*, 1890, 57–63.

Coleman, D., *The Life and Work of John Hall Gladstone (1827–1902) with particular reference to his contribution to elementary science education at the London School Board*, Unpublished Ph.D. thesis, King's College London, 1991.

Committee of Council in Scotland, *Report of the Committee of Council in Scotland with Appendix, 1907–1908, Memorandum on Nature Study and the Teaching of Science in Scottish Schools*, London, HMSO, 1908.

Committee of Council on Education, *Annual Reports*, London, HMSO.

Committee of Council on Education, *Minute Establishing a New Code of Regulations*, PP, 1882, XXIII, 111–44.

Committee of Council on Education, *New Code of Regulations for Elementary Schools*, PP, 1875, LVIII, 1–36.

Connell, L., *A Century of Teacher Training in Leeds, 1875–1975*, Leeds, Leeds Metropolitan University, 1996.

Connell, L., *Carnegie. A History of Carnegie College and School of Physical Education, 1933–1976*, Leeds, Carnegie School of Physical Education, 1983.

Conran, J., Primary Science 1950–82: A Personal View, in Richards, C. and Holford, D. (eds), op. cit., 17–27.

Cowham, J.H., The School Journey (London to Caterham etc.) Made by Students at the Westminster Training College, in Board of Education, *Special Reports on Educational Subjects*, Volume VIII, London, HMSO, 1902.

Cox, C.B. and Dyson, A.E. (eds), *Fight for Education*, London, Critical Quarterly Society, 1961.

Craft, M., A Broader Role for Colleges of Education, in Tibble, J.W. (ed.), op. cit., 7–38.

Crewe College of Education, *A College in Green Fields. The Story of Crewe College of Education 1908–1974*, Crewe, The College of Education, 1974.

Crossland, R.W., An Individual Study of the Nuffield Foundation Primary Science Project, *School Science Review*, 53 (1972), 628–38.

Crowther, H., Discussions on Sir Henry Miers' Report, *Museums Journal*, XXVIII, 1928–9, 224.

Cunningham, P., *Curriculum Change in the Primary Schools since 1945, Dissemination of the Progressive Ideal*, London, Falmer Press, 1987.

Curtis, S.J. and Boultwood, M.E.A., *An Introductory History of English Education since 1800*, London, University Tutorial Press, 1960.

Curtis, S.J. and Boultwood, M.E.A., *A Short History of Educational Ideas*, London, University Tutorial Press, 1965.

Darroch, A., Modern Education. Second Period. From Rousseau to the Present Time, in Laurie, A.P., op. cit., Volume VII, 173–4.

Dearden, R., The Aims of Primary Education, in Peters, R.S., op. cit., 21–41.

Dent, H.C., *The Training of Teachers in England and Wales, 1800–1975*, London, Hodder and Stoughton, 1977.

Department for Education and Science, *Teacher Education and Training, A Report of a Committee of Inquiry under the Chairmanship of Lord James of Rusholme*, London, HMSO, 1972.

Department of Education and Science and Welsh Office, *Science 5–16: A Statement of Policy*, London, HMSO, 1985.

Department of Education and Science, *Better Schools*, London, HMSO, 1985.

Department of Education and Science, *Curriculum 11–16*, London, HMSO, 1977.

Department of Education and Science, *Designated Courses in Mathematics and Science for Primary Teachers, April 1990–April 1991, A Report by HMI*, London, DES, 1992.

Department of Education and Science, *Primary Education in England: A Survey by HM Inspectors of Schools*, London, HMSO, 1978.

Department of Education and Science, *Science in Primary Schools. A Discussion Paper prepared by the HMI Science Committee*, London, HMSO, 1984.

Department of Education and Science, *Science: Key Stages 1, 2, and 3, A Report by HM Inspectorate on the Second Year, 1990–91*, London, HMSO, 1992.

Department of Education and Science, *Teaching Quality*, London, HMSO, 1983.

Department of Education and Science, *The School Curriculum*, London, HMSO, 1981.

Department of Education and Science, *Children and their Primary Schools. A Report of the Central Advisory Council for Education (England)*, London, HMSO, 1967.

Desmond, A., *Huxley, The Devil's Disciple*, London, Michael Joseph, 1994.

Desmond, A., *Huxley: Evolution's High Priest*, London, Michael Joseph, 1997.

Devitt, M., *Realism and Truth*, Oxford, Blackwell, 1991.

Dodd, C.I., A School Journey in Germany, *The National Review*, XXX, 1897–8, 445–52.

Donnelly, J.F., Jenkins, E.W., Buchan, A., Welford, A.G. and Laws, P., *Investigations by Order: Policy, curriculum and science teachers' work under the Education Reform Act*, Studies in Education, Driffield, 1996.

Eaglesham, E., *Foundations of Twentieth Century Education*, London, Routledge and Kegan Paul, 1967.

Edwards, A. and Collison, J., Taking Teacher Education to task: an examination of primary school subject studies in school-based teacher training, Paper presented at the Annual Meeting of the American Educational Research Association, New York, 1996.

Ellis, G.H., The Social Value of Gardening, *School Nature Study*, 1, 43 (1916), 35.

England, J.M., Three School Journeys in Yorkshire, in Board of Education, *Special Reports on Educational Subjects*, 21, London HMSO, 1902.

Ennever, L. and Harlen, W., *With Objectives in Mind: Guide to Science 5–13*, London, Schools Council/Macdonald Educational, 1972.

Ennever, L., A Case Study of a Project, *Secondary Education*, 4, 2, 1974, 87.

Fearn, E. and Simon, B., *Education in the Nineteen Sixties, Proceedings of the 1979 Annual Conference of the History of Education Society of Great Britain*, Leicester, History of Education Society, 1980.

Fennell, M., *Notes of Lessons in the Herbartian Method*, London, Longmans Green, 1902.

Fensham, P.J., Science and Technology, in Jackson, P.W. (ed.), op. cit.

Froebel Foundation, *Children Learning Through Scientific Interests*, London, Froebel Foundation, 1966.

Furneaux, W.S., *A Nature Study Guide*, London, Longmans, 1912.

Galton, M., Change and Continuity in the Primary Schools; the research evidence, *Oxford Review of Education*, 13, 1, 1987, 81–93.

Galton, M., Simon, B. and Croll, P., *Inside the Primary Classroom*, London, Routledge and Kegan Paul, 1980.

Gammage, J., *Science 5–13 Project*, Wollongong Institute of Education Monograph No. 1, Wollongong, 1976.

Gardner, D.E.M., *Experiment and Tradition in Primary Schools*, London, Methuen, 1966.

Gibby, B., Curriculum evaluation with reference to some projects, in Lawton, D. *et al.*, op. cit., 166–75.

Goodson, I. (ed.), *Social Histories of the Secondary Curriculum: Subjects for Study*, Lewes, Falmer Press, 1985.

Goodson, I., *Studying Curriculum: Cases and Methods*, Buckingham, Open University Press, 1994.

Gordon, P. and Lawton, D., *Curriculum Change in the Nineteenth and Twentieth Centuries*, London, Hodder and Stoughton, 1978.

Gosden, P.H.J.H. and Taylor, A., *Studies in the History of a University, 1874–1974*, Leeds, Leeds University Press, 1975.

Gosden, P.H.J.H., *The Evolution of a Profession. A Study of the Contribution of Teachers' Associations to the Development of School Teaching as a Professional Occupation*, Oxford, Blackwell, 1972.

Graham, D. and Tytler, D., *A Lesson for Us All: The Making of the National Curriculum*, London, Routledge, 1993.

Graves, N.J., *Initial Teacher Education. Policies and Progress*, London, Kogan Page/Institute of Education, 1990.

Griffiths, B.M., *A Study of the Effectiveness of Different Methods of Inservice Education and Training Designed to Introduce the Schools Council Science 5–13 Project into Primary Schools*, Unpublished M.Phil. thesis, University of Nottingham, 1978.

Hall, J.S., *Experience, Experiment and Research: English Primary Science 1959–1967*, Unpublished Ph.D. thesis, University of Liverpool, 1993.

Halsey, A.H. and Sylva, K., Plowden: History and Prospect, *Oxford Review of Education*, 13, 1, 1987, 3–11.

Hampson, B.L., Science from the beginning for the Primary School, *School Nature Study*, 52, 209 (1957), 66.

Harlen, W., Darwin, A. and Murphy, P., *Match and Mismatch: Raising Questions: Leader's Guide*, London, Schools Council/Oliver and Boyd, 1977.

Harlen, W., Science and Scientific Thinking across the Curriculum, *Cambridge Journal of Education*, 7, 3, 1977, 131.

Harlen, W., Ten Years On: the Past and the Future of Research in Primary Science, *Primary Science Review*, 47, 1997, 6–7.

Harlen, W., *The Teaching of Science in Primary Schools*, London, David Fulton,1996.

Harris, S., *Science in Primary Schools*, Slough, The National Foundation for Educational Research, 1996.

Harvey, T.J., Science in the Primary school – an estimate of the amount taught and the teacher's attitude towards it, *School Science Review*, 57, 210, 1976, 770–73.

Hayward, F.H., *The Secret of Herbart, an Essay on the Science of Education*, London, Watts, 1907.

Henriques, J., Holloway, W., Urwin, C., Venn, C., Walkerdine, V., *Changing the Subject: Psychology, social regulation and subjectivity*, London, Methuen, 1984.

Hill, M.D. and Webb, W.M., *Eton Nature-Study and Observation Lessons*, London, Duckworth, 1903.

Hilliard, F.H., The Moral Instruction League 1897–1919, *Durham Research Review*, III, 12 (1961), 53–63.

Hindshaw, B., The Young Visitor, *Museums Journal*, XXIX, 1919–30, 227–8.

Hirst, P.R. (ed.), *Educational Theory and Its Foundation Disciplines*, London, Routledge and Kegan Paul, 1983.

Hodson, F.H. (ed.), *Broad Lines in Science Teaching*, London, Christophers, 1909.

Holford, D. and Richards, C. (eds), *The Teaching of Primary Science: Policy and Practice*, London, Falmer Press, 1983.

Holmes, E.G., *What Is and What Might Be*, London, Constable, 1911.

Holroyd, C. and Harlen, W., Teachers' Understanding of Science: A Cause for Concern? *Primary Science Review*, 39, 1995, 23–5.

House of Commons Education Committee, Fourth report, *Science and Technology in Schools*, Volume 1, London, HMSO, 1995.
Howes, F.H., Rubber: Past and Present Sources, *School Nature Study*, 37, 148 (1942), 33.
Huggins, Sir W., *The Royal Society in the State and in the Schools*, London, The Royal Society, 1905.
Hutchinson, J., Museum Examinations, *The Nineteenth Century*, LXII, 1907, 248–53.
Huxley, T.H., *Physiography, An Introduction to the Study of Nature*, London, Macmillan, 1877.
Ingle, R. and Jennings, A., *Science in Schools, Which Way Now?*, London, Institute of Education, 1981.
Isaacs, N., *The Growth of Understanding in the Young Child: A Brief Introduction to Piaget's Work*, London, Ward Lock Educational, 1961.
Isaacs, S., *Intellectual Growth in Young Children*, London, Routledge, 1930.
Jackson, P.W. (ed.), *Handbook of Research on Curriculum*, New York, Macmillan, 1992.
Jeffreys, M.V.C., *Revolution in Teacher Training*, London, Pitmans, 1961.
Jenkins, E.W. and Swinnerton, B., The School Nature Study Union 1903–94, *History of Education*, 25, 2 (1996), 191.
Jenkins, E.W., *A Magnificent Pile: A Centenary History of the Leeds Central High School*, Leeds, City of Leeds School, 1985.
Jenkins, E.W., *Policy Issues and School Science Education*, Leeds, Centre for Studies in Science Education, University of Leeds, 1989.
Jenkins, E.W., *From Armstrong to Nuffield: Studies in Twentieth-century Science Education in England and Wales*, London, Murray, 1979.
Jenkins, E.W., Science for Professionals: Scientific Method and Secondary Education, in Price, M.H., op. cit., 156–81.
Johnson, C.M., Freedom in Junior Schools, in Cox, C.B. and Dyson, A.E. (eds), op. cit., 48–50.
Joint Advisory Committee of the Association of Education Committees and the National Union of Teachers, *Examinations in Public Elementary Schools*, London , AEC/NUT, 1930.
Joint Standing Committee of The Headmasters' Conference and the Incorporated Association of Preparatory Schools, *Guide to Science Teaching in the Preparatory Schools*, Revised edition, Lymington, C.E. Publications, 1973.
Jolly, W., *Education: Its Principles and Practice as Developed by George Combe*, London, Macmillan, 2 volumes, 1879.

Jones, L.G.E., *The Training of Teachers in England and Wales, A Critical Survey*, London, Oxford, Oxford University Press, 1924.

Keys, W., Harris, S. and Fernandes, C., *Third International Mathematics and Science Study, First National Report, Part 1*, Slough, The National Foundation for Educational Research, 1996.

Keys, W., Harris, S. and Fernandes, C., *Third International Mathematics and Science Study, Second National Report, Part 1*, Slough, The National Foundation for Educational Research, 1997.

Kirby, N., *Personal Values in Primary Education*, London, Harper and Row, 1981.

Kogan, M., The Plowden Report Twenty Years On, *Oxford Review of Education*, 13, 1, 1987, 13–21.

Lane, H., *Talks to Parents and Teachers*, London, Allen and Unwin, 1928.

Laurie, A.P., *The Teacher's Encyclopaedia of the Theory, Method, Practice, History and Development of Education*, 7 volumes, London, Caxton Publishing Co., 1912.

Lawson, J. and Silver, H., *A Social History of Education in England*, London, Methuen, 1973.

Lawton, D. and Chitty, C. (eds), *The National Curriculum*, London, 1995.

Lawton, D., Gordon, P., Ing, M., Gibby, B., Pring, R. and Moore, T., *Theory and Practice of Curriculum Studies*, London, Routledge and Kegan Paul, 1978.

Layton, D., *Interpreters of Science: A History of the Association for Science Education*, London, ASE/Murray, 1984.

Layton, D., *Science for the People. The Origins of the School Science Curriculum in England*, London, Allen and Unwin, 1973.

Lewis, G.G., Possibilities of Nature Study in a London Elementary School, *School Nature Study*, 9, 33 (1914), 6.

London School Board, *Final Report of the School Board for London, 1870–1904*, London, 1904.

Lowe, R. (ed.), *The Changing Primary School*, London, Falmer, 1987.

Lowe, R., *Education in the Post-War Years, A Social History*, London, Routledge, 1988.

Lowndes, G.A.N., *The Silent Social Revolution, An Account of the Expansion of Public Education in England and Wales, 1895–1935*, London, Oxford University Press, 1937.

MacDonald, B. and Walker, R., *Changing the Curriculum*, London, Open Books, 1976.

MacGilchrist, B., A Primary Perspective on the National Curriculum, in O'Hear, A. and White, J. (eds), *Assessing the National Curriculum*, Paul Chapman, London, 120–26.

Magnus, P., *Educational Aims and Efforts 1890–1910*, London, Longmans, 1910.

Manzer, R.A., *Teachers and Politics*, Manchester, Manchester University Press, 1970.

Mark, H.T., *Modern Views on Education*, London, The National Library, 1914.

Matthews, M.R., *Challenging NZ Science Education*, Palmerston North, Dunmore Press, 1995.

McCulloch, G., 'Spens v. Norwood': Contesting the educational state? *History of Education*, 22, 2 (1993), 163–80.

McGabe, G.I., *Museums in Education: the educational role of museums in the United Kingdom*, Unpublished M.Ed. thesis, University of Sheffield, 1975.

Ministry of Education, *Education 1900–1950. The Report of the Ministry of Education and Statistics of Public Education for England and Wales for the Year 1950*, London, HMSO, 1951.

Ministry of Education, *Science in Secondary Schools*, Pamphlet No. 38, London, HMSO, 1961.

Ministry of Education, Central Advisory Council (England), *Half Our Future*, London, HMSO, 1963.

Ministry of Education, *Higher Education, Report of the Committee Appointed by the Prime Minister under the Chairmanship of Lord Robbins, 1961–3*, London, HMSO, 1963.

Ministry of Education, *Primary Education, Suggestions for the Consideration of Teachers and Others concerned with the Work of Primary Schools*, London, HMSO, 1959.

Ministry of Education, *Science in Primary Schools*, Pamphlet No. 42, London, HMSO, 1961.

Ministry of Education, *15 to 18*, London, HMSO, 1959.

Misselbrook, H., *Nuffield Secondary Science: Teacher's Guide*, London, Longmans, 1970.

More, C., *The Training of Teachers 1847–1947. A History of the Church Colleges of Cheltenham*, London, Hambledon Press, 1992.

Morgan, E.J., The Richness of Parsley in Vitamin C (Ascorbic Acid), *School Nature Study*, 37, 149 (1942), 60.

Morrell, D.H. and Potts, A., *Britain's New Schools*, London, Longmans, 1960.

Morris, T., A Critique of School Nature Study: A View from the Antipodes, *School Nature Study*, 47, 189 (1953), 58.

Mowat, C.L., *Britain Between the Wars 1918–1940*, London, Methuen, 1955.

National Curriculum Council, *The Teaching of Science at Key Stages 1 and 2*, York, National Curriculum Council, 1993.

Neill, A.S., *Summerhill*, London, Gollancz, 1962.

Niblett, W.R., Humphreys, D.W. and Fairhurst, J.R., *The University Connection*, Windsor, National Foundation for Educational Research, 1975.

Norris, S.P., Intellectual Independence for Non-Scientists and Other Content-Transcendent Goals of Science Education, *Educational Researcher*, 81, 2, 1997, 239–58.

Nunn, T.P., *Education, Its Data and First Principles*, London, Edward Arnold, 1925.

Office for Standards in Education, *Science and Mathematics in Schools: A Review*, London, HMSO, 1994.

Office for Standards in Education, *Science: A Review of Inspection Findings 1993/4*, London, HMSO, 1995.

Office for Standards in Education, *The Annual Report of Her Majesty's Chief Inspector of Schools, 1995–96*, London, HMSO, 1996.

Official Report of the Nature Study Exhibition and Conferences, Glasgow, Blackie, 1903.

Ogborn, J., Constructivist Metaphors of Science Learning, *Science & Education*, 6, 1–2, 121–33.

Osborn, M. with Croll, P., Broadfoot, P., Pollard, A., McNess, E. and Triggs, P., Policy into Practice and Practice into Policy: Creative Mediation in the Primary Classroom, in Helsby, G. and McCulloch, G. (eds), *Teachers and the National Curriculum*, Cassell, 1997, 53–65.

Osborne, J. and Simon, S., Primary Science: Past and Future Directions, *Studies in Science Education*, 27, 1996, 99–147.

Paler, E.L., Fifty Years of Nature Study and the American Nature Study Society, *Nature Magazine*, 50 (1957).

Parker-Jelly, S., Science 5–13, Reflections on its Significance, in Richards, C. and Holford, D. (eds), op. cit., 147–58.

Parkinson, M., *The Labour Party and the Organisation of Secondary Education, 1918–1965*, London, Routledge and Kegan Paul, 1970.

Part, A., *The Making of a Mandarin*, London, Deutsch, 1990.

Perkins, W.H. (ed.), *The Place of Science in Primary Education, Proceedings of the BAAS Conference, September, 1961*, London, British Association for the Advancement of Science, 1962.

Peters, R.S., *Perspectives on Plowden*, London, Routledge and Kegan Paul, 1969.

Phillips, D.C., The Good, the Bad and the Ugly: The Many Faces of Constructivism, *Educational Researcher*, 24, 7, 1995.

Pollard, H.M., *Pioneers of Popular Education 1760–1850*, London, Murray, 1956.

Potter, F.F., *Educational Journey, Memories of 50 Years in Public Education*, London, Pitman, 1949.

Price, M.H. (ed.), *The Development of the Secondary Curriculum*, London, Croom Helm, 1986.

Rattansi, A. and Reeder, D. (eds), *Rethinking Radical Education: Essays in Honour of Brian Simon*, London, Lawrence and Wishart, 1992.

Raymont, T., *The Principles of Education*, London, Longmans Green, 1904.

Redman, S. *et al.*, Young Children and Science: The Oxford Primary Science Project, in Richards, C. and Holford, D. (eds), op. cit., 131–8.

Renshaw, P., The Objective and Structure of the College Curriculum in Tibble, J.W. (ed.), op. cit., 53–67.

Reynolds, D. and Farrell, S., *Worlds Apart: A Review of International Surveys of Educational Achievement Involving England*, Ofsted Reviews of Research, London, HMSO, 1996.

Richards, C. and Abell, B., Science 5/13 ; an evaluation of an evaluation? *School Science Review*, 54, 188, 1973, 579–83.

Richards, R., A Bumpy Ride: the Progress of Primary Science, *Primary Science Review*, 47, 1997, 3–5.

Richards, R., The Swinging of a Pendulum: Discovery science with young children, *Education 3–13*, 1, 1, 1973, 28.

Richards. C. and Holford, D. (eds), *The Teaching of Primary Science: Policy and Practice*, London, Falmer Press, 1983.

Riley, J., Nature Study Introductory to the Study of Light, *School Nature Study*, 7, 25 (1912), 50.

Royal Commission Appointed to Inquire into the Elementary Education Acts, *Final Report*, PP, 1888, XXXV, 1–406.

Royal Commission on Scientific Instruction and the Advancement of Science, *Sixth Report*, PP, 1875, XXVIII, 59–473.

Royal Commission on Secondary Education, *Report, Volume III*, PP, 1895, XLVIII, 1–260.

Royal Commission on Technical Instruction, *First Report*, PP, 1882, XXVII, 401–567.

Royal Society, *The Public Understanding of Science*, London, The Royal Society, 1985.

Sandiford, P, *The Training of Teachers in England and Wales*, New York, Teachers College Press, 1910.

Saville, J., *Rural Depopulation in England and Wales, 1851–1951*, London, Routledge and Kegan Paul, 1957.

Schools Council, *Curriculum Development*, Working Paper No. 10, London, Schools Council, 1967.

Schools Council, *Learning Through Science, Formulating a School's Policy*, London, Schools Council, 1980.

Schools Council, *The First Ten Years*, Schools Council, Bath, n.d.

Seaborne, M. and Lowe, R., *The English School, its Architecture and Organisation*, Vol. 1, 1971, Vol. 2, 1977, London, Routledge and Kegan Paul.

Seeley, J.R., *Ethics and Religion*, London, Society of Ethical Propagandists, 1900.

Selleck, R.J.W., *The New Education, The English Background 1870–1914*, London, Pitman, 1968.

Selleck, R.J.W., *English Primary Education and the Progressives, 1914–1939*, London, Routledge and Kegan Paul, 1982.

Selleck, R.J.W., The Hadow Report: A Study in Ambiguity, *Melbourne Studies in Education*, 145 (1972), 148–51.

Shapin, S. and Thackray, A., Prosopography as a Research Tool in the History of Science: the British Scientific Community 1700–1900, *History of Science*, XII, 1974.

Shaw, P., *Science*, London, Macmillan, 1972.

Shorney, D., *Teachers in Training, 1906–1985. A History of Avery Hill College*, London, Thames Polytechnic, 1985.

Shulman, L.S., Knowledge and Teaching: Foundations of the new reform, *Harvard Educational Review*, 57, 1, 1987, 1–22.

Silver, P. and Silver, H., *The Education of the Poor. The History of a National School, 1824–74*, London, Routledge and Kegan Paul, 1974.

Simon, B. and Willcocks, J. (eds), *Research and Practice in the Primary Classroom*, London, Routledge and Kegan Paul, 1981.

Simon, B., *Education and the Labour Movement 1870–1920*, London, Lawrence and Wishart, 1965.

Simon, B., *The Politics of Educational Reform 1920–1940*, London, Lawrence and Wishart, 1974.

Simon, B., The Primary School Revolution: Myth or Reality? in Fearn, E. and Simon, B., op. cit.

Skilbeck, M, *School-based Curriculum Development*, London, Harper and Row, 1974.

Smith, F., *A History of English Elementary Education*, London, University of London Press, 1931.

Smith, L.A.H., *To Understand and to Help: The Life and Work of Susan*

Isaacs (1885–1948), New Jersey, Associated University Presses, 1985.

Snow, C.P., *The Two Cultures and the Scientific Revolution*, Cambridge, Cambridge University Press, 1959.

Standing, E.M., *Maria Montessori, Her Life and Work*, London, Hollis and Carter, 1957.

Sutherland, M.B., *Theory of Education*, London, Longman, 1988.

Syfret, R.H., Some Early Critics of the Royal Society, *Notes and Records of the Royal Society of London*, 8, 1970, 65–7.

Thomas, E., The Scope of Nature Study, in Hodson, F.H., op. cit., 16–22.

Thomas, E.J., *Views on Science Education 1900–1960 with particular reference to the primary schools*, Unpublished M.Ed. thesis, Chelsea College, London, 1978.

Thompson, D., General Science: its origin and growth, *School Science Review*, 140, 1958, 109–22.

Thomson, J.A. and Geddes, P., *Life: Outlines of General Biology*, 2 volumes, London, Williams and Norgate, 1931.

Tibble, J.W. (ed.), *The Future of Teacher Education*, London, Routledge and Kegan Paul, 1971.

Toulson, S., The Influence of Science 5–13, *Dialogue*, 18, 1974, 5.

Trades Union Congress/Labour Party, *The Training of Teachers*, London TUC/Labour Party, 1922.

Tropp, A., *The Schoolteachers. The Growth of the Teaching Profession in England and Wales from 1800 to the Present Day*, London, Heinemann, 1957.

Turner, D.M., *A History of Science Teaching in England*, London, Chapman and Hall, 1927.

Unesco, *Meeting of Experts on the Incorporation of Science and Technology in the Primary School Curriculum, Final Report*, Paris, Unesco, 1980.

van Praagh, G. (ed.), *H.E. Armstrong and Science Education: Selections from the Teaching of Scientific Method and Other Papers on Education*, London, Murray, 1973.

von Wyss, C., Some Suggestions for Autumn Nature Lessons, *School Nature Study*, 1, 1 (1906), 1.

von Wyss, C., The School Nature Study Union: Looking Backward and Forward, *School Nature Study*, 10, 38 (1915), 3.

von Wyss, C., The Teaching of Nature Study, in Hodson, F.H., op. cit., 23–36.

von Wyss, C., Wild Life Held Captive, *School Nature Study*, 13, 51 (1918), 25.

Walker, L., *Cusack's Object Lessons, Mineral and Vegetable World and Common Objects*, London, City of London Book Depository, 1895.

Walkerdine, V., Developmental Psychology and the Child-centred Pedagogy: the insertion of Piaget into early education, in Henriques, J. *et al.*, 153–202.

Ware, F., *Educational Reform, The Task of the Board of Education*, London, Methuen, 1900.

Waring, M., *Social Pressures and Curriculum Innovation: A Study of the Nuffield Foundation Science Teaching Project*, London, Methuen, 1979.

Wastnedge, E.R., *Nuffield Junior Science: Teacher's Guide, 2 Volumes*, London, Collins, 1967.

Webb, W.M., Nature Knowledge: its progress and interpretation, *The Record of Secondary and Technical Education*, XI, 1902, 413.

Weber, L., *The English Infant School and Informal Education*, New Jersey, Prentice Hall, 1971.

Wellington, J.J. (ed.), *Skills and Processes in Science Education: A Critical Review*, London, Routledge, 1989.

Whitehead, A.N., *Science and the Modern World*, Cambridge, Cambridge University Press, 1929.

Wilson, D., The Nature Study Section of the Children's Holiday Fund, *School Nature Study*, 3, 7 (1908), 3.

Index

Index

Other Woburn Education Series Titles

General Series Editor: Professor Peter Gordon

Educational Policy Studies

Education and Policy in England in the Twentieth Century
Peter Gordon, Richard Aldrich and Dennis Dean

A Significant Social Revolution: Cross-Cultural Aspects of the Evolution of Compulsory Education
edited by J.A. Mangan

The State and Higher Education
Brian Salter and Ted Tapper

Educational Reconstruction: The 1944 Education Act and the Twenty-first Century
Gary McCulloch

Fee-paying Schools and Educational Change in Britain: Between the State and the Marketplace
Ted Tapper

Going Comprehensive in England and Wales: A Study of Uneven Change
Alan C. Kerckhoff, Ken Fogelman, David Crook and David Reeder

Education Policy-making in England and Wales: The Crucible Years, 1895–1911
Neil Daglish

Her Majesty's Inspectorate of Schools since 1944: Standard Bearers or Turbulent Priests?
John E. Dunford

Educational Practice

Slow Learners. A Break in the Circle: A Practical Guide for Teachers
Diane Griffin

Games and Simulations in Action
Alec Davison and Peter Gordon

Music in Education: A Guide for Parents and Teachers
Malcolm Carlton

The Education of Gifted Children
David Hopkinson

Teaching and Learning Mathematics
Peter G. Dean

Comprehending Comprehensives
Edward S. Conway

Teaching the Humanities
edited by Peter Gordon

Teaching Science
edited by Jenny Frost

The Private Schooling of Girls: Past and Present
edited by Geoffrey Walford

International Yearbook of History Education, Volume 1
edited by Alaric Dickinson, Peter Gordon, Peter Lee and John Slater

A Guide to Educational Research
edited by Peter Gordon

Social History

The First Teenagers: The Lifestyle of Young Wage-earners in Interwar Britain
David Fowler

James Kay Shuttleworth: Journey of an Outsider
R.J.W. Selleck